# Praise for *Understanding Zionism*

*Understanding Zionism* is a masterfully written guidebook through one of the most contested subjects in modern history. Any reader searching for clarity about Zionism and its many interlocutors, historical and contemporary, will benefit from Perez's steady, fair, and compelling account.

—Daniel G. Hummel, author of *Covenant Brothers: Evangelicals, Jews, and U.S.-Israeli Relations*

Drawing from cutting-edge scholarship, and yet free of academic jargon, *Understanding Zionism* is a thoughtful and concise history of Zionism and the modern Jewish experience. Deftly explaining the multiple varieties of Zionism, and particularly its Christian versions, the book is crucial reading for laypeople and clergy of any faith. I especially recommend it for those interested in contemporary Jewish-Christian relations as well as the place of religion in the Israeli-Palestinian conflict.

—Shayna Weiss, associate director of the Schusterman Center for Israel Studies at Brandeis University

*Understanding Zionism* is a comprehensive, nuanced, and accessible history that reveals the diversity both within Zionist movements and among Zionism's critics. In her balanced account of a hotly debated subject, Anne Perez demonstrates that it is possible to understand and tell the truth about historical traumas on both sides without losing sight of our shared humanity—a spark of hope seventy-five years into the Israeli-Palestinian conflict.

—Deanna Ferree Womack, associate professor of history of religions and interfaith studies at Emory University; author of *Protestants, Gender and the Arab Renaissance in Late Ottoman Syria*

UNDERSTANDING
# ZIONISM

# UNDERSTANDING
# ZIONISM

*History and Perspectives*

Anne Perez

**Fortress Press**
Minneapolis

UNDERSTANDING ZIONISM
History and Perspectives

Cover design: Kristin Miller
Cover image: Jewish National Fund KKL Stamp Theodor Herzl Psalm 137 (1916)

Print ISBN: 978-1-5064-8116-6
eBook ISBN: 978-1-5064-8117-3

To Grandma Polly

# CONTENTS

# INTRODUCTION

The word "Zionism" can evoke many things for many people—from liberation of the oppressed all the way to oppression itself, from a divine outworking in history to the violation of the Word of God. For many others, "Zionism" simply invokes confusion, something you know is controversial without knowing exactly why. Coined in the 1880s by a secular Jewish author, the word "Zionism" initially described a movement to invigorate Jewish cultural, linguistic, and national identity. Zionism has since evolved into a movement with many streams, brought about the establishment of the State of Israel in 1948, and captured the attention of different communities around the globe into the twenty-first century.

Despite being a Jewish nationalist movement, Christians have engaged with Zionism since its emergence, and continue this engagement in various ways today. Christian organizations supporting Zionism now include membership numbers into the millions, while Christian organizations opposing aspects of Zionism operate as well. Christians of all denominations, nations, and political persuasions regularly flock to Israel for vacations and Bible tours. Christians constitute "a third of American visitors to Israel," and increasing numbers of tourists and pilgrims visit from the Global South.[1] Most of these Christians go to Israel to enrich their engagement with the Bible by seeing its sites, sights, and geographical context. But while the pages of Scripture may come alive, the pages of the region's contemporary history do not read as easily. As Israeli anthropologist and tour guide Jackie Feldman asserts, many tour programs often "ignore current events completely."[2] The intersections of these histories are not self-evident, so Christians can come and go from Israel without a clear understanding of how the modern state came to be, the values it holds, or the challenges it faces. Most visitors will not have the desire, time, or ability to synthesize the vast historical-political context of the place they are visiting for devotional purposes. Even without a visit to Israel, Christians might notice news from Israel and the Middle East peppered with familiar names like "Jerusalem," "the Jordan River," and the "Temple Mount." They may see these alongside less recognizable terms and wonder how they relate (where is "Tel Aviv" in the Bible?).

## KEY TERMINOLOGY

### Zionism

Perhaps the most basic definition of Zionism is the view that Jews should have political, cultural, and national autonomy (self-rule) in part or whole of the land of ancient Israel and Judea, known for the last two millennia as multiple names: Palestine, *Eretz Israel* (the Land of Israel), and the Holy Land. The pieces of this basic definition have been the subject of robust debate and evolution among both Zionist supporters and their opponents. They contested whether the autonomy that Jews should pursue should be political or cultural (or both), and the best means by which they would attain this autonomy. On a more fundamental level, Zionism highlighted questions surrounding the boundaries of the Jewish nation itself, with some insisting it is a group defined by religion; others a cultural group based on shared values, customs, texts, and experiences; still others an ethnic category based on birth and bloodlines; and others espousing different constellations of all of the above. In many ways the definition of Zionism and its component parts are still under dynamic political, social, and cultural construction.

## Israel

In biblical periods *Israel* was a specific geographic and political entity—the kingdom of the ten northern tribes of Israel, distinct from the kingdom of Judah. Under King David and his heir Solomon, the northern tribes united with Judah as one monarchy "collectively known as Israel."[3] The term is also used as a "nickname" for God's people as a whole; the biblical patriarch Jacob was famously renamed Israel in Genesis 32, and all twelve tribes descended from Jacob's sons. Furthermore, the foundational prayer the *Shema* (from Deuteronomy 6:4 and cited in Jesus's own teaching in Mark 12:29)—"Hear, O Israel: the Lord our God, the Lord is one"—calls on all Israelites and not just those of the ten northern tribes. When the State of Israel was established in 1948, many names were considered (such as Judah), but the founders thought that "Israel" had the strongest emotional and historical resonance.

## The Land of Israel/*Eretz Israel*

*The Land of Israel* is a loose term referring to some or all of the land in which ancient Israelites lived, and can include some or all of the ancient Kingdom of Israel and the Kingdom of Judah, the Galilee region, the Negev Desert region, the southern hill country of Judea (surrounding Jerusalem), the northern hill country of Samaria, and the Mediterranean coast from ancient Philistia/modern-day Gaza through the Tyre area (contemporary southern Lebanon). Until the establishment of Israel in 1948, most Zionists referred to this general area as *Eretz Israel*, Hebrew for the Land of Israel (or in common shorthand, *ha'aretz*, Hebrew for *the Land*). *Eretz Israel* was used both during the Ottoman and British Mandate administrations, and is still used today to refer to Israel as a modern country in its 1948 borders, as well as to what is called *Greater Israel*, which generally includes the 1948 borders, the West Bank, and the Gaza Strip.

## Palestine

Since Antiquity, the term *Palestine* (from the name *Philistia* of the ancient Philistines) has been used as another name for the territory around the Land of Israel, with varying geographical boundaries, though most commonly referring to the area south of present-day Lebanon and Syria and west of the Jordan River. Today the name Palestine is used in different ways and with different ideological connotations. For instance, it can be the umbrella term for both Gaza and the West Bank, which the United Nations has recognized as an Arab Palestinian (observer) state and under which different Palestinian administrative bodies have certain degrees of authority (these areas are also known collectively as the "Occupied Palestinian Territories," "Palestinian Territories," or even just "the territories"; the term "occupied" is itself disputed). Those who deny the legitimacy of the modern State of Israel and want to highlight the historical unity of the whole territory of Gaza, Israel, and the West Bank refer to all of Israel as "Palestine." In most scholarly literature on this subject, the word "Palestine" (or the term "historic Palestine") is used when describing this whole area before Israel was established in 1948, in which case it is not an explicitly political or ideological term but a historical and geographical one.

## Israel/Palestine

The use of the combined *Israel/Palestine* can be both ideological and geographical. On the one hand it is used to acknowledge the historical complexities that would lead certain groups of people to call the same place both Israel and Palestine. But it can also be used to refer to the geographic area that includes both the Palestinian Territories and Israel according to its borders upon establishment in 1948 (also known as the "Green Line"—colloquially referring to the color of the pen drawing armistice lines on a map). It can therefore serve as a shorthand version of "Israel and the Palestinian Territories."

## Israeli

*Israeli* is the term describing a citizen of the modern State of Israel. It includes anyone who is a citizen of Israel and can thus include Jews, Arabs, and others. "Israelite" is the adjective for descendants of Jacob and members of the ancient Kingdom of Israel, and is thus anachronistic when used in the modern context.

## Palestinian

A Palestinian is someone born in or descending from historic Palestine. Most Palestinians are Arabs, but the term encompasses people from other ethnic backgrounds as well, such as Armenians or Circassians. There is no official state of Palestine, and so while there are no "citizens" of Palestine, any Arab living in the West Bank and Gaza is generally considered Palestinian. Many Palestinians also live as refugees (including the descendants of refugees) in other countries like Jordan and Lebanon. Arab Israelis oftentimes identify as Israeli Palestinian to emphasize that while their citizenship is Israeli they also maintain a distinctly Palestinian ethnic identity.

## Jew/Jewish

Jewishness is both a religious and a cultural identity, and it can be both ascribed (given automatically) and adopted (through conversion). Many Christians misunderstand this, assuming that Judaism (and other religions for that matter) function in the same way as faith and identity according to Christianity. Evangelical Christians tend to maintain that someone is a Christian when they consciously believe in the gospel of Jesus, choosing to make him the Lord of their life and to be united to him by the Holy Spirit (also known as becoming "born again," taking Jesus's words from John 3). Someone can therefore become a Christian regardless of national, ethnic, or racial identity or citizenship status; these things don't change if someone adopts the Christian faith. For most of church history, and for many large branches of the church today, someone is generally identified as a Christian when they are baptized (usually as an infant) and receive the other sacraments of the church (like communion, marriage, and last rites); these practices are applicable to members of any ethnic or national group. Churches in the Eastern Orthodox tradition are somewhat unique in that they do identify more closely with an ethnic and territorial identity, especially since many have used ethnic languages (Syriac, Greek, Russian, etc.) in their official liturgies. While it certainly does happen that in practice Christian groups will conflate their faith and their ethnicity or nation, theologically speaking, Christians generally understand Christianity as a religious and spiritual identity, and thus assume other religious categories operate in a similar way.

Jewish identity is not a purely religious identity, both according to the tenets of Judaism as a religion and according to historical circumstances. In the biblical period, Jewishness was mainly determined by birth and by circumcision. The term "Jews" came into common usage after the Babylonians expelled the Judeans from Jerusalem in the sixth century BCE. After the exiles' return and the rebuilding of the Second Temple, "Jew" applied both to those who lived in Judah and its surroundings, as well as those in the Diaspora (concentrated mainly in Babylon and Egypt).

Rabbinic Judaism developed over the first few centuries CE as rabbis developed Jewish law, known as *halakha* (Hebrew for *"way/path"*), based on both the laws of the Torah and rabbinical interpretation and commentary. The predominance of rabbinic Judaism can be traced in part to the establishment of a rabbinic community in Yavne (Jamnia in Greek) in the wake of the Roman destruction of the Second Temple. Tradition holds that esteemed Rabbi Yohanan Ben Zakkai did not support the Jewish uprising against Rome and escaped Jerusalem in exchange for Roman permission to establish in Yavne a center of rabbinic learning and transmission that could thrive without imperial interference. Together the rabbis of Roman Palestine and those in Persian Babylon created the corpus of Jewish law known as the Talmud. Over the years Judaism developed a vast heritage and network of religious traditions, cultural customs, and folk practices. The broadest classifications of these are the Ashkenazi and Sephardic traditions that originate in central/eastern Europe and the Iberian Peninsula, respectively. Both these traditions, and the various streams within them, generally maintain that someone is a Jew if they are born to a Jewish mother, and that the status is permanent (more contemporary forms of Judaism, like Reform Judaism, also acknowledge someone as a Jew if born to a Jewish father even if the mother is not Jewish). A famous declaration in the Talmud assures that "a Jew, though he sins, remains a Jew," meaning no matter how unobservant or outright rebellious someone might be, no Jew can lose his or her Jewish identity.[4] Jewish law also makes provisions for conversion to Judaism, so that even those not born into the Jewish people can become Jews.

While Judaism itself has defined Jewishness as something that is generally conferred through descent or conversion, the societies and governments Jews have lived among have historically considered Jews both a religious group and a distinct ethnic group. This treatment promoted (or enforced) social, linguistic, legal, economic, and other cultural differences between Jews and the communities in which they lived. Some of the most extreme cases of "difference" were the forcing of Jews to live in ghettos or even expelling them from areas altogether. One of the largest expulsions of this kind was from Catholic Spain and Portugal in the fifteenth century, but it happened on smaller scales throughout medieval and early modern history. Many Jews spoke their own languages as their mother tongue—Yiddish in central and eastern Europe; Ladino (Judeo-Spanish) in Spain and the Sephardic Diaspora; and Judeo-Arabic in the Arab world. Jews were frequently barred from owning land or from certain occupations, and were therefore funneled into others. Historians of Jewish history have shown that Jews in different parts of the world, in both Christian and Islamic societies, have adopted, resisted, and influenced the cultures in which they have lived.[5] Therefore, while Jews have been an integral part of the cultures and societies they have shared with non-Jews, they have also created and maintained distinct cultures (by choice and/or by force) that designated them not only as a separate religious group but as a separate cultural and/or linguistic group as well.

The process known as Emancipation, in which Jews attained equal legal and political status to those around them, took place at different rates and in different ways across the world in the late eighteenth through the nineteenth centuries (in Russia, equal political rights for Jews took place—at least formally —as late as the 1917 communist revolution). With Emancipation, Jews were invited—and generally speaking, required—to assimilate to the majority of societies they were part of, and Jewish communities across Europe created new ways of preserving and nurturing their religious and cultural institutions and values.

By the time Zionism emerged in the late nineteenth century, Jewish identity could ultimately mean a variety of things: a religion, an ethnic group with shared ancestry and language, and a cultural group with shared values, customs, and texts. The words used in Modern Hebrew reflect these different categorizations: 'am (pronounced ahm) means "*a people*" and is a term used in the Bible and in more religious contexts (*Am Yisrael*/the people of Israel), but since the emergence of Zionism the Modern Hebrew term *le'om* (leh-OHM) is used for the modern sense of "nation" as an ethnic group seeking political autonomy. While these words are used in the Hebrew Bible, the modern Hebrew word *le'umiyut* (leh-oom-ee-YOOT) was coined only in the late nineteenth century to denote modern nationalism. The variation of Jewish identity is also indicated with Modern Hebrew parlance that describes Jews or Jewish institutions as "religious" or "secular" (increasingly, the term "traditional" is also used to connote those not strictly observant of Jewish law but more

8

intentionally observant of Jewish customs and holidays). When talking about Jewish nationalism, then, it is important to keep this historical context in mind. Zionism is not a nationalism based directly on Judaism, though Judaism is a key link that has unified Jews both historically and into the present, regardless of whether they practice Judaism as a religion.

## Understanding Zionism

Understanding the history of Zionism requires the use of a historian's approach, such as engaging with a variety of sources and perspectives, placing them in their various contexts, and acknowledging change over time rather than viewing Zionism as unchanging or unchangeable.[6] A historical approach examines the context in which Zionism emerged, as well as the different and competing political, cultural, economic, or strategic priorities and influences within and around the Zionist movement over time. When Zionism became institutionalized in the new State of Israel, it bore different implications for Israeli politics, society, and identity, both among Jews and non-Jews (most notably Palestinians). Many values and goals of the earlier decades of the Zionist movement both affected and were affected by the establishment of a Jewish State.

Understanding the different perspectives on Zionism requires discussions of different stages of Zionist history, and at times, of disparate groups and individuals. Christian Zionism has origins, influences, theological emphases, and key leaders and institutions distinct from the Zionist movement as a whole. Opposition to Zionism, particularly since the establishment of Israel, has energized major movements both in the Middle East and globally, and has prompted contentious questions about the differences and similarities between anti-Zionism and antisemitism. Diverse perspectives exist on possibilities and visions for the future of Zionism, especially regarding a peace process between Israel and the Palestinians and the ongoing and vibrant discussions surrounding Jewish and Israeli national identity in this context.

# 1 | THE FOUNDATIONS OF ZIONISM

"If I were to sum up the Congress in a word . . . it would be this: At Basel I founded the Jewish State." Theodor Herzl penned these words in an 1897 journal entry, adding, "If I said this out loud today I would be greeted by universal laughter. In five years perhaps, and certainly in fifty years, everyone will perceive it."[1] Herzl is known as the father of Zionism, and his prediction of fifty years for his efforts to come to fruition was indeed astonishingly accurate. Herzl wrote this entry after the First Zionist Congress that had just taken place in Basel, Switzerland. He had originally planned to convene the congress in Munich, Germany, but the city's Jewish community objected (earning them Herzl's nickname for them, "protest rabbis"); such a gathering, they thought, would be fodder for the growing antisemitism that considered Jews inherently separate from the German race. Basel it was, then, and for the nearly 200 Jews who came from fifteen countries, "the inward note was that of a gathering of brothers meeting after the long Diaspora," according to Herzl's colleague and (first) biographer Jacob de Haas.[2] The congress launched the Zionist Organization (ZO), which remained the main Zionist body until the establishment of Israel in 1948, and is still in existence today as the World Zionist Organization.

Despite Herzl's grandiose claims for founding the Jewish state, Zionist activity had already been underway for well over a decade by the time the Basel Conference convened. In the 1880s eastern European Jewish literary and cultural figures had been forging new genres of Jewish cultural expression and exploring their political implications. At this same time, antisemitic violence and political discourse was rising throughout Europe, compelling around 2.5 million Jews to leave eastern Europe between 1881 and 1914. While most resettled in the United States or in other central or western European countries, a small proportion set their sights on a new life in Palestine under the Ottoman Empire.[3] By the time Herzl wrote his landmark book *The Jewish State* in 1896, European Jews had already established agricultural settlements in Palestine and started to retool the Hebrew language from a holy tongue to a daily vernacular. Jews around the world had a range of responses to the crystalizing Zionist movement; while there was an enthusiastic contingent willing to flock to Herzl's conference and perhaps even to Palestine, others supported the cause without adopting it themselves. Others vehemently opposed it on political or religious grounds. Within this diverse landscape of early Zionist thinking and organizing emerged the Zionist Organization and adjacent organizations, transforming political options for Jews amid other major political and social shifts across Europe and the Middle East.

## A LAND AND ITS PEOPLES

Since the Roman conquest in the first and second centuries CE, there have been many changes in political sovereignty in Palestine, from Byzantine, Arab, Crusader, and Ottoman empires— with some more short-lived claimants as well. Throughout these shifts Jewish communities have been continuously living in Palestine, concentrating mainly in what were considered Judaism's four "holy cities": Jerusalem, Hebron, Tiberias, and Safed. These Jews mostly led lives of study and prayer, and drew meager stipends through *halukah*, an alms system from Jewish communities in the

Diaspora who supported these communities as a pious remnant in the land of their heritage. To be sure, these small communities generated significant traditions and texts that impacted Jewish thought and life in the Diaspora as well—most notably the mystical kabbalah forming around the thirteenth century. A trickle of particularly devout and usually aged individuals migrated to the land as a personal step of devotion, ideally to be buried on the Mount of Olives where the Messiah is believed to first appear at the promised redemption. Even though the Jewish Passover liturgy famously declares "next year in Jerusalem," Jewish communities worldwide simply did not consider a mass Jewish immigration to the Holy Land to be a realistic or desirable prospect, and especially did not envision any kind of Jewish political sovereignty over the land.[4] Jewish sovereignty in Eretz Israel was largely considered to be completely in the purview of the future Messiah. In fact, the Talmud issued specific commands against encroaching on the divine chain of events, in what was known as the Three Oaths binding upon Israel, two of which forbid Israel from "ascending the wall" (which was generally interpreted to mean immigrating *en masse* or by force) or antagonizing the nations/Gentiles.[5] "Next year in Jerusalem" was therefore more shorthand for the hope of a speedy dawn of the messianic age than it was any kind of geopolitical goal.

When Zionism emerged in the late nineteenth century, Palestine had been part of the Ottoman Empire, which had been undergoing changes in both domestic and international policies. Its territorial holdings started to shrink with Russia's annexation of Crimea in 1774, the Greek Revolt of 1821, and a separatist uprising by Ottoman governor of Egypt Muhammad Ali, which intensified by the late 1830s. Ottoman officials sought out European aid and enacted imperial reforms in an attempt to strengthen the empire. In what is known as the Tanzimat, or reorganization, the Ottoman Empire canceled the millet system, under which religious communities had different laws, tax rates, and access to certain forms of education and employment, and which had reserved certain privileges and benefits for Muslims.[6] This declaration of equality for religions was in part meant to encourage loyalty and integration into the wider Ottoman state, as well as to adapt to European norms since the French Revolution. The Ottoman government also enacted land reforms in an attempt to increase cash flow and to streamline property tax revenue, consolidating and subsidizing state lands for sale to private landholders. The peasants on these properties continued to live and work on the land after changes in ownership, a custom so established as to be known as "customary rights," which were not explicitly protected by law—a legal reality that later had major implications for tenants when Zionist entities were able to purchase property.

Despite Ottoman reforms to strengthen and centralize its government, other influences impeded social and political cohesion across the empire. Ottoman officials solicited European economic and military aid with a series of agreements known as the Capitulations. In return for loans and military assistance, the Ottoman Empire offered significant trade and legal privileges to European countries. Europeans would not be subjected to heavy tariffs and could import and export freely; they were also allowed to purchase land at the same property tax rates as Ottomans. These trade agreements created a significant economic impact in the Ottoman Empire. Major companies that were primarily European owned, such as the Suez Canal Company, were able to operate within Ottoman territory. Moreover, these European powers were allowed to act as "protectors" of certain religious communities in the Ottoman Empire (France, for instance, claimed protection for Roman Catholics, and Russia over the Eastern Orthodox); members of these protected communities could receive benefits of citizenship of these European countries and could thus become subject to foreign rather than Ottoman law. Protected Christian communities were thus positioned to become main agents for growing European trade and investment.

Social and political responses to these Ottoman reforms varied. Some Ottomans wanted to push the more liberalizing trends of the Tanzimat toward the establishment of a robust parliamentary democracy and an Ottoman civic identity shared by the state's multi-ethnic population. There were also burgeoning ethnic nationalist movements, such as the Arab *Nahda* (Arabic for *"awakening"*), which promoted Arab ethnic identity through literature, journalism, and science. Some nationalist movements had strong separatist goals, and the Russo-Turkish War of 1877–78 led to the Ottoman loss of Romania, Serbia, Montenegro, and Cyprus. The crystallizing Turkish nationalist movement excluded, exploited, and in some regions, violently persecuted non-Turkish groups; Arabs were marginalized, and Ottoman operations carried out ethnic cleansing against Armenians through massacres, expulsion, and forced conversion. Between its territorial losses, socio-political fault lines, and growing debt, European countries gave the Ottoman Empire the epithet "the Sick Man of the East," and competed as beneficiaries should the empire succumb to these ailments.

Considering these major shifts in the Ottoman Empire, Ottoman Palestine was a patchwork of economic and political interests when the Zionist movement began. The European patronage system had ushered a stronger European presence in and around Palestine's holy sites, and its tourism industry increased with a steady stream of officials, investors, and an increasing number of pilgrims. Prominent Arab families served as government intermediaries and ensured collection of Ottoman taxes. Most of the Arab Palestinians engaged in agrarian or pastoral livelihoods (citrus and olive growing were common), though there was also urban commerce, particularly in the coastal cities of Jaffa and Haifa.[7] While Jewish communities throughout the Ottoman Empire (such as in Istanbul, Salonica, Cairo, Beirut, Damascus, and Baghdad) engaged in various forms of commerce and scholarship, the Jewish communities in Ottoman Palestine mostly still eked their living through *halukah*, and mostly spoke Arabic. While Zionists were to poetically refer to the Holy Land as "a land without a people," in reality Ottoman Palestine was certainly not empty.

# HISTORICAL CONTEXT OF THE EMERGENCE OF ZIONISM
## Emancipation

Zionism emerged during a particularly transformative time in European history, what historians call the "Long Nineteenth Century," between the French Revolution in 1789 and the outbreak of World War I in 1914. It was also a time of major shifts within Jewish history in particular. These included the Emancipation, the Jewish Enlightenment known as the Haskalah, the rise of nationalism, and the increase and evolution of antisemitism. A watershed event was the French Revolution's Declaration of the Rights of Man, in which Jewish men were included in equal citizenship of the new French Republic. Until then, Jewish communities across Europe had been administered within *kehillot* (singular *kehillah*, Hebrew for *community*), with separate and limited legal, economic, and cultural autonomy. After Napoleon Bonaparte consolidated his power over the French Empire, he summoned Jewish leaders as a "Sanhedrin" (a term borrowing the legitimacy of the ancient governing council) to ensure they would recognize French legal and political authority over Jewish law. These Jewish leaders assured Napoleon of the compatibility of Jewish religious life and French civic life, declaring the epochal formulation that they were "Frenchmen of the Mosaic faith." As one French official said regarding the civil integration of French Jews, "we must refuse everything to the Jews as a nation and accord everything to Jews as individuals," meaning the legal and economic autonomy the *kehillot* exercised was to dissolve in favor of equal rights and responsibilities among individual French citizens.[8] With the expansion of the Napoleonic Empire spread the civic inclusion of the Jews, and this process, known as Emancipation, happened at various rates across Europe, especially during a revolutionary period in the mid-nineteenth century.

Jewish communities in Europe grappled with the interrelationships between their Jewish identities—both religious and cultural—amid the shifting geopolitical climate. With Jewish communal autonomy weakened in favor of the state, Jewish cohesion was at stake. As a result, Jews identified not primarily as Jews but as members of their nation who were Jewish by religion only—in the words of a famous dictum, living as "a Jew in the home and a man on the street." Some Jewish leaders developed Reform Judaism, which differentiated the religious tenets of Judaism from national ones. Reform congregations adopted architectural and musical elements from Christian churches, rewrote liturgies to be in national vernacular languages, and even removed prayers and references regarding a return to Zion. Other European Jews repudiated Judaism altogether; many converted to Christianity, changed their names, and married non-Jews. As German Jewish author (and convert to Christianity) Heinrich Heine pithily concluded, conversion was the entry ticket for European civilization.

An influential subset of Jewish intellectuals strove to broaden Jewish scholarship, education, and identity beyond Judaism to include the pursuit of Enlightenment philosophy and science. This proliferation of Jewish intellectual and literary activity is known as the Haskalah, or Jewish Enlightenment, and was meant to incorporate Jews into the European intelligentsia, preserve and highlight the distinctive philosophical and cultural strengths of Jewish thought, and synthesize these strengths with a growing body of scientific knowledge. Following the tradition of eighteenth-century German Jewish philosopher Moses Mendelssohn, as well as the earlier influence of Dutch Jewish philosopher Baruch Spinoza, Jewish *maskilim* (Hebrew for *disciples*, but referring specifically to adherents of the Haskalah) promoted Enlightenment science and philosophy into Jewish curricula, education in European languages, and the cultivation of Hebrew from a language of religious texts to a language of modern literature. *Maskilim* integrated European science and languages without yielding their Jewish identity or communal membership, though their "freethinking" deviation from rabbinic authority at times cost them their livelihoods or even estranged families. The strengthening of Jewish knowledge and literature through adopting wider European texts and disciplines created fertile ground for new thinking about Jewish cultural and political identity.

## Nationalism

Another trend that was an important influence for the formation of Zionism was the increasingly prominent role of nationalism, by which groups identified as nations and desired a corresponding governing entity as a nation-state. Historians have postulated that the rise of print media in the sixteenth century and its wider availability in different vernacular languages led linguistic groups to imagine themselves as distinct communities, even from those with whom they shared an economy, history, and imperial language.[9] Within the major empires of Europe and Western Asia—such as the Napoleonic Empire, German states, Austro-Hungarian Empire, and Russian Empire—identity and authority began to shift from religion (Catholic, Protestant, Jewish, Eastern Orthodox, Muslim) or class (peasant, nobility, merchant, professional) to language or region. The achievement of a nation-state—a political entity to be ruled primarily by and for distinct nations, as compared to multinational empires—grew in demand, as countries like Greece and Bulgaria sought independence (or in the significant case of Germany, independent German states united to form a larger German state). As early as 1862, Polish Rabbi Zvi Hirsch Kalischer, now considered a "forerunner" of Zionism, exhorted his fellow Jews "to hear the examples of the Italians, Poles, and Hungarians."[10] Zionism thus drew inspiration from other movements toward ethnic, religious, and territorial cohesion that was crystallizing in nineteenth-century Europe.

While there is significant debate and controversy around the subject, it is also worth noting the context of European colonialism that influenced Zionism. Many nations viewed the acquisition of territory as an important vehicle for bolstering national unity, resources, and markets. The widespread European perception that land occupied by non-Europeans was available for the taking was evident in the so-called Scramble for Africa that took place between the 1884 Berlin Conference and the turn of the twentieth century. One significant form of European expansion was settler colonialism, in which Europeans not only controlled an overseas territory but relocated with the aim of replacing its political, economic, and cultural institutions and norms. South Africa, Australia, and North America were some of the major European settler destinations, but there were other smaller-scale instances as well.

Unfortunately, the term "settler colonialism" oftentimes serves a "shibboleth" or gatekeeping function in discussions of Zionism, so that its introduction shuts down any further exchange; on one end of the spectrum it is viewed as such an egregious label that whoever wields it is immediately discredited, and on the other end it obscures unique factors in the Zionist context so that anything associated with Zionism is considered inherently effacing to indigenous populations. Yet early Zionist rhetoric indeed reveals some widespread colonialist assumptions; Herzl envisioned that Zionists "can be the outpost of civilization against barbarism," and his colleague Max Nordau announced at one gathering that, "we will endeavor to do in the Near East what the English did in India . . . It is our intention to come to Palestine as the representatives of culture and to take the moral boundaries of Europe to the Euphrates River."[11] Israel Zangwill, who advocated for a Jewish state in any viable territory and not necessarily in Palestine, asserted, "the world still holds—though it will not long hold—vast tracts of comparatively unexploited or neglected territory," noting that "British East Africa is only one instance."[12] Even the German Jewish intellectual Moses Hess, who predated the Zionist movement, thought if the Jews returned to the Holy Land they would be "bearers of civilization to peoples who are still inexperienced," mediators in "unknown regions which must ultimately be open to civilization," and that their "capital will again bring the wide stretches of barren land under cultivation."[13] These examples are some of many that indicate that the notion of gathering people on a mass scale to create a new society, economy, and government in a place where a different culture's society, economy, and government already existed undoubtedly influenced Zionists' worldviews, even if Zionists did not generally envision achieving this in the same ways as European colonial powers.

## EUROPEAN ANTISEMITISM, FROM EAST TO WEST

As Jewish Emancipation unfolded by varying degrees throughout Europe, the Russian Empire remained especially closed to Jewish integration or equality. Occasionally Russian reforms removed some of the more draconian policies against Russian Jews, but Jews still faced many restrictions: Jews in the Russian Empire needed special permits to reside outside the region in the westernmost part of the empire known as the Pale of Settlement (the coastal Ukrainian city of Odessa was the noteworthy exception to this rule), universities maintained strict Jewish quotas, and certain professions remained closed to Jews. Jews were also popularly scapegoated and vilified in the Russian press, and religious prejudices tended to heighten during Christian holidays (especially Holy Week, with its remembrance of the crucifixion, recalling the antisemitic charge of Jewish deicide), or with recurrent accusations of blood libel, a centuries-old (and completely unfounded) belief that Jews kill Christian children to use their blood for ritual purposes like baking matza. This hatred and prejudice fomented pogroms, a term for mob violence and pillaging against Jewish communities. Jews were largely unprotected by

Russian security forces, and at times the czarist regime even instigated pogroms to deflect possible unrest against itself (conversely,
anticzarist groups also believed the pogroms could help destabilize
the government, and therefore Jewish communities were at times
thrown in the crossfire of opposing forces). In the chaos of the assassination of Czar Alexander II in 1881, pogroms erupted across 160
eastern European towns. This scale of persecution, and the widespread poverty that accompanied it, constituted a major push factor
for massive Jewish emigration.

The increasing antisemitic social unrest and inequality also cat-
alyzed other Jewish efforts of social change. Many Russian Jews
embraced the growing communist and socialist platforms and associations. Some established the Bund, a Jewish socialist organization that
addressed the specific challenges, opportunities, and cultural assets of
the Jews in eastern Europe and promoted Jewish national and cultural
autonomy within a socialist framework. Many other Russian Jews did
their best to adhere to Orthodoxy and religious education even amid
the poverty, violence, and communal emigration. *Maskilim* hoped that
improved education, adoption of the Russian language, and even agricultural development in Jewish communities could catalyze social uplift
by which they would not be viewed as much as "backward" outsiders
and could earn wider societal acceptance. These *maskilim* were devastated when their increased education and assimilation did not stop them
from being the same targets of attacks as the "alien" Orthodox Jews.

In western and central Europe, it was not *in spite of* increasing
inclusion of Jews into European society that antisemitism accelerated
in the nineteenth century, but in many ways *because of* it. Early Zionist
Max Nordau surmised that emancipatory policies toward Jews were
adopted throughout Europe not because Europeans valued them but
because it was just considered part of being an advancing European
nation, comparing it to the inclusion of a piano in a full furniture
set even if it is never played. Successful Jewish inclusion into the

professions and government was thus viewed by many conservative and nationalist sectors as a sign of revolutionary social disintegration.

As race increasingly became a feature of national ideologies, influential scholars and journalists began to propagate the idea that Jews were a separate race altogether, inassimilable into various European nations. Moses Hess, writing as early as 1860, claimed that "even an act of conversion can not relieve the Jew of the enormous pressure of German antisemitism. The Germans hate the religion of the Jews less than they hate their race—they hate the peculiar faith of the Jews less than their peculiar noses."[14] A racially motivated antisemitism cultivated by those like German politician Wilhelm Marr, who coined the term "anti-Semitism" and formed the League of Anti-Semites in 1879, did not distinguish between Jews who practiced Judaism or those who may have even converted to Christianity; in fact, Marr claimed that "it is precisely the baptized Jews who infiltrate furthest, unhindered in all sectors of society and political life." Marr believed that "Jewry's control of society and politics, as well as its practical domination of religious and ecclesiastical thought, is still in the prime of its development," thus advancing a fear-mongering worldview that Jews, as a race, were a growing threat to all areas of life.[15] In Vienna, Karl Lueger, another figurehead of German antisemitic politics, was elected mayor in 1895 on a heavily antisemitic campaign. Suspected racial differences went in tandem with suspected national differences; Russian Zionist Moshe Leib Lilienblum described the Jews' position thus: "the opponents of nationalism see us as uncompromising nationalists, with a nationalist God and a nationalist Torah; the nationalists see us as cosmopolitans, whose homeland is wherever we happen to be well off . . . the liberals say we are conservative and the conservatives call us liberal . . . Officialdom accuses us of circumventing the laws of the land—that is, of course, the laws directed specifically against us."[16] As Max Nordau reflected, this phenomenon of political, national, and racial antisemitism "revealed to a mortified Jew, who thought anti-Semitism was gone forever, the true picture of his situation."[17] Even though the process of Emancipation lifted social, political, and legal barriers against Jews in various European countries, Jews—regardless of their practice of Judaism—became targets of racial exclusion, vitriol, and scapegoating.

The apparent inescapability of persecution led many Jews to consider what it would look like to have their own state, like those emerging that century. In 1882 Russian Jewish writer Leon Pinsker called for the creation of a Jewish homeland in one of the earliest and most influential Zionist texts, *Auto-Emancipation*. Pinsker was one of the well-educated Russian Jews who experienced the pogroms of 1881 as a point of no return for eastern European Jews. He observed that even outside Russia, "*legal emancipation* is not *social* emancipation, and with the proclamation of the former the Jews are still far from being emancipated from their exceptional *social position*."[18] This left Jews existing in an inherently disturbing category: "that of a people without a body . . . the frightening form of one of the dead walking among the living."[19] He reasoned that even if "regular" foreigners are not fully accepted by a society, they are at least understood as belonging to another, whereas Jews are permanently alien because they do not belong to another place. Pinsker's solution for this problem was that "we finally must have a home, if not a country of our own," and Jews must organize to achieve this themselves.[20] Pinsker's text was pivotal for the emergence of the idea that Jews might congregate into an independent political entity similar to those of other European nation-states.

Over a decade later, Theodor Herzl arrived at the same conclusion as a response to his continual exposure to antisemitic prejudice and exclusion, despite his middle-class status and the fact that he did not practice Judaism (Herzl's nonobservance was almost conspicuous—he famously did not circumcise his son, and would even put up a Christmas tree in his home). Herzl recalled the 1894 Dreyfus trial in France, at which he served as a newspaper correspondent, as a turning point for his politics. Alfred Dreyfus was a Jewish officer in the French army who was framed for treason and sentenced to prison. He served almost five years of his sentence, after which he was eventually retried after many substantiated appeals for his innocence, and ultimately exonerated. The whole affair displayed the depth and popularity of antisemitic assumptions in France – the ostensible birthplace of Jewish Emancipation – and exposed a wider fault line in French society on issues of religion and the state. Herzl's description of his awakening has become a founding myth in the history of Zionism, since most of his biographers have taken Herzl's diary reflections at face value, though French Historian Jacques Kornberg has convincingly debunked the Dreyfus trial as Herzl's epiphany. Even if the trial was not the revelation Herzl claimed it was, the pervasive antisemitism that the Dreyfus Affair exemplified certainly spurred Herzl to his historic movement. As he declared in *The Jewish State*, "the decisive factor is our propelling force. And what is that force? The plight of the Jews."[21]

# EARLY ZIONIST ORGANIZING

At this time of increasing persecution, eastern European Jewish writers formed the earliest organized efforts to develop Zionist ideas and aims. The network Hibbat Zion (Hebrew for "Love of Zion," also known collectively as the Hovevei Zion, "Lovers of Zion") established branches throughout eastern Europe to cultivate modern Hebrew language and literature, especially through founding various periodicals, as well as the first Zionist publishing house. Eliezer Ben Yehuda, known as the father of Modern Hebrew, moved to Jerusalem in 1881 to establish the first Hebrew-speaking household and develop a Modern Hebrew dictionary. He insisted that Hebrew literature could only emerge in a Hebrew-speaking society: "the more I endeavored to speak Hebrew, the more I expanded my conversational boundaries, the more suffocated I started to feel," Ben Yehuda recalled. "It's a lovely language for spiritual matters . . . but . . . when we hit more trivial and vulgar matters, we were struck mute!"[22] The term "Zionist," coined by Nathan Birnbaum, was initially in reference to these cultural activities of the Hovevei Zion. The organization convened its first conference in 1884 (under the presidency of Leon Pinsker) and established branches in eastern and central Europe as well as in Ottoman Palestine.

Arguably the foremost proponent of the cultural aspirations of Hibbat Zion was Ahad HaAm, Hebrew for "One of the People" and the pen name of Russian Jewish writer Asher Ginsburg. Despite the humble and homogenizing pen name by which he is known, he urged the cultivation of a literary elite that would gradually reform Jewish culture from the top down, rather than for a popular mass movement. In his classic 1894 essay "Torah [Law] of the Heart," he wrote that "the function of literature is to plant the seed of new ideas and new desires."[23] Once the literary vanguard sows these seeds, "in time the new idea or desire becomes an organic part of consciousness, an independent dynamic force, no more related to its literary origin than is the work of a great writer to the primer from which he learned at school." For the previous two millennia, Ahad HaAm argued, Jews had been constrained by a slavish dependence on "the written word" to which they responded only by "a prearranged and artificial plan."[24] However, the Jewish Haskalah, he suggested, placed undue blame on the written word itself and on the rabbis who transmit it, when the root problem lay in the assumptions prevalent across Jewish culture. Ahad HaAm aimed to revitalize the culture in total, and asked "the paramount question" of "whether there is any possibility of curing this long-standing disease; whether the Jewish people can still shake off its inertia, regain direct contact with the actualities of life, and yet remain the Jewish people."[25] Instead of a straightforward infusion of Enlightenment thinking into Jewish thought, which could inadvertently destroy distinctive Jewish culture altogether, Zionism would transform the Jewish people while also keeping its culture intact. "True Hibbat Zion [Love of Zion] is not merely a part of Judaism, nor is it something added on to Judaism; it is the whole of Judaism, but with a different focal point," Ahad HaAm declared.[26] Crucially, he did not want to reject or change Jewish texts, but to center "the ideal of our nation's unity [and] development through the expression of universal values in the terms of its own distinctive spirit."[27] Ahad HaAm and fellow Lovers of Zion therefore did not want to reject Judaism outright but to refocus it to prioritize a Jewish national spirit that did not rely exclusively on *halakha*.

Taking place alongside the cultural efforts of the 1880s was the establishment of small Jewish agricultural colonies in Palestine. Many of the immigrants to these colonies imbibed the value, common in eastern Europe at the time, that there was a symbiotic relationship between a nation and the cultivation of its land. The most preeminent of these groups was the Bilu, which began settlement activities in 1882. Bilu was an acronym from Isaiah 2:5, "House of Jacob, come let us go" (their earlier name was based on a similar exhortation in Exodus 14:15, "tell the children of Israel to go forth"). The Bilu completely rejected European emancipation as a viable future for Jews; as their founding document proclaimed: "Sleepest thou, O our nation? What hast thou been doing until 1882? Sleeping, and dreaming the false dream of Assimilation."[28] They emphasized the need to join cultural efforts together with agricultural ones, specifically in the territory of Eretz Israel, and traveled the Russian Empire for recruitment and fundraising, eventually establishing offices in Istanbul and Jaffa to facilitate the immigration of primarily young, able-bodied Jewish men. They also required members to be religiously observant, though their piety was under great suspicion by more traditional leaders. Even though the group was strikingly small—they usually had between ten and thirty members operating in Palestine at any given time, and only had around sixty overall—the Bilu are considered the forerunners of the first wave of Zionist immigration, and their colony in the inland town of Gedera remains an icon of Jewish return to the land. The Bilu's motto, building upon the Shema, illustrates their synthesis of biblical and religious tradition with territorial aspirations, proclaiming: "Hear O Israel! The Lord is our God, the Lord is One, and our land Zion is our only hope."[29]

Many other early Jewish agricultural settlements procured funds from European Jewish philanthropists who acknowledged the sentimental value of the Holy Land and wanted to alleviate poverty and danger for fellow Jews (and as some of the more cynical observers claimed, did not want these impoverished coreligionists resettling in their own European backyards). Many of these colonies employed not only the Jewish immigrants themselves but also Arabs who had more expertise in local agricultural conditions and could oftentimes work for lower wages. This model of philanthropic dependence and use of cheaper Arab labor became a major flashpoint for inter-Zionist politics in its first decades. This first wave of Jewish agricultural settlement is known in Zionist history as the First *Aliyah*, or first wave of Jewish immigration. *Aliyah* literally means "ascent" or "going up," and Modern Hebrew still uses the word for immigration to the Land of Israel. The most significant waves of immigration before the establishment of Israel are referred to as successive *aliyot* (plural of *aliyah*).

As efforts toward Jewish immigration to Palestine grew alongside the increasing cultural impact of Hovevei Zion, many Orthodox Jews raised serious concerns. Along with the belief that any mass mobilization to immigrate to the Holy Land violated the Three Oaths, rabbis viewed the Zionist goal to transform Hebrew into an everyday language and a secular literature as a profanation of *lashon hakodesh,* or the holy tongue, to be used only for prayer and study. Moreover, since Zionist leaders and ideologues were predominantly not devout observers of *halakha,* the movement stood to threaten the status quo of Jewish communal leadership. Ahad HaAm's essay "Torah of the Heart" seemed to confirm fears of the Zionist desire to overhaul Judaism completely. In 1900, leaders from different streams of Orthodoxy detailed their position against immigration to Eretz Israel in the publication *Light to Those on the Straight Path*. Some rabbis threatened to place their students or community members under a ban (excommunication) for supporting the Zionist movement or even for reading its literature.[30] One rabbinical proclamation in Poland warned, "the core of the Zionist idea was no less than the uprooting of the religion of Moses and Israel. . . . Zionism is liable too to bring upon our nation a greater material disaster than all the disasters brought upon the people by false prophets and disseminators of lies about the Redemption of Israel."[31] They insisted that collaborating with unfaithful leaders would prove ineffectual or even harmful, citing 2 Chronicles 20:35–37, in which the otherwise righteous king Jehoshaphat allied with the wicked king Ahaziah to build a fleet of trading ships and God destroyed the ships as a punishment for such an alliance. Along with this strident Orthodox opposition to Zionism, leaders from the much more liberal stream of Reform Judaism criticized Zionism as well; the Rabbinical Association of Germany objected to Zionism's insinuation that Jews constituted a different nation than the nations to which they already belonged.[32]

Despite a generally widespread opposition among Orthodox (and Reform) Jews, there was an active segment of Orthodox Jews who were compelled by early Zionist aims. Key religious Zionist leaders pursued Jewish settlement in a variety of ways; Rabbi Samuel Mohilever helped to establish a branch of Hovevei Zion in Warsaw and urged Baron Edmond de Rothschild to channel philanthropic efforts toward settling Jews in Palestine. Mohilever was able to attend the First Zionist Congress but died soon after. He was supportive of Herzl's aims and strove to emphasize support for Zionism as a humanitarian and political movement unrelated to divine redemption. He did not consider the Zionists' irreligiosity a disqualification for cooperation, comparing the effort to a rescue from a burning building—the humanitarian situation of the Jews was so dire that it was beside the point whether those who saved them observed Jewish law or not.[33]

Other early religious Zionists were more inclined to align Zionism with halakhic requirements or even with broader redemptive implications. From 1878 Yehiel Michael Pines lived in Palestine as a manager of settlement funds, a writer, and a teacher, and maintained high religious expectations for the new communities of Jewish immigrants. The secularists do not have "a monopoly on the Zionist sentiment," Pines insisted; "I am as much a Lover of Zion as you are, not a whit less. But mine is not the Love of Zion which you have abstracted from the whole Jewish tradition to set it up in a separate existence."[34] In 1892, *Shivat Ziyon* (*Settling Zion*) was published as a collection of texts affirming biblical and halakhic support for settling the Land of Israel. A prestigious Tunisian rabbi, Moshe HaCohen, praised the Zionist movement not only because it saved secular Jews from assimilation to humanism but also for heralding God's coming redemption. He loftily wrote, "and it came to pass that the spirit of the Lord settled in the heart of a hero and warrior who fought ferociously for our brethren. Herzl was his name."[35] For those like HaCohen and other later influential Zionist rabbis, political Zionism could not only coexist with a divine plan but was inextricably linked to it.

## THEODOR HERZL AND THE ZIONIST ORGANIZATION

Zionist organizing entered a pivotal era with the efforts of Theodor Herzl. Herzl's 1896 book *Der Judenstaat* (which is most commonly translated from the German as *The Jewish State* but can also be translated as *"the State of the Jews"*) "came like a lightning bolt in the darkness of night."[36] In this book Herzl outlined the need and strategy for large-scale efforts to achieve a Jewish state. He dismissed earlier small agricultural Jewish settlements, admirable as they were, as "teakettle phenomena" in which steam will rattle a lid, whereas his proposal was more akin to harnessing the same power for a steam engine. Herzl devoted himself to obtaining an internationally recognized charter that would deed a large swath of land to Jews in order for them to establish a national home or a state. He thus sought audiences with high-ranking officials to pitch his vision for a Jewish homeland, which would in turn benefit its diplomatic and financial investors and supporters. Herzl met with the pope and the German kaiser, and after tireless networking, eventually met with the Ottoman sultan himself. While he never obtained his charter, he was the figurehead who envisioned and created the most widely known platform for Jewish nationalism.

After releasing *The Jewish State*, Herzl started the Zionist newspaper *Die Welt* and, most consequentially, created the Zionist Organization, which convened for the first time in 1897. Members attempted to gather annually (not always possible during times of crisis like the world wars) to share progress and opportunities and to vote on organization leadership and policies. Its executive committee, elected by ZO delegates and based out of London, served as the political leadership for the movement in the international arena. The organization also established a number of action committees. Any Jew could become a member of the ZO by "paying the Shekel," which were modest membership dues named after the biblical-era currency.

Herzl and the ZO sought to achieve several sweeping objectives but the details of attaining them were not immediately apparent. In *The Jewish State*, Herzl admitted that "I do not profess to have discovered the shape it may ultimately take," but that "the world needs the Jewish State; therefore it will arise."[37] Herzl insisted that if "sovereignty be granted us over a portion of the globe adequate to meet our rightful national requirements," Zionists will "attend to the rest."[38] The First Zionist Congress ratified the Basel Program, which established the organization's mission statement and four broad tasks. "The aim of Zionism is to create for the Jewish people a homeland in Palestine secured by public law," declared the program.[39] The first task was "the settlement in Palestine of farmers, artisans and laborers."[40] This was in line with Herzl's assumption that the poorest and most desperate Jews would immigrate first and create the infrastructure for ever-increasing absorption of Zionist immigrants of higher socio-economic classes. The second and third points of the Basel Platform concerned unifying Jews worldwide and promoting "Jewish national feeling and national consciousness." The last aim called for the more general "preparatory steps to obtain governmental consent necessary to achieve the goals of Zionism."[41]

Shortly after its formation the ZO established the Jewish Colonial Trust and the Anglo-Palestine Bank in order to raise capital, and the Jewish National Fund to purchase land. Coin boxes for the Jewish National Fund became an icon of grassroots support for Zionism across the Diaspora. The ZO opened the Palestine Information Office in Jaffa in 1908 to better facilitate Jewish immigration and settlement in the region. This movement that began as a small literary awakening and somewhat scattershot settlement program coalesced into an international diplomatic and financial campaign, generating its own cultural and political branches. As one historian writes, "as an ideology, Zionism offered members a guide for analyzing the world, a blueprint for changing it, and a culture for living in it. Zionist culture included archetypes, vocabulary, myths, heroes, villains, and styles."[42] These archetypes, vocabulary, myths, heroes, villains, and styles continued to mature, clash, and transform as the Zionist movement grew and as it confronted broader geopolitical forces in its first decades.

# 2 | CULTURE WAR, WORLD WAR, AND THE MANY TYPES OF ZIONISM

## INTRODUCTION

During the Sixth Zionist Congress in 1903, delegates debated a proposal so loudly and long into the night that they were warned several times not to wake the residents of Basel.[1] At some points during the meeting, people allegedly wept; some staged walkouts from meeting sessions. This 1903 congress is widely accepted as a decisive moment in Zionist history, and for Zionist leaders and delegates it was certainly viewed as an unprecedented crisis within the movement. The rupture was due to Theodor Herzl's news that he was considering an offer for the Jews to settle in British East Africa in pursuit of their Zionist project.

Britain had claimed control of the territory of what is now Kenya since the 1880s, and had been looking to establish there a nonindigenous population amenable to British economic and political interests. When Herzl got the opportunity to meet with the British colonial secretary Joseph Chamberlain, the latter suggested the Zionists take East Africa into consideration as an autonomous zone within the British Empire. The Ottoman sultan had already rejected Herzl's proposal of a charter for the Zionists in Palestine, and Herzl had also reached a dead end on the possibility of negotiating British-controlled territory on the Sinai Peninsula, just outside Palestine. In Herzl's view, the offer in East Africa was the most tangible gain the

Zionists had made to date.[2] While it was not Palestine or even in its close proximity, Herzl believed the proposal offered key advantages: it would provide an open refuge for the increasing numbers of Jews fleeing pogroms and discrimination, and it could be a base from which to establish and implement a Jewish government and to campaign for a charter in Palestine at a later stage (in the words of Herzl's colleague, it would be "a drill ground for our national forces"[3]). Perhaps more importantly for Herzl, taking the East Africa offer into serious consideration meant keeping the lines of negotiation open with the British Empire, and that was a door he did not want to close. Furthermore, Herzl hoped that a British offer of a piece of its empire might prompt the Ottoman Empire to reconsider an offer to the Zionists as well; "our road to Zion will have to be paved with charters," he justified to a colleague concerned about such a plan.[4]

As it turned out, many other Zionists thought even the consideration of such an offer was a betrayal from Herzl, and some even called his leadership and vision into question. Many "Zion Zionists," as they called themselves, argued it flatly contradicted the Basel Platform, which was to obtain "a homeland in Palestine secured by public law," and they were unconvinced that it would be a waystation to Palestine. Ahad HaAm lambasted Herzl for presenting the proposal to the congress, declaring, "the deed you have done at Basel is no less in my eyes than a public change of religion."[5] When the 1903 Zionist congress controversially compromised to approve an expedition to East Africa before turning down Britain outright, key Zionist leaders still fought against it and viewed the decision as destabilizing for the movement. Chaim Weizmann, who would later serve as the first president of Israel, wrote "a man comes along and transforms our entire programme at one go and here we are, all confused, devising stratagems to escape from the predicament."[6] In response to the controversy, Herzl drafted a letter of resignation from the organization he founded, but after many mediation meetings and conciliatory letters the various sides reconciled. Moreover, when the Zionist expedition

in East Africa did take place, it proved thoroughly unpromising, clos-
ing the possibility of a Jewish settlement in East Africa once and
for all.

It was not long after this affair that Herzl died of heart disease—
likely brought on by severe stress—at the young age of forty-four.
Zionism thus lost its key diplomat and visionary, and even though the
ZO continued to operate from London, the Zionist center of gravity
shifted in many ways back to eastern Europe. Even though the East
Africa debates came to naught for the Zionist movement, the fault
lines of this controversy represented deeply rooted differences among
Zionists regarding the movement's overall goals and strategies. As
the Zionist Organization grew in number and stature, these various
streams and emphases continued to vie for influence and direction of
the movement. When World War I broke out in 1914, the geopolitical
landscape in which Zionism operated shifted even further, creating
new challenges and opportunities.

## THE PROBLEM OF THE JEWS VERSUS THE PROBLEM OF JUDAISM

Zionism is not a monolith, and in fact many proponents of the same
goal—a Jewish homeland—pursued it with conflicting and at times
even diametrically opposed methods and motivations. The various
streams of Zionism can be categorized by their various diagnoses of
the problems Jews faced, the solutions they offered, and the means
by which the Jewish nation could establish a successful homeland.[7] A
major underlying cleavage of Zionism was whether the diagnosis was
for the "problem of the Jews" or the "problem of Judaism"—in other
words Zionists debated whether their movement was primarily meant
to save Jewish individuals and populations from poverty, danger, and
discrimination, or to prevent Judaism and Jewish culture from disap-
pearing. Different diagnoses thus prompted different solutions—those
who emphasized physical Jewish survival tended to support mass
migration and establishment of a state in any inhabitable territory,

while those focused on revitalizing Jewish thought, culture, and education stressed a connection to their ancient homeland, even if it was not as politically or logistically expedient. Subgroups of Zionists also disputed whether or not the Jewish nation needed to solve their existential and political problems in alliance with other countries—even those in which Jews were heavily persecuted.

The rivalry between Herzl and Ahad HaAm represented divergences on the answers to the problem of the Jews versus the problem of Judaism. Ahad HaAm had long derided the concept of mass Jewish immigration to Palestine. His famous 1891 article "Truth from Eretz Yisrael" detailed his trip to Palestine and his impression that the local Arab society would not be receptive to large-scale European Jewish settlement, and that therefore Zionists should not or could not pursue mass settlement. Instead, Ahad HaAm maintained that the main task of Zionism was to establish a Jewish cultural elite in Palestine as a "spiritual center," a cultural spring in the Jewish ancient homeland from which Jews in the Diaspora would draw for national identity and development. He preferred that "[Eretz] Israel . . . would constitute a centre for our national life as a whole and exert a spiritual influence on all other parts of the people, those who would remain in foreign lands, to cleanse them of the filth of their inner slavery and to unite them into a single national body with a single spirit."[8] In this way the Jews losing their national identity through assimilation or persecution could become "so molded by [the spiritual center] that its imprint will be recognizable in all their way of life and thought, individual and social."[9] Zionism would thus serve as a centripetal force for Jewish culture as a whole, regardless of whether Jews remained in Diaspora and whether they followed *halakha*.

Ahad HaAm continued his insistence on cultural pursuits rather than mass migration even as Herzl launched the Zionist Organization. In his 1897 article "The Jewish State and the Jewish Problem," Ahad HaAm criticized the First Zionist Congress for its emphasis on a

Jewish state rather than a Jewish national center. He wondered if the broad invitation to the first congress for simply anyone "who expresses his agreement with the general programme of Zionism" was perhaps a red flag for the new organization's cultural anemia. Ahad HaAm also considered Herzl's goal for an international charter wildly unrealistic and therefore an unviable path for solving the material problems of the Jews like poverty and discrimination.[10] He warned that Herzl's logic "implies that failure to end the dispersion would mean extinction," an ultimatum that Ahad HaAm refused to accept.[11] Zionists should therefore commit themselves to the task of national renewal regardless of "any [political] condition, because the condition might not be fulfilled."[12] Ahad HaAm also insisted that the ZO's political platform essentially reproduced the problem of Jewish assimilation on a national scale by trying to create a Jewish version of another European nation-state. He cited Herzl's 1902 utopian novel *Altneuland* (German for *"Old-New Land"*), which depicted what Herzl called the "New Society" in Palestine. Ahad HaAm accused this envisioned society of lacking any specifically Jewish character, since it would be characterized primarily by technological know-how, business acumen, and liberal values born of the European Enlightenment. All members of society would have freedom of conscience and religion regardless of their national background—much like the post-Emancipation poetic slogan of "be man in the streets, and Jew in the home."[13] No one depicted in this new society spoke Hebrew. For Ahad HaAm, then, Herzl's diplomatic approach was not only logistically unviable but culturally bankrupt and was therefore impotent to solve *either* the problem of the Jews or the problem of Judaism.

Despite criticism like Ahad HaAm's, Herzl sincerely believed the Zionist movement could feasibly solve the "problem of the Jews" by improving their material condition and possibly by ending antisemitism altogether.[14] He insisted that the Zionist movement was capable of addressing the causes of antisemitism at their roots.[15] For one,

Herzl believed that Zionism allowed Jews to assert their own national pride and thus escape antisemitic accusations that Jews were culturally, politically, or economically rootless, thus either dependent upon other nations or bent on destabilizing them. If the Jews obtained an internationally recognized charter and built a strong, scientific society, Herzl maintained, the world would respect the Jews' independence and contributions. In this scenario, Jews could therefore leave countries in which they lived "as honored friends" in a "gradual [and] well-regulated" process.[16] Herzl also asserted that Zionism would stem antisemitism that arose when "we [Jews] naturally move to those places where we are not persecuted, and there our presence soon produces persecution."[17] He reasoned that if impoverished and/or religious Jews instead had a Jewish state to which they could immigrate, they would not move to established Jewish Diaspora communities and in so doing stir prejudice and xenophobia against Jews as a whole. Herzl stridently believed that by reasserting Jewish national identity in the community of nations, and by physically resettling Jewish populations elsewhere so that Europeans would not view them as alien or burdensome, Zionism would alleviate or even solve the physical and social impact of antisemitism.

Despite his focus on alleviating antisemitism, Herzl did not, as Ahad HaAm had claimed, only want to solve the material "problem of the Jews," but anticipated that Jews would thrive culturally if their material suffering was resolved. At the First Zionist Congress Herzl famously announced that Zionism was a return to Judaism before it was a return to land; he did not just want to create a Jewish state but to stop the cultural drift of assimilated Jews like himself from the Jewish people.[18] However, Ahad HaAm had some grounds to complain that Herzl seemed largely unconcerned with and even unaware of the condition of Judaism or Jewish culture itself. Herzl thought Hebrew as a modern language was an unrealistic goal. He suggested a Jewish state could be a multilingual society comprised of the languages of its immigrants, and whatever became the state's dominant language (in his diary he even speculated German) would be purely practical and culturally inconsequential.[19] But for Herzl, if a Jewish state were established with freedom of conscience and religion, citizens would be guaranteed freedoms to pursue Hebrew literature or observance of various streams of Judaism without it being a necessary feature of the state. Solving the practical "problem of the Jews," then, would provide the freedom for Jews to address the cultural "problem of Judaism."

## ZIONIST FACTIONS

Herzl had a pragmatic reason to avoid cultural and religious objectives in his movement: solidifying the role of Judaism in a Jewish state could potentially sow division among different cultural and religious constituencies that might otherwise support the Zionist cause. However, Herzl's preference to keep cultural and political questions separate often underscored how the two were in many ways inextricable from one another. Zionists did not fit into neat political and cultural camps, since those who foregrounded a diplomatic solution to the problem of the Jews cared about the problem of Judaism as well, and conversely those who prioritized national culture as a solution to the problem of Judaism also sought tangible, political goals. Making matters more complicated were differences within these priorities, such as which political goals were desirable, or what form national culture should take—and particularly its relationship to Judaism. In 1901 the Zionist Organization bylaws changed to allow the creation of different parties or affiliate branches within the organization to better represent the different constituencies' approaches to these cultural and political questions. This structural change facilitated a shift in activity from regional Zionist branches to association by parties or factions with different interpretations of how Zionism intersected with religion, economics, culture, and diplomacy. These parties allowed groups to pursue their respective agendas within the overarching objectives of the Zionist Organization, but their differences loomed at Zionist gatherings as possible sparks of controversy or, even worse, dissolution.[20]

One of the earliest and most prominent groups to form was the Democratic Faction, which advocated within the ZO to cultivate and foreground modern Hebrew language and literature, education, science, and technology. They also strove to prevent religion from interfering in these areas. While many prominent members of the group did not oppose religion itself or the practice of Judaism, their founding program deemed it "inconsistent with the national character of Zionism."[21] Education was a particularly contentious issue, as Zionists of the Democratic Faction did not want traditional rabbinical teaching and scholarship (and its widespread repudiation of non-Jewish disciplines) to chart the direction of education in the movement. Ultimately Ahad HaAm, as a major early figurehead for this faction, proposed the enduring compromise that there should be two tracks of education to accommodate both the "modernists" and Orthodox within the Zionist movement. He exhorted that "each shall make the ideal of national revival, in the modern sense, the basis of education; but on this foundation each is at liberty to erect its own superstructure in its own way."[22] The Democratic Faction also wanted to address the tumultuous sociopolitical situation of the Jews of eastern Europe, and in 1906 passed a platform endorsing what they called "present work"—advocating for improvement of Jewish conditions in their various countries of residence. While this decision seemed to deflect from the Zionist goal of removing Jews *from* the Diaspora, the group viewed it as advancing the Basel Platform's task of uniting the Jewish nation by balancing the need to protect and strengthen Jewish society as it was in the present, regardless of how close it was to endorsing or achieving Zionist aims in the future.

## RELIGIOUS ZIONISM

While cultural Zionists coalesced into a formal faction, religious Zionists also established their own party within the ZO. A contingent of Orthodox delegates had as early as the First Zionist Congress tried to demand a rabbinical council to oversee cultural and propaganda activities of the movement, but their request was denied by the majority of delegates.[23] When the Democratic Faction formed to fulfil essentially that same purpose, religious Zionists formed the Mizrahi Party (an acronym of the Hebrew for "*Spiritual Center*") in 1902 to steer either the ZO from cultural matters altogether or to guard cultural developments against extreme secularization. Religious Zionists found themselves as a double minority of sorts—religious among predominantly secular Zionists, and Zionist among predominantly anti-Zionist Orthodox. Mizrahi hoped to establish further inroads within Orthodox communities, who continued to largely oppose the Zionist movement. Rabbi Yitzhak Yaakov Reines presided over Mizrahi, and published a new religious Zionist manifesto, *A New Light on Zion*, in 1902. Reines framed the religious Zionists as the fullest manifestation of the movement, since "a fundamental basis of faith is to believe in the return of the people of Israel in their land."[24] In a statement that encapsulates the charged polarization that took place among Zionists at the time, Reines wrote that "the Zionists say that every Jew who is not a Zionist is not a Jew. I say that every Zionist who is not a Jew is not a Zionist."[25] Mizrahi remained the main representative body of religious Zionists, and later became its own political party in the early State of Israel.

Perhaps the most significant leader and ideologue of religious Zionism was Rabbi Avraham Isaac Kook (1865–1935), who considered the mobilization of Jewish nationalism to be a sign of approaching messianic redemption. Kook maintained that the Land of Israel was the "essence of [Jewish] nationhood," and that the Jewish people must be united with the Land as requisite component not only of

Jewish redemption but world redemption as a whole. "All the civilizations of the world will be renewed by the renaissance of our spirit," Kook taught; "all quarrels will be resolved, and our revival will cause all life to be luminous with the joy of fresh birth. All religions will don new and precious raiment, casting away whatever is soiled, abominable, and unclean."[26] Kook's ideology toward secular Zionists was not as defensive as the Mizrahi Party, because in Kook's interpretation, Zionists were not rebels against God's will who threatened the cohesion of the nation but were rather unassuming instruments of God. "The spirit of Israel is so closely linked to the spirit of God that a Jewish nationalist, no matter how secularist his intention may be, must, despite himself, affirm the divine," Kook concluded.[27] They may think their nationalism is like any other nationalism, but this is a "grave error" that leads them to try, unsuccessfully, "to sever the national from the religious element of Judaism."[28] In 1905, Kook agreed to serve as a rabbi for a Zionist community in Jaffa, and became the first Ashkenazi Chief Rabbi of Palestine under the later British administration. He wrote many texts and also established the religious Zionist school Mercaz HaRav Yeshiva, which is influential to this day. The conciliatory posture toward secular Zionism that those like Kook and Rabbi Samuel Mohilewer espoused influenced religious Zionism to gradually adopt practices and values of the wider Zionist movement, such as the importance of agricultural labor and the formation of international youth networks.

## NEGATION OF THE EXILE

Some Zionists sought radical solutions to the problem of the Jews and the problem of Judaism, demanding total revolution for both. Those in this stream of Zionism called for "negation of the exile [galut]": leaving the Diaspora to settle in Eretz Israel was only a start, these Zionists wanted to also purge Jewish national culture of what they viewed as diasporic traits and institutions. Micah Joseph

Berdichevski, a poet and influential exponent of the notion of negating the Diaspora, proclaimed that the Jews' fate as a nation depended on breaking their dependence on religious tradition propagated by "erring shepherds."[29] "The resurrection of Israel depends on a revolution—the Jews must come first, before Judaism—the living man, before the legacy of his ancestors," Berdichevski urged, emphasizing an irreconcilable dichotomy between the well-being of the Jewish people and the continuation of their religion. This shift in emphasis from Judaism to the Jews, Berdichevski insisted, would require "fundamental transvaluations in the whole course of our life, in our thoughts, in our very souls."[30] Another Zionist figurehead posited that simply relocating to the Land of Israel would not itself negate the exile, since "*Galut* [Exile] . . . is a way of life which requires radical change, a complete revolution in our *Galut* notions and attitudes and in our *Galut* view of life."[31] These radical thinkers upheld Zionism as the necessary catalyst for this Jewish cultural revolution.

Calls for negation of the exile often spoke of Judaism and Jewish life in diaspora not as a reservoir of national culture but at times in disparaging or even damning terms. Russian Zionist philosopher Jacob Klatzkin pronounced severe judgment: "The Galut does not deserve to survive," he concluded. "The Galut has a right to life for the sake of liberation from the Galut," Klatzkin grimly asserted; "without the goal of a homeland, the Galut is nothing more than a life of deterioration and degeneration, a disgrace to the nation and a disgrace to the individual, a life of pointless struggle and futile suffering, of ambivalence, confusion, and eternal impotence. It is not worth keeping alive."[32] In other words, the only value in the Jews' exile was their desire to end it. These radical Zionists especially condemned the esteemed role religious study had played in Jewish life, arguing that the emphasis on study promoted physical weakness, creative inertia, and passive resignation to divine purposes even in the face of mortal threat. A statement from the Zionist youth group HaShomer

HaTzair (Hebrew for "the Young Guard") declared that, "we strive for an end to the idolatrous worship of books which is typical of us. Everything we say or write or think gives off the odor of mold on worn-out pages."[33] Hayim Nachman Bialik, considered the first Zionist national poet, depicted a similar critique through one of his most famous poems, in which a man seeks advice from a rabbi whether his wife was still ritually pure if she was raped during a pogrom—an indirect yet seething critique of those who prioritize religious conformity in the midst of communal tragedy.[34]

Many Zionists believed that one of their major flaws in exile was physical weakness, and the concept of the "Muscle Jew" or "Muscle Judaism" grew in prominence in Zionist discourse and community organizing. Max Nordau introduced the term in a speech at the Second Zionist Congress, during which he promoted the importance of Zionist physical education. In a later article "Jewry of Muscle," Nordau floridly declared that "too long, all too long, we have been engaged in the mortification of our own flesh. Or rather, to put it more precisely— others did the killing of our flesh for us. Their extraordinary success is measured by hundreds of Jewish corpses in the ghettos, in the churchyards, along the highways of medieval Europe."[35] He urged the development of "new muscle Jews"— specifically males—who would display heroism, athleticism, and strength. Nordau's call for muscle Judaism provided the impetus for the creation of the Zionist Bar Kochba Gymnastics Association, the name of which invoked the ancient precedent of a Jewish warrior and political leader Simon Bar Kochba, who led the final Jewish military uprising against the Roman government in Palestine in 132 CE. The platform of the Zionist youth group HaShomer HaTzair expressed similar sentiments, asserting that "we hope that nature will . . . straighten our crooked back, stretch our muscles and strengthen our resolve . . . Our ideal is a young Jew of strong body and courageous spirit."[36] A Zionism imbued with "Muscle Judaism" would replace the legacy of suffering violent persecutions in exile with a culture of physical fitness and defensive readiness.

The emphasis on masculine bodily and military strength as a transformation of exilic life was evident in other areas as well. In his aforementioned poem "The City of Slaughter" (1903), Bialik presents a heartbreaking depiction of the Kishinev Pogroms in 1903, and seems to indict the Jews (and particularly Jewish men) of exile with passivity in the face of violence. Amid gruesome details of bloodshed and rape, the poem states: "Note also, do not fail to note, / In that dark corner, and behind that cask / Crouched husbands, bridegrooms, brothers, peering from the cracks, / Watching the sacred bodies struggling underneath . . . Crushed in their shame, they saw it all; / They did not stir nor move . . . Perhaps, perhaps, each watcher had it in his heart to pray: / *A miracle, O Lord,—and spare my skin this day!*"[37] There were in fact growing numbers of self-defense units in eastern European Jewish communities, some of which were spearheaded by Zionists. The act of training the body and taking up arms was a common theme across the Zionist spectrum, but it was particularly so among those who took a more revolutionary stance toward Judaism and Jewish national culture.

While many of these more radical Zionists condemned the Diaspora as irredeemable, they believed the seeds of revolution were already planted within their pre-exilic Jewish history in the Land of Israel. Zionists otherwise vitriolic toward rabbinic Judaism in Diaspora valorized biblical-era figures like Joshua, Samson, and David as exemplars of national strength and progress. The Bible, being composed in and taking place in ancient Israel, was therefore a source of national rather than religious inspiration. HaShomer HaTzair declared that "for us the Bible stands above all; we wish to make it our primer, for it is the never-failing source of idealism, and will forever remain the spring from which the thirsty may drink."[38] The group claimed that through the Bible they would "absorb the spirit of the ancient

Hebrews, the spirit of the prophets, the spirit of a moral world view."[39] While Berdichevski wrote some of the strongest Zionist criticism against religion, he also conceded that the Bible contained examples of physical flourishing, stating that "many things were bequeathed us by our ancestors which deaden the soul and deny it freedom [but] we also have the 'Song of Songs', we have paeans to life and its bounty."[40] Negation of diaspora was thus considered a reclamation of pre-exilic life, with its examples of military success, fertile agriculture, and literary beauty, as much as it was a rejection of the cultural influences of rabbinic Judaism underlying Jewish life in diaspora.

## LABOR ZIONISM

Many members and sympathizers with the radical streams discussed above were simultaneously proponents of Labor Zionism, which became the most influential stream of the Zionist movement in both culture and politics. Labor Zionism had many influences: the concept of negation of the exile, and the emphasis on physical strength and biblical heritage that came with it, spurred Labor Zionists to idealize manual labor, the agrarian lifestyle of biblical Israelites, and a retreat from vocations considered "exilic" like finance or law. Labor Zionists were also influenced by wider European class politics, especially the socialist and communist movements in their European countries of origin. While pure Marxism condemned nationalism as a form of bourgeois control of the working class, Labor Zionism synthesized nationalism and aspects of communism and socialism in a variety of ways, such as workers' collective management of the means of production (land and property) and the dignity and protection of the worker against the interests of capital. Labor Zionists also varied among themselves regarding the desirability or even applicability of class struggle in the Jewish context. Since there was not a single nation in which Jews composed both a bourgeoisie and proletariat,

Labor Zionists like those in the early group HaPoel HaTzair (Hebrew for *the Young Worker*) maintained that the Marxist insistence on class struggle was not relevant for a people who aimed to create a society from scratch. Others, on the other hand, envisioned Jewish immigrants to Palestine cooperating with indigenous Arab workers to prevent an exploitative capitalist economy. Labor Zionists therefore also differed on whether to cooperate with the Zionist Organization, with its emphasis on capital investment and diplomatic progress rather than grassroots development.

While only a minority of immigrants to Palestine became agricultural workers, this minority influenced the values and strategies of what became the dominant Zionist parties. The earliest of these parties were the more centrist HaPoel HaTzair and the more leftist Poalei Zion (*Workers of Zion*). Along with these parties was the Hehalutz (*Pioneer*) movement that organized agricultural training colonies in various European countries for young Zionists, with the aim of immigrating to Palestine ready to cultivate land. The formation of these groups and proliferation of their ideologies occurred during the period of the Second Aliyah (1904–14), and thus this Aliyah is most closely associated with Labor Zionism in Zionist history and collective memory.

Labor Zionism not only espoused economic and political goals and ideals but cultural goals as well. It was common for Labor Zionists to change their names from European and Ashkenazi names to Hebraicized ones, such as David Green (Ben Gurion), Yitzhak Shimshelevech (Ben Zvi), and Golda Myerson (Meir). Labor Zionist groups established their own newspapers and social clubs. Labor even came to be effectively regarded as a religion, with varying degrees of synthesis with Judaism. The "grandfather" figure of the Labor Zionist movement, A. D. Gordon, is regarded as pioneering the concept of "religion of labor." In 1904, a nearly fifty-year-old Gordon immigrated to Palestine and, without any prior agricultural experience, dedicated himself to farm labor. He wrote extensively on the subject and acted as a mentor for younger Jewish immigrants adopting this way of life. In his 1911 essay "People and Labor," Gordon stressed that the Jews' exclusion from owning and cultivating agricultural lands in diaspora was a form of economic and cultural persecution, and he urged that "from now on our principal ideal must be Labor . . . Only by making Labor, for its own sake, our national ideal shall we be able to cure ourselves of the plague that has affected us for many generations and mend the rent between ourselves and Nature."[41] Gordon touted a certain mystic connection between Jews and the Land, teaching that "there is a cosmic element in nationality . . . best described as the blending of the natural landscape of the Homeland with the spirit of the people inhabiting it."[42] He agreed that Zionism must include cultural pursuits, but maintained that culture could not be expressed by ideologies or "abstract spirit," but had to be enacted through labor, which would restore the mystical connection between a nation and its land. "Farming, building, and road-making—any work, any craft, any productive activity—is part of culture and is indeed the foundation and the stuff of culture," Gordon insisted.[43] Gordon and fellow Labor Zionists furthered this belief that manual labor was not only essential for a successful national economy but for a legitimate and vibrant national culture.

An early tenet of Labor Zionism was known as conquest of labor, a pillar for both major Labor Zionist parties despite their differences. HaPoel HaTzair, for instance, made it part of their platform that "a necessary condition for the realization of Zionism is the conquest of all branches of work in Eretz Israel by Jews."[44] Labor Zionists viewed privately owned Jewish farms, plantations, and burgeoning industries as their key battleground for realizing this. Many Zionist farm owners would hire Arabs as both regular and seasonal employees, since indigenous Arab peasants newly evicted from lands had very few job prospects and were generally more desperate to work for lower wages than immigrant Jews. These Zionist farm owners reasoned that Jewish-owned industries that yielded higher profits were part of building the Jewish national infrastructure as a whole, and thus the nationality of the workers creating it was not decisive. Labor Zionists, however, demanded that Jewish-owned industries should exclusively hire Jewish laborers, since the Jewish immigrants needed secure employment as well as the opportunity to develop the physical and cultural characteristics of a legitimate working class.

The conquest of labor was joined with the Labor Zionist call for the conquest of land. In the period before World War I, this "conquest" took the form of promoting smaller scale and gradual land purchases. This piecemeal approach was not generally endorsed during the leadership of Herzl, who pressed to instead obtain a land charter. But the change in leadership after his death and the ascendance of Labor Zionism paved the way for the creation of *kvutzot* (singular *kvutzah*, literally *group* in Hebrew), communal farms, which were the precursor of the *kibbutz*, or collectively run agricultural community. The kibbutz is still one of the most signature features of Israeli society and history, but it was a minority of Zionist settlement. Degania, the first kibbutz, was established in 1909 near the Sea of Galilee in conjunction with the ZO Palestine Office and a small group of workers. While kibbutzim (plural of kibbutz) are known for their more communistic features of worker governance, community over individual, limitation of private property, and rejection of bourgeois domination (in some more radical kibbutzim even raising children in children's homes instead of as nuclear families), they were not initially collective for idealistic reasons but rather practical. Few Jewish immigrants had the capital to own and operate their own farms, and Zionist leaders believed that communally run farms would be more cost-effective. Even so, the kibbutz became an important economic, strategic, and cultural institution in the course of the Zionist movement, furthering the Labor Zionist emphasis on agriculture, self-sufficiency, and communalism.

Labor Zionists of the Second Aliyah did not consider a physical conquest of territory to be feasible or desirable, but as Zionist land ownership in Palestine increased, so did the need for private security of landholdings. Property security was frequently privately contracted in Ottoman Palestine, but instead of employing indigenous residents, kvutzah and kibbutz members began to organize their own defense. The Labor Zionist group HaShomer formed in 1909 as a network of trained defense units, and was for a time contracted by the ZO Palestine Office, which also funded many of HaShomer's arms purchases. While not all Labor Zionists were involved in HaShomer or trained in armed defense, the group furthered the image of the Second Aliyah as the vanguard for Muscle Judaism and securing the broader project of Hebrew labor and land. As HaShomer's motto asserted, "in blood and fire Judea fell; in blood and fire Judea shall arise."[45]

## ZIONISM IN PALESTINE

It perhaps goes without saying that growing momentum among a movement that stressed conquest of land and labor, as well as imperial diplomacy, raised concerns for the Ottoman subjects already living in the land under consideration. Not long after Zionism emerged, the Ottoman administration officially banned Jewish immigration to Palestine to forestall any possible separatist agitation (Jews were still allowed to immigrate to any other part of the empire). Ottoman administrators also tried to prevent land sales to foreign Jews presumed to be Zionists. However, the Ottomans' ability to enforce this was tenuous at best; Jews in Palestine could simply immigrate under the jurisdiction of European powers who had capitulation agreements with the Ottomans. Land sales, whether by Arab landlords or Ottoman officials, often succeeded for the highest offer. This was especially destabilizing for Arab peasants, since Zionists' purchase contracts generally stipulated that tenants would not remain on the land, thus breaking the chain of customary rights by which Arab peasants stayed through changes in ownership. Evicted tenants were forced to find new landlords or, in many cases, new livelihoods altogether. Despite Palestinian Arabs' frequent attempts to prevent land sales or eviction orders, as well as some complaints to higher Ottoman officials, Arab displacement continued. One Israeli politician later posited that given the scale of economic displacement that took place under the campaign to conquer land and labor, "it is no exaggeration to say that the struggle for Hebrew Labor was the real beginning of the Israeli–Arab war."[46]

Palestinian Arabs raised early concerns about the potential scope of Zionist political goals. Naguib Azoury, an Arab Christian in Beirut and advocate of Arab independence from the Ottoman Empire, was one of the first to comment on the bourgeoning movement. In 1905 Azoury asserted that Arab nationalism was diametrically opposed to the "latent effort of the Jews to reconstitute on a very large scale the ancient Kingdom of Israel." "The fate of the entire world," Azoury (somewhat hyperbolically) continues, "will depend on the final result of this struggle between these two peoples representing two contrary principles."[47] Arabic newspapers *Al-Karmil* (founded 1908) and *Falastin* (founded 1911) conveyed support for a Palestinian national identity and raised caution about the development of the Zionist movement. One Arab Ottoman political activist stated that "we see the Jews excluding themselves completely from the Arabs in language, school, commerce, customs, in their entire economic life. They cut themselves off in the same way from the indigenous government, whose protection they enjoy, so that the population considers them a foreign race."[48] While Zionists recognized and anticipated considerable opposition to their aims, they also maintained a studied ignorance of the scope or magnitude of the opposition. Zionists regularly expressed the assumption that the benefits brought to the area by Zionist development would in time quell any opposition, or alternatively, that opposition could be overpowered.

Jews of the "Old Yishuv," as the Jewish communities before the First Aliyah were known, were in an ambiguous position as Zionism forged more of a presence in Palestine. Those in religious Jewish communities subsisting on *halukah* were less than impressed with the incoming Zionists' immodesty, apparent disregard of religion, and ignorance of local Jewish leadership. Some progressive Ottoman Jews in Palestine had enlisted in movements to democratize the Ottoman Empire, which European Zionists dismissed as naïve or unwelcome attempts in light of similar attempts in Europe. Some Ottoman Jews in Palestine who supported causes for an Ottoman parliamentary revolution would embrace Zionism as a cultural movement compatible within a more democratic Ottoman Empire. The breakup of the Ottoman Empire after World War I made these Ottoman political possibilities moot, and the Old Yishuv drew administratively and politically closer with what became known as simply the Yishuv (the Hebrew word for "*settlement*," in this context used specifically for the Jewish population and governing bodies established in Eretz Israel with the rise of the Zionist movement).

## WORLD WAR I

World War I was a turning point for the trajectory of many nationalist movements, and Zionism was no exception. Most significantly, the entrance of the Ottoman Empire into the war on the side of the Central Powers in 1914 meant that the empire's sovereignty and territory was potentially at stake in the event of a loss. During the war the Ottomans expelled or detained all citizens of enemy nations, which included many Zionists in Palestine who had not become Ottoman citizens. Like many other fronts of the war, most residents of Palestine suffered famine, shortages of supplies, conscription, and tensions with Ottoman military and administrative officials. The outbreak of war thus brought to a halt the normal operation of many communities and initiatives, including Zionism, which relied on international communication and travel. However, Chaim Weizmann, a British Jewish chemist who was high in the Zionist leadership in Britain, occupied an important position in the British war effort by heading the British Admiral laboratories. His contributions gave him privileged access to British affairs, so that while there were not many gains on the ground in Palestine, the Zionist Organization made diplomatic gains abroad.

The Allied forces, as it turns out, had an unclear vision for what should happen in Ottoman Palestine after the war. Britain had incentives to gain some type of control of Ottoman territory, including Palestine—it bordered the Red Sea, which was vital for stability through the Suez Canal, a necessary outlet for international shipping and administration of further parts of the British Empire (particularly India). Palestine also could be an important connection to the growing European oil industry in Iran (and oil under exploration elsewhere in the region). But direct acquisition of Palestine was not a priority for the British or other Allied countries, and thus the Allies remained open to a range of outcomes favorable to their interests. Britain, France, and Russia thus agreed to "spheres of influence" that each would claim over Ottoman territory. This agreement between British and French diplomats Mark Sykes and François Georges-Picot (thus known as the Sykes–Picot agreement) allotted the area of Lebanon and Syria to France; Palestine, Transjordan (now Jordan), and Iraq to Britain; Istanbul/Constantinople and parts of Armenia to Russia; and agreed to an international administration of Jerusalem.

To aid the war effort against the Ottomans and to prevent a disastrous encroachment of German forces from North Africa, the Allies cultivated alliances with Husayn Sharif of Mecca (governor of Muslim areas of Mecca and Medina) and his son Faisal Husayn to combat and sabotage their Ottoman government in exchange for support of an independent Arab government after the war (these Arab rebel forces were those the famed T. E. Lawrence "of Arabia" fought alongside). The 1915–16 correspondence between British official Henry McMahon and Sharif Husayn reveals emphatic—yet carefully vague—assurances of European support for Arab independence in all or part of "Greater Syria" (the umbrella term for the area of contemporary Palestine, Jordan, Lebanon, and Syria and, in some schematics, stretching outward to include the Arabian Peninsula and contemporary Iraq). However, the British assurances at worst contradicted or at best overlapped with the Allies' Sykes–Picot agreement on the European spheres of influence in the region. In a particularly cynical evaluation of the agreement with the Arabs, one British official asserted, "after all what harm can our acceptance of his proposal do? If the embryonic Arab state comes to nothing all our promises vanish and we are absolved from them—if the Arab state becomes a reality we have quite sufficient safeguards to control it."[49] To the Allies' horror, when Russia exited from the war after the 1917 Soviet revolution, the communist Soviets, in an anti-imperialist gesture, leaked Allied wartime agreements, including Sykes–Picot. This revelation contradicted the assurances given to the Arab rebels and sowed doubt into future Arab–European relations.

In a further attempt to strengthen the Allied war effort, the British also pursued strategic alliances with the Zionist movement. While the Arabs under Ottoman control were in the position to fight the Central Powers' forces directly, British administrators considered how Zionists might support the war effort in diplomatic ways. The motivations for this British support are still debated today, but there were likely a combination of reasons. A major one was antisemitic assumptions about Jewish international influence—perhaps if Britain offered Palestine to the Zionists, American Jews would convince the United States to join the Allies in the war and the Russian Jews would force Russia to remain.[50] British willingness to grant Palestine to the Jews was also reflective of Christian restorationist views among British officials. Ultimately, in November of 1917, the British Foreign

Secretary Arthur Balfour gave historic assurances to the Zionists in what became known as the Balfour Declaration. It was essentially the charter that Theodor Herzl had hoped to see in his lifetime, stating: "His Majesty's Government view with favour the establishment in Palestine of a national home for the Jewish people, and will use their best endeavours to facilitate the achievement of this object, it being clearly understood that nothing shall be done which may prejudice the civil and religious rights of existing non-Jewish communities in Palestine, or the rights and political status enjoyed by Jews in any other country." Like the Husayn–McMahon correspondence, however, the wording left significant leeway for interpretation. The support for a national home did not specify the form such a home would take; it could therefore mean anything from support for Jewish minority rights and protections, including rights to immigrate and settle, to a separate autonomous region or government for Jews in a broader regional federation, or could even mean an independent Jewish state. The Balfour Declaration was both celebrated and highly controversial, and despite disagreements on its meaning or implementation, it arguably remained the compass for British–Zionist relations until the establishment of Israel in 1948.[51]

World War I ended in 1918 and changed the map of Europe and the Middle East. Allied victors Britain and France established "mandatory governments" in what had been most of the Ottoman Empire. Great Britain, now the sponsor of the Zionist movement, gained control of the desired territory, and the existing "non-Jewish inhabitants" referred to in the Balfour Declaration—and who had been enticed to aid the British in return for a favorable postwar settlement—faced drastically new social and political possibilities.

The different Zionist streams—cultural, religious, Labor—and their broader values and agendas regarding the problem of the Jews, the problem of Judaism, and the "negation of the exile" contributed to how Zionism continued to develop in the context of these massive changes. Zionists negotiated what Jewishness would mean in the context of their movement, including whether Judaism would impact its content or leadership, and if not, what forms of Jewish national identity would replace it. Even among secular Zionists, answers ranged from what Gideon Shimoni called "laissez-faire" Zionist secularism, such as that of radicals like Berdichevski, to "normative" secular identity like that of Ahad HaAm who was far less iconoclastic.[52] For some Zionists, the establishment of the British Mandate and the momentum of Labor Zionism called for major revisions to the direction of the Zionist movement. Ultimately, with British support in place, the Zionist Organization could now establish a recognized administrative entity for the Jewish community of Palestine, in which these existing streams and questions continued to grow, compete, and change.

# 3 | ZIONISM IN THE MANDATE PERIOD

In 1919 the Paris Peace Conference was about to establish the outcome of the recent "war to end all war," as World War I was sometimes
called. Ahead of the conference, Zionist leader Chaim Weizmann and
Arab nationalist leader Faisal Husayn drafted conditional support of
each other's movements. They agreed their respective movements
were related by "racial kinship and ancient bonds existing between the
Arabs and the Jewish people," and that they should therefore collabo-
rate toward achieving their nationalist aims in tandem.[1] Faisal, corresponding with another Zionist official, wrote that, as his delegation
headed to the Peace Conference, they would support the Zionist cause,
and in so doing would "wish the Jews a most hearty welcome home"
to the land of their ancient origins. He asserted that since neither of
their movements were imperialist, but rather nationalist, "there is a
place for both of us [in Greater Syria]. Indeed, I think that neither
of us can achieve real success without the other."[2] Years later, Faisal
claimed he did not remember writing any letter to this effect.[3] In any
case, his support for Zionism had been explicitly noted as conditional
upon the achievement of an independent Arab state, as expected per
the wartime Husayn–McMahon agreement. As it turned out, neither
a Jewish nor an Arab state resulted from the conference proceedings,
a process that historian David Fromkin laconically dubbed, "a Peace
to end all Peace."[4]

In several commissions of inquiry to discern the political will and conditions of the Arab inhabitants of the former Ottoman Empire, Arab leaders insisted upon an independent Arab constitutional monarchy. They specifically noted they "reject the claims of the Zionists for the establishment of a Jewish commonwealth . . . in Palestine, and we are opposed to Jewish immigration into any part of the country."[5] These Arab leaders noted that while the Jews native to the recently dissolved Ottoman Empire should "enjoy the rights and [bear] the responsibilities which are ours in common," they regarded the aims of the Zionist movement "as a grave menace to our national, political and economic life."[6] Despite Arab leaders' support for an independent Arab country, the new League of Nations ultimately chose to place these former Ottoman territories under mandate governments, so that "advanced nations who by reason of their resources, their experience or their geographical position" can take these populations under their "tutelage . . . until such a time as they are able to stand alone."[7] Areas of Greater Syria fell under French and British administrations, along boundaries similar to those established in the 1916 Sykes–Picot agreement. It was in this context of political uncertainty, frustration, and hope among Arabs, Zionists, and European administrators that Zionists carried the cultural and political legacies from the movement's formative decades into new opportunities and unprecedented challenges.

## THE BRITISH MANDATE FOR PALESTINE

The British Mandate for Palestine was officially established in 1922 under the authority of the League of Nations. While it aimed to "so far as circumstances permit, encourage local autonomy," the Mandate specified that the British administration "shall have full powers of legislation and of administration."[8] Its charter included a commitment to "[put] into effect the [Balfour Declaration]," meaning Britain was "responsible for placing the country under such political, administrative, and economic conditions as will secure the establishment of the Jewish National Home."[9] The Mandate only indirectly referred to the Palestinian Arabs, stating it will "[safeguard] the civil and religious rights of all the inhabitants of Palestine, irrespective of race and religion."[10] Even though the Jewish National Home was enshrined in its purpose, the Mandate government had a blank slate for what this would mean in practice, and how it would affect its other commitments to civil and religious rights for the rest of the population.

The British Mandate operated as an executive umbrella over a variety of legal and administrative institutions. English, Arabic, and Hebrew were the new official languages of the government. Throughout the Mandate, Zionists, Palestinian Arabs, and British administrators pursued the possibility of a joint legislative assembly of both Jewish and Arab representatives, but this kind of governing body never materialized. Zionists created their own elected representative National Assembly under an executive National Council (Vaad Leumi) to administer policies specific to the Yishuv (the word used for the Jewish population of Palestine). The Jewish Agency was established in 1929 to enlist the cooperation of non-Zionist organizations and individuals worldwide, as well as to coordinate between the Zionist Organization and Vaad Leumi.

The British encouraged other separate Jewish and Arab institutions in Palestine. Schools were separate among Jews and Arabs (though there were several foreign missionary schools that included students from both groups). Separate administration was especially pronounced in religious jurisdiction. The British allowed religious groups to retain control of personal status law, including marriage, divorce, child custody, conversion, and inheritance, with the intention of honoring the religious status quo from Ottoman rule. Not only did they retain the model of separate personal status law, but they ironically introduced new religious administrative roles to administer it.

For the Jews of Palestine, the British recognized two chief rabbis, over the Ashkenazi and Sephardi communities respectively. The leadership structure for the Muslims of Palestine was especially novel, with the British creating the role of grand mufti to oversee a Supreme Muslim Council, neither of which had been entities in Islamic law or tradition. By restructuring religious authorities, the British both disrupted existing dynamics among Muslim leaders, and created positions where, in the absence of a general assembly representing the population of Palestine as a whole, government-sanctioned power would be consolidated on religious rather than civil lines.

Most importantly for the Zionist movement, the British Mandate government recognized the Zionist Organization as "a public body for the purpose of advising and co-operating with the Administration of Palestine in such economic, social and other matters as may affect the establishment of the Jewish National Home and the interests of the Jewish population in Palestine."[11] Even though the functions of advising and co-operating were vague—as was what constituted the Jewish National Home or the "matters" and "interests" pertaining to it—this recognition of the ZO in official British policy gave the Zionists formal stature in the Mandate government. This amenable posture to Zionism manifested in various ways in the British administration. The first high commissioner, for instance, was a British Jewish Zionist, as was the attorney general for much of the 1920s. Jews were hired in government positions at a higher rate than Arabs, and were paid more as well (with the rationale that as Europeans they had higher living standards). Far fewer Arabs than Jews were employed by the police force, since it was assumed the Arabs would be unable to uphold the Mandate government commitment to the Balfour Declaration.

However, despite the favorable position that the Zionist movement had within the Mandate charter, Zionists could not pursue their own policies completely unhindered. Jewish immigration was limited to British administrators' discretion, and generally constrained by what they deemed the economic capacity of Palestine. The British at times limited Jewish immigration for political reasons as well. This was particularly challenging after the United States Immigration Act of 1924, which severely curtailed US immigration; many Jewish immigrants who would have been demographically much likelier to choose America as a destination now had to consider a visa for Palestine. Along with limits on immigration, the British prohibited Jews from organizing their own defense force, even when British police and military forces were not able or willing to protect Jewish areas more vulnerable to attack or theft. Finally, Britain's refusal to explicitly endorse a Jewish state rather than the murkier goal of a Jewish homeland was considered by many Zionists, when taken together with other limitations, to mean that the Mandate government was generally antagonistic to their ultimate aims. While there were certainly individual British administrators less sympathetic or even hostile to Zionism, British policies largely depended not only on the inclinations of specific governors and administrators on the ground in Palestine, but on various political and military interests of the British government as a whole.

## EARLY CHALLENGES

By most measures the Mandate had a difficult start. The Arabs of Palestine were already suspicious of British intentions after the failure to establish an Arab state in the postwar settlement, and the Mandate's explicit endorsement of the Balfour Declaration was particularly objectionable. Palestinian Arabs viewed the increase in Jewish immigration and land purchases under the British administration as especially threatening, and Muslim Christian Associations (MCAs) formed to consolidate and advance Palestinian Arab interests in the face of the changing political atmosphere. The 1920 congress of MCAs voted to reject the Balfour Declaration and to establish an Arab Executive. These early political associations of both Muslims and Christians, along with the earlier establishment of Palestinian newspapers by Arab Christians, indicated the extent to which Arabs of the former Ottoman Empire considered themselves to be undergoing a national struggle rather than a religious one; however, these categories would become increasingly blurred.[12]

In the early transition to the British Mandate there were episodic outbursts of violence between Jews and Arabs, and isolated planned attacks. One of the most infamous attacks was on the Jewish settlement of Tel Hai in the Galilee in 1920, during which hundreds of Arabs fought against just dozens of Jewish settlers, who ultimately had to abandon the settlement for several years. One of the casualties was Yosef Trumpeldor, a war veteran and a former member of the Second Aliyah defense group HaShomer. His reported last words—"it is good to die for your country"—became a Zionist mantra, and Trumpeldor and Tel Hai became symbols of sacrifice for the Yishuv even when outnumbered.[13]

Instances of spontaneous intercommunal violence spurred greater concern for strong self-defense. One of the earliest popular riots broke out in 1921 in Jaffa, where clashes between rival leftist Zionist groups ignited into days of intercommunal fighting between Jews and Arabs. The British administration conducted the first of what would be several major commissions of inquiry into the causes of Arab–Jewish violence. Their reports identified the initial inter-Zionist brawls, but noted that more systemic social and political tensions underlay the riots' escalation. High Commissioner Herbert Samuel, despite his sympathy to the Zionist cause, paused Jewish immigration altogether in response. Additionally, in an attempt to assuage the fears of both Jews and Arabs in Palestine, then-colonial secretary Winston Churchill issued the 1922 White Paper clarifying that while Britain still embraced the Balfour Declaration it was not intended to support the creation of a Jewish state or to allow "the disappearance or the subordination of the Arabic population, language or culture in Palestine."[14] This clarification did little to reassure either side, both of which considered the British to be giving too much credence or amnesty to the concerns or crimes of the other. While Zionists strongly condemned this initial immigration freeze, they continued to more or less cooperate with the British administration.

## LABOR ZIONIST HEGEMONY

Under the British, Zionists acquired far greater permission to develop national institutions than they had had during the Ottoman Empire, and the most significant of these institutions were heavily influenced by Labor Zionism and its leaders. The Histadrut, short for the General Federation of Hebrew Labor in Palestine, was the Labor Zionist workers' federation that owned and operated a wide range of enterprises and functions. The federation ran an employment agency, sick fund and medical insurance, a bank, construction company, and marketing agency. The Histadrut also built a number of cultural institutions, including schools, libraries, sports clubs, a newspaper, and a prominent theater group. These initiatives not only strengthened the economic and social life of the Yishuv, they also allowed Labor Zionists to influence the development of Zionism as a whole. In 1930 the two dominant Labor Zionist parties merged to form Mapai (the Hebrew acronym of *"Workers' Party of Eretz Israel"*), and prominent Labor Zionists joined the Jewish Agency Executive, including Mapai head David Ben Gurion, cofounder of the Histadrut and its general secretary. As head of Mapai and the Histadrut, as well as a member of the Jewish Agency Executive, Ben Gurion was able to steer the interests of Mapai and the ZO as a whole closer together. His 1933 book, aptly titled *From Class to Nation*, upheld Labor Zionists not only as one Zionist stream of several, but as "the nucleus of the future nation" since they embraced and mobilized all Jews regardless of their economic means, and prioritized fundamental institutions such as the Jewish labor market and Jewish agricultural settlement.[15]

The Histadrut also oversaw the formation of the Haganah, the defense organization that absorbed and replaced the Second Aliyah Labor-Zionist HaShomer. Physical assertiveness remained a key tenet of Labor Zionism, and with the regularity of violence between Arabs and Jews, along with growing landholdings, Zionists prioritized training and arming organized defense units. The Haganah was technically an illegal underground organization, since the British Mandate had forbidden independent militias. But the organization succeeded in steadily procuring arms by smuggling them from British police forces and also by purchasing them in Europe and smuggling them in cargo shipments to Palestine. By 1937 Mandate officials estimated the Haganah could arm up to 10,000 soldiers.[16] While the continued growth of this armed organization caused tensions with British administrators as well as with Palestinian Arabs, it also lay a foundation for future military readiness and ultimately the army of the State of Israel.

## REVISIONIST ZIONISM

Not all Zionists were supportive of the ever-growing influence of Labor Zionism. There was a large percentage of General Zionists, for instance, who did not identify with Labor platforms and eventually organized themselves into a distinct party within the ZO. The most oppositional challenge to Labor Zionism came, however, with the establishment of the Revisionist Party in 1925. Revisionism emerged under the leadership of Vladimir Jabotinsky (1880–1940), whose iconic status among followers is nearly comparable to Theodor Herzl's. Jabotinsky had a more secular education than many of his Russian Zionist counterparts. He had a history of armed defense efforts—in 1903 organizing a defense unit during pogroms in his hometown of Odessa, and mobilizing Jewish battalions for the British forces in Palestine during World War I. During riots in Jerusalem in 1920, Jabotinsky was arrested for illegal possession of weapons, but after being sentenced to ten years in prison he was pardoned by High Commissioner Herbert Samuel on the condition that he did not settle in Palestine permanently, since he was considered a possible threat to public safety. Jabotinsky thus campaigned for Zionism abroad. After serving on the Zionist Executive, Jabotinsky resigned in protest at the organization's policies. In 1925 he established the Revisionist Party, so named for its call to revise Zionist Organization tactics and values. By 1935 the Revisionists broke with the ZO altogether and established the New Zionist Organization.

Revisionism rejected key goals and tactics of the Zionist Organization, most significantly its emphasis on the working class and its acquiescence to British interests. The Revisionists condemned what they saw as the Zionist Organization's "cringing before England as if she had given us a refuge out of compassion," and they refused to consider the Balfour Declaration an act of charity or a license to dictate Jewish affairs. Instead, the Revisionists insisted that "our relations with Great Britain should be, and, in our own view, could be based on a foundation of mutual loyalty," since a strong Jewish state would serve wider British interests in the region.[17] The British certainly did not, according to Jabotinsky, have the right to dictate the Jews' immigration to their own homeland, and Jabotinsky objected to the prohibition on Jewish defense units when their need was so obvious. Jabotinsky especially resented the British creation of a separate Transjordanian mandate east of the Jordan River, and was determined to reclaim the territory for Zionist expansion. Revisionists insisted the land was necessary for absorbing Jewish immigrants and that it was part of the territorial promises of Scripture (such as in Genesis 15:18, that states "to your descendants, I shall give this land, from the River of Egypt to the great Euphrates River"). Followers of Jabotinsky would later expand upon his views to not only reject cooperation with Britain but to actively take up arms against the British if it was deemed necessary.

Jabotinsky also rejected the Labor Zionists' synthesis of social-ism and Zionism, calling it a "cancer" on the nation and comparing such an "admixture of various ideals" with the Torah's prohibition of *scha'atnez* (mixing wool and linen, noted in Leviticus 19:19 and Deuteronomy 22:11).[18] Like other Zionist streams, Revisionism was not only committed to achieving a state but transforming Jewish cul-ture as well. For Jabotinsky, however, Jewish national culture should embody excellence and glory (the Hebrew word *hadar*), rather than valorizing manual labor and prioritizing workers' rights against capi-talist expansion.[19] The Revisionist movement established its own youth movement, Beitar, to advance and exemplify Revisionist political and cultural values, and to "create the type of Jew which the nation needs in order to create the Jewish state as quickly as possible and in the best way possible."[20] Establishing a rival Revisionist organization and youth movement was meant to check the ascendance of Labor Zionist influence on Zionist economic and cultural developments, as well as on executive leadership.

Revisionists also contested the Zionist Organization's emphasis on diplomacy, instead advocating the use of force, both demographi-cally and militarily. Neither the British nor the Arabs would simply hand the Zionists a Jewish state, Revisionists maintained, and thus Zionists must create a Jewish majority to force its possibility.[21] This goal shaped Jabotinsky's approach to the Palestinian Arabs, which was one of coexistence (in his words, "polite indifference" and even "sincere goodwill") upon the condition of Jewish cultural, numeric, and military strength.[22] Jabotinsky did not think creating a Jewish majority was inherently oppressive to Palestinian Arabs, especially since he explicitly condemned expulsion as a means of achieving a majority. He even claimed to support Arab equality and autonomy in areas of "communal affairs, education, cultural activities and politi-cal representation," echoing the Revisionist Party platform, which asserted that "the economic welfare of the non-Jewish population

[was] one of the fundamental conditions for the welfare of the country."[23] While Jabotinsky espoused these ideals of Arab equality in the context of a Jewish majority, his offer of inclusion came with the not-so-veiled threat that resistance would be met with force: "we nevertheless firmly believe that the transformation of Palestine into a Jewish state is a postulate of the highest justice and that all opposition to it is unjust. One may neither come to terms with injustice or make any concessions to it," he concluded.[24] He believed that while the goal of a Jewish state was "completely peaceful," Zionists could only "achieve our peaceful aims through peaceful means" if the Arabs accepted Jewish authority.[25] The Revisionist founding document applied this same logic to the British, declaring unequivocally that "if the activity or the inactivity of the British Administration in Palestine prove harmful to us, our fight against it is justified."[26] In other words, they believed they had no choice but to resort to force in the face of opposition to a Jewish state.

Jabotinsky expounded upon this militant perspective in his article, "On the Iron Wall," which "became one of the cornerstones of Revisionist Zionist thought."[27] Jabotinsky believed that the Arab Palestinians had aspirations for their own state, breaking rank with the long-standing Zionist claim that outbursts of Arab violence were the result of manipulation by Arab elites or a misunderstanding of the ultimate benefits of the Zionist project in Palestine. He insisted that Arabs would not surrender these aspirations "as long as they see any hope of ridding themselves of the danger of foreign settlement . . . [or] as there remains a solitary spark of hope that they will be able to prevent the transformation of 'Palestine' into the 'Land of Israel.' "[28] Zionism must therefore create "an iron wall which the native population cannot break through."[29] Jabotinsky described the iron wall as "the strengthening in Palestine of a government without any kind of Arab influence," and openly admitted this meant a government "against which the Arabs will fight." "Only when not a single breach [in the iron wall] is visible" would moderate Arabs convince extremists to stop resisting and subsequently forge meaningful compromises with the Zionists.[30] Building this iron wall of a purely Jewish government would thus require the Revisionist tenets of a Jewish majority, strong military deterrence, and refusal to sign agreements until the Palestinian Arabs fully accepted Zionist aims for a Jewish state.[31]

In 1931 the Revisionists established their own paramilitary force, the National Military Organization in the Land of Israel, known as the Irgun or Etzel. The Irgun operated separately from the Labor paramilitary Haganah. Prominent Revisionist leaders served in and oversaw the Irgun, such as Menachem Begin, who was considered the successor of Jabotinsky and, much later, the first non-Labor prime minister of Israel. The Irgun maintained that "it is essential . . . that we prove to the world that our right to a Jewish state is not only an historical and human right but that we are ready and prepared to back it with military force, rather than relying on British bayonets."[32] In 1940 an even more radical military force, the Lehi (the Hebrew acronym for *Fighters for the Freedom of Israel*), also known as the Stern Gang (for its founder Avraham Stern), formed to escalate offensive tactics against the British administration. Several of their "Eighteen Principles of Rebirth" emphasize the use of arms; one principle was "War: Constant war against those who stand in the way of fulfilling the goals"; another was "Conquest: The conquest of the homeland from foreign rule and its eternal possession."[33] The Revisionist exaltation of physical strength and military assertiveness was not unique, as Labor Zionism had upheld these traits since HaShomer and the battle of Tel Hai, and Max Nordau even earlier issued the call for "Muscle Judaism." However, conflicts between Labor and Revisionist Zionists over the proper use of force were significant challenges until the establishment of Israel, when both militias were disbanded.

## BINATIONALISM

In this period, during which the Jewish National Home still did not have an official pragmatic interpretation, some Zionists advocated that a Jewish home should not mean a Jewish nation-state but rather part of a binational arrangement for the Arabs and Jews in Palestine. In 1925 the Brit Shalom (Hebrew for *"Covenant of Peace"*) formed as an "independent association for fostering Jewish–Arab understanding."[34] Binationalism was numerically marginal, but some of its key proponents were major cultural figures in Mandate Palestine: Judah Magnes, the founder and president of the Hebrew University of Jerusalem; renowned philosopher and writer Martin Buber; and Henrietta Szold, tireless activist and founder of the women's Zionist organization Hadassah. Brit Shalom was not a political party but a cultural association whose members envisioned and supported policies toward a shared government and economy between both Jews and Arabs, in which both populations had freedom to preserve national distinctions such as language, religious institutions, holidays, and education. The group believed that, if national autonomy was ensured for both groups, neither Jews nor Arabs would need a numerical majority, and could conduct wider civil, economic, and foreign policies based on shared interest, with the same laws and legal authority applying to both peoples. This binational model thus conflicted with the Labor Zionist tenets of conquest of land and labor to the exclusion of the Arabs. Binationalists were especially opposed to the rising Revisionist movement and its demand for a Jewish majority. Martin Buber argued that seeking a Jewish majority or an exclusively Jewish nation-state would simply reverse conditions that Jews sought to escape in diaspora, and he was thus sympathetic to the motivations behind Arab resistance.[35] While Buber regretted there was not a parallel Arab movement seeking binationalism, he reasoned that, as the ones entering the country, the onus was on the Zionists to build trust by aiming to create a nation *with* the inhabitants rather than *alongside* them (which he thought would ultimately mean *against* them).[36] In a way the Revisionists and Binationalists both believed that a Jewish state would rightfully provoke resistance from the Palestinian Arabs, but the former concluded it could be overcome by force whereas the latter believed it could be overcome by forfeiting a nation-state in favor of a binational one.

In 1942, Brit Shalom members formed the political party Ichud (Hebrew for *Union*) to try to salvage a binational path in the face of growing Zionist unanimity for a Jewish state. Ichud never gained a significant following, but isolated political groups and leaders continued to espouse aspects of their platform. For instance, in 1946 HaShomer HaTzair, the left-most wing of the Labor movement, published "The Case for a Bi-National Palestine." They proposed that Jews should be able to immigrate to Palestine, while the Palestinian Arabs could concurrently preserve their "profound attachment to their soil and culture." If political structures could be put in place to protect these rights and facilitate joint sovereignty and shared economy, HaShomer HaTzair asserted, "we fail to see what meaning the controversy of a Jewish versus an Arab State would then still possess and why it could not be resolved instead in a form that might be termed a Jewish–Arab State."[37] Despite the ultimate impotence of binational political platforms, their formation played a gadfly role in the strengthening Zionist movement and attested to the diversity within Zionist ideologies.

## THE 1929 RIOTS

In 1929 a major outbreak of violence over the Wailing (or Western) Wall escalated the national tensions between Jews and Arabs in Palestine. The Wailing Wall is located under what was during the biblical era the Temple Mount, which has been since the seventh century CE an Islamic holy site comprising both the Dome of the Rock and the Al-Aqsa Mosque. The Western Wall itself was not part of the actual Temple, but rather part of an outer retaining wall. Still, its proximity to the Temple's original site has made it an especially sacred place of prayer for Jews over the centuries. While the Al-Aqsa complex remained under Islamic administration into the British Mandate, the Western Wall was in an alleyway of the Mughrabi neighborhood (named after residents originating from Morocco), and Jews and Muslims disputed whether changes made at the Western Wall constituted a violation of the status quo per the Mandate policy on religious administration. Tensions built in smaller ways together raised larger disputes about this space—Jewish worshipers brought chairs and dividing screens to the wall and, more significantly, the Jewish National Fund initiated attempts to purchase the area with the wall. Hajj Amin al-Husseini, the appointed grand mufti, circulated propaganda that framed these developments as Zionist encroachments on the Al-Aqsa complex and, by extension, toward all of Islam. In 1929 tensions mounted around Tisha B'Av, the Jewish holiday commemorating the destruction of the Temple, after which the Revisionist youth group staged a march through the neighborhood. In this charged atmosphere a misunderstanding as minor as a ball kicked in a yard triggered an outbreak of violence lasting a week and spreading to different parts of the country. The massacres during these riots were particularly devastating for indigenous Jewish communities such as those in Hebron, who had not been affiliated with Zionist institutions. To both Labor and Revisionist Zionists the episode proved that the British administration both could not and would not sufficiently defend Jews, and therefore the Yishuv must continue to strengthen its own defensive forces. Through another British commission of inquiry, it became clear that Arabs, Jews, and British administrators in Palestine viewed the episode as a sign of worsening political gridlock and intercommunal animosity.[38]

# RISE OF NAZISM AND THE FIFTH ALIYAH

Jewish demographics in Palestine underwent major shifts when Adolf Hitler's rise to power in Germany brought some of the most organized persecution against European Jews to date, tragically only foreshadowing the Nazi genocide of the Jews that would take place under the wartime conditions of World War II. The first of the Nazi regime's many exclusionary policies was the 1933 "Aryan paragraph," which terminated employment for many German Jews. By 1935 the Nazis legislated the Nuremberg Laws, including the Law for the Protection of German Blood and the Reich Citizenship Law, which stripped German Jews of their citizenship rights and criminalized marriages and sexual relationships between Aryans and non-Aryans. In this social and political environment, even the most assimilated of German Jews faced threats to their livelihood or basic safety. Other European countries, such as Hungary, Romania, and Poland, initiated their own versions of the Nuremberg Laws and harbored rising popular violence against Jews. Many Jews tried to flee from these conditions, but very few countries were open to large numbers of Jewish refugees; Palestine was one of the only places for which Jews could receive visas. In this Fifth Aliyah, comprised mainly of German and other central European Jews, the Jewish population of Palestine doubled between 1933 and 1935 alone. Many of these immigrants had little to no prior interest in Zionist activity or in settlement in Palestine. This group of immigrants became known in the Yishuv as the *yekkes*, German-speaking Jews known for more bourgeois taste and appearance who hardly adopted the persona of a *halutz*. These refugees established their own newspapers and several immigrants' organizations. Since these immigrants had generally more wealth than previous waves of eastern European immigrants, investment in the country's industries rose in this period as well. This surge of Jewish population and economic investment in Palestine not only created new cultural and economic challenges and opportunities within the Yishuv, but it also strained the already volatile political and economic dynamics among the British, Jews, and Palestinian Arabs.

## ARAB RESISTANCE

By the early 1930s Palestinian Arabs had formed several political parties and factions, nearly all of which opposed the strengthening Zionist administration and rising Jewish population in Palestine. The Istiqlal (Independence) Party advocated for a more pan-Arab movement, and Grand Mufti Hajj Amin al Husseini continued to build support for his own leadership with a more specifically Islamic bent. In 1937 the British exiled him from Palestine, but he continued his anti-Zionist campaigns among other leaders in the Arab world and Europe, most infamously even meeting with Hitler. Izz al-Din al-Qassam became another prominent advocate for blending Islamic piety with violent opposition to Zionism. Al-Qassam attained the status of martyr in 1935 after he killed kibbutz members and a British police sergeant before being killed by British forces. A growing fusion of Islam and anti-Zionist sentiment—which had grown significantly since the earlier formation of Muslim–Christian Associations—was evidenced by Islamic names adopted by groups opposing British rule and Zionism, such as "Central Committee for Jihad" and "Army of Holy Jihad."

Between 1936 and 1939, in what became known as the Arab Revolt, Palestinians organized a general strike and series of attacks against the British administration and Jewish settlements and property. Many factors led to the revolt; tensions had been growing since the 1929 riots, Arab unemployment was rising, and a Palestinian representative council was repeatedly delayed or rejected in discussions between British, Zionist, and Arab leaders. Under these wider circumstances, a British interception of arms smuggled by Zionists raised alarm about the extent of Jewish armament. Various Palestinian political parties and local leaders formed the Arab Higher

Committee to coordinate resistance. Their initial revolt took the form of a general workers' strike from British and Jewish institutions (especially those working directly for the British administration), boycotting business with Jews, and using guerilla and terror tactics against both Jewish settlements and British military targets. At later stages of the revolt, militants targeted British civil administrators as well. Palestinian authors and musicians of the time popularized nationalist aspirations through literature and songs.

Jewish armed groups were divided on how to respond—the Haganah officially endorsed a policy of *havlaga* (restraint), but in practice allowed selective retaliatory attacks. The Revisionist Irgun, on the other hand, initiated offensive attacks, even using terror, such as placing bombs in crowded Arab areas. By 1938 the Mandate administration officially legalized the Haganah's use of arms so they could aid in suppressing the ongoing revolt. Zionist leader Uri Avnery later reflected on this period, concluding in retrospect that "these 'disturbances', as we called them in Hebrew, were in fact an Arab rebellion, a last desperate, and wholly inefficient, try of the Palestinian Arab nation to get rid of the British overlords and Jewish immigrants, who looked to them like a rabble of foreigners trying to take over their country." From his perspective in a Revisionist group, however, he "saw only that our people were being killed, that the hypocritical British were doing nothing to stop them, and . . . as if our established leaders, preaching havlaga, or self-restraint, were acting like cowards."[39] His experience exemplified the growing conflict not only between Zionist and Arab armed groups but between the Labor and Revisionist Zionist militias themselves.

It was amid this violence that British policymakers considered partitioning Palestine between Jews and Arabs, concluding that the current arrangement was proving untenable. The 1937 Peel partition plan (named for Lord Peel who oversaw an investigation into the Arab Revolt) was not ultimately carried out, but the Zionists had been ambivalently willing to accept part of the territory if it meant formally obtaining an independent Jewish state. Ben Gurion and other Zionist officials also assumed that they would expand upon initial territory. Ben Gurion envisioned that with a Jewish state in part of Palestine, "we'll establish a multifaceted economy . . . we'll build sophisticated armed forces, an excellent military . . . and then we'll be able to settle in the other parts of the country, either through mutual agreement with our Arab neighbors or through other means."[40] The Palestinian Arabs, however, refused to agree to divide their land, especially when they still constituted the majority in both proposed states. The Zionist binationalists objected to partition as well; not only had they consistently opposed an exclusively Jewish state, but, as Judah Magnes argued, "wherever you draw those boundaries, you create an irredenta on either side of the border. An irredenta almost invariably leads to war."[41]

As the likelihood of war with Germany and its allies increased, Britain considered an oppositional Arab population a serious liability; they simply could not afford to divert troops to Palestine to quell uprisings or protect personnel, and certainly could not risk the Arabs choosing to aid the Germans against Britain and its allies. To try to neutralize the ongoing conflict in Palestine, Britain issued the White Paper of 1939, in which it stated, "His Majesty's Government declare unequivocally that it is not part of their policy that Palestine should become a Jewish state," and announced it would begin to institute strict limitations on Jewish immigration. Jews could come to Palestine for five more years so long as the Jewish population would not exceed a third of the country's population (this amounted to an average of around 1500 people a month).[42] It also limited land transfers from Arabs to Jews. Zionists across the political spectrum were devastated and enraged at what was effectively a cancellation of the Balfour Declaration, particularly at a time with unprecedented numbers of Jewish refugees. The Arab Revolt, however, subsided, perhaps in part from the British assurances in the White Paper, though also due to a variety of other reasons, including increasingly harsh reprisals from British forces and Palestinian Arab elites who cooperated with the British in order to restore their own normalcy.

## WORLD WAR II

The outbreak of world war between the Allies—Britain, France, Russia, and later the United States—and the Axis powers—Germany, Italy, and Japan—placed Palestine in the geographical middle of an intercontinental war effort. In 1940 Italy bombed key sites along the Palestinian coast, and through 1942 there was a real possibility that Nazi forces would successfully control North Africa as far as Egypt, jeopardizing Allied access to the Southeast Asian war front via the Suez Canal. Meanwhile, Zionists struggled with the growing awareness of the genocide being carried out against European Jews in Nazi concentration camps and death camps and by death squads. David Ben Gurion thus famously declared that "we will fight the White Paper like there is no war, and we will fight the war like there is no White Paper." Jews in Palestine enlisted in the British war effort and it was at this time the Haganah created an elite unit called the Palmach (Hebrew acronym for *Shock Forces*), which fought on behalf of the British against Vichy France in Syria. Revisionists were divided; the Irgun under Menachem Begin agreed to pause attacks on British personnel so as to not interfere with their war on the Nazis, but Lehi opted to take advantage of British vulnerability and continue militant efforts to gain control of Palestine. By 1944 the Irgun resumed open revolt against Britain as well.

Even though the Haganah and Palmach aided the British against the Axis powers, they also launched operations to increase illegal Jewish immigration to Palestine beyond the White Paper restrictions. Some attempts had particularly notorious and tragic outcomes; during the war the ship *Struma* was denied entry at Istanbul and refused British visas for Palestine, ultimately sinking with all 300 refugees aboard. The *Patria* succeeded in landing in Haifa but was given a deportation order by the British and, when the Haganah tried to prevent deportation by planting a bomb on board, there were hundreds of accidental casualties (those who survived were ultimately able to stay in Palestine). In the face of the massive persecution of European Jews, Zionist and Jewish leaders from the United States and around the world met at the Biltmore Hotel in New York, where they agreed on the 1942 "Biltmore Program," urging support for a Jewish state in a postwar arrangement, an explicit contradiction of the 1939 White Paper.

The Allied victory in 1945 left Britain with a gargantuan postwar recovery, and administering the Palestine Mandate, with its militant unrest, was considered prohibitively costly, even though the Mandate's original purpose of establishing an independent government had not yet been achieved (and was arguably more elusive than ever). Meanwhile, Holocaust survivors were destitute, most either languishing in displaced persons camps under the protection of Allied forces, or attempting to find new refuge. Zionists continued to mobilize illegal immigration to Palestine, and many of those who were caught were usually sent to detention camps, sometimes in Palestine but oftentimes offshore to Cyprus or distant Mauritius. Perhaps most infamous of these attempts was by the ship *Exodus*, the story of which has been adapted into a historical novel and later a Hollywood film. This shipload of refugees was denied entry to Palestine and multiple ports of entry in Europe, and was ultimately forced to land in Germany where the refugees were shamefully held in a former concentration camp.

After British success against the Axis powers, the Irgun and Lehi escalated coordinated attacks on British forces in Palestine. One of the most shocking of these was the 1946 bombing of the British administrative headquarters at the King David Hotel in Jerusalem, in which ninety-one people were killed and dozens wounded. Extreme terror activities such as these, as well as assassinations of British officials, were consistently condemned by the Haganah, since they targeted civilians, destabilized relations with the British Mandate government, and, significantly, challenged the Haganah's monopoly on the use of force. There were thus occasional skirmishes between Labor and Revisionist forces. Lehi consistently issued scathing critiques of Ben Gurion's leadership in the Yishuv, accusing him of inciting civil war and expressing a willingness to fight against the Haganah if necessary.[43]

By 1947, Britain was looking for a way to transition Palestine from its Mandatory government, and brought the issue to the consideration of the recently formed United Nations, which created a UN Special Committee on Palestine (UNSCOP). In 1947 UNSCOP concluded that "the basic conflict in Palestine is a clash of two intense nationalisms. Regardless of the historical origins of the conflict, the rights and wrongs of the promises and counter-promises . . . there are now in Palestine some 650,000 Jews and 1.2 million Arabs who are dissimilar in their ways of living and, for the time being, separated by political interests which render difficult full and effective political cooperation."[44] It therefore proposed a partition of Palestine into two states for the Jews and Palestinian Arabs, respectively, and an international administration of Jerusalem. These two states were to have "economic association" such as common customs, currency, and infrastructure. The UN General Assembly voted 33–13 (with 10 abstentions) on Resolution 181 for the partition of Palestine. The Yishuv celebrated official international approval for a Jewish state, but Palestinians rejected the international dissection of their homeland; one Palestinian called the proposed border a "line of blood and fire."[45]

In the aftermath of the UN partition plan and the British announcement of their withdrawal from Palestine, violence continued to escalate. Zionists mobilized to secure the land recognized by the UN plan but also to possibly expand their territory to retain prominent Jewish settlements slated to fall within the Palestinian state. The Palestinians also prepared for war against the Zionists, and coordinated with other Arab countries, forming the Arab Liberation Army under the auspices of the newly constituted Arab League. One of the most notorious and terrorizing instances of intercommunal violence at the close of the Mandate was the massacre of Deir Yassin, an Arab village outside Jerusalem. Despite the fact this village had a nonaggression agreement and mutual defense pact with a neighboring Jewish village, the Irgun and Lehi planned to attack it as a key location to prevent blockades of Jerusalem, and—in character with Jabotinsky's "iron wall" paradigm—to set an example to other Arab villages of the fate of those who resist Jewish occupation. The militias killed over one hundred residents, the rest of whom were permanently displaced. This episode succeeded in terrifying Arabs as to what could happen in an ensuing war. It also provoked retaliatory efforts, such as an Arab attack on a Jewish convoy of civilians (accompanied by Haganah forces) on its way to Jerusalem in which nearly eighty people were killed. Deir Yassin significantly exacerbated the circulating fears of forced population transfers against the political uncertainty of the ending Mandate (the 1947 case of the partition of India and Pakistan was one recent, and harrowing, example). With the increasing violence, the thought that Jewish or Arab populations would be safe in a country controlled by the other seemed unlikely. Historical scholarship has hotly debated references to transfers or expulsion in Zionist records or Arab propaganda in this period, but has yet to unanimously conclude whether Jews (or Arabs) had an explicit or detailed agenda for ethnic cleansing.[46] Nevertheless, wartime conditions, combined with the sociopolitical cleavages that had formed over decades, led to many instances of both intentional and inadvertent displacement or destruction of Palestinian Arab neighborhoods, villages, and towns.

On May 14, 1948, hours before the official end of the British administration, Zionist leaders gathered in Tel Aviv while David Ben Gurion read out the Declaration of Independence of the State of Israel. The United States offered unofficial recognition of the new state soon after, and was followed by many other countries. This declaration prompted the Arab Liberation Army to invade the new State of Israel, and waves of fighting continued until armistice agreements were signed in 1949 between Israel and different Arab countries. These armistice borders left Israel with more territory than had been proposed in the UN plan (78% instead of 55% of British Mandate Palestine), and included all of the Negev, the entire coast between the Gaza Strip and Lebanon, and the Galilee. The area known as Judea and Samaria became part of the Kingdom of Jordan, and the Gaza Strip fell under Egyptian administration. No longer simply a homeland, Zionists had officially created a state.

# 4 | ZIONISM IN THE STATE OF ISRAEL

In 1958, Oswald Rufeisen, also known as Brother Daniel, rescinded his Polish nationality and immigrated to Israel to become a citizen under the Law of Return. Rufeisen was not only a Holocaust survivor but also a hero. As a Polish Jew who had learned German from his German Jewish mother, he was able to pass as a non-Jew during the German occupation and to work as a translator in a Nazi office. By doing this he not only avoided the ghetto and certain death, but used his position to smuggle information, supplies, and even people in and out of the nearby Jewish ghetto of Mir. He was eventually discovered and fled to a monastery where he ended up embracing Catholicism. By the end of the war Rufeisen had fought in an anti-Nazi partisan militia and had chosen to become a monk and a priest. Even as a convert to Christianity, Rufeisen maintained the Jewish nationalism he espoused since his youth, and hoped to immigrate to Palestine where his brother had already fled. He had joined the Carmelite order precisely because they had a monastery in Haifa, and he hoped to serve the Catholic community there while living as a proud member of what ultimately became the Jewish State of Israel.

According to the 1952 Israel Nationality Law, all Israeli residents had to register their nationality and their religion and to display these on their identification cards. "Israeli" was not (and is still not) a recognized category for nationality, so most Jewish residents registered both their religion and their nationality as "Jewish." Rufeisen, however, tried to register his nationality as "Jewish" and his religion as "Catholic." The minister of the interior refused to honor this registration—how could a national Jew be a Catholic monk? Rufeisen insisted, and brought his case to the Israeli Supreme Court in 1962. The judges were torn. For example, after a lengthy retelling of Rufeisen's acts of service during the war and his strong loyalty to the Jewish people, Justice Zvi Berenson confessed that, "if I could follow my own inclination I too would grant the request of the petitioner," since "at my own convictions I would not have the slightest hesitation in regarding this particular petitioner as a member of the Jewish people."[1] But as a judge, he could not grant legal precedence to Rufeisen's national identity. Other judges expressed similar sympathies. All but one judge ruled that even though Rufeisen was Jewish according to *halakha* (Jewish law) as the son of a Jewish woman, the state could not use a religious litmus test for his national inclusion. Ironically, though, it was the petitioner's religion that disqualified him from nationality. The court's majority opinion was that the "man on the street" would not call someone a Jew who had also become a Catholic monk, and they would thus not contradict the "common use" of the term "Jewish." The court thus upheld the minister of the interior's decision to forbid Rufeisen's Jewish nationality and Catholic religion. Rufeisen could still keep his naturalization as a citizen, and could still register his religion as Catholic, but his nationality was officially registered with a word that perhaps fittingly described the status of religious and national identity in Israel: "unclear." Rufeisen served as a priest in Haifa until his death in 1998. His experience as a Holocaust refugee, an immigrant under the Law of Return, a petitioner of the Israeli Supreme Court, a Catholic in Israel, and a self-professing national Jew is reflective of the unique challenges, opportunities, and uncertainties that came with the establishment of the State of Israel.

In 1948 the signatories of the Declaration of Independence in Israel announced "the establishment of the Jewish State in Palestine, to be called Israel."[2] This declaration of Israel as a Jewish state meant that an independent government and diverse society now had to answer enduring and even contentious questions of the Zionist movement: How does a Jewish state work? And even more fundamentally, who is a Jew? Israel was not only established as a Jewish state, but also as a democratic one; the Declaration of Independence promised "elected bodies of the State in accordance with a constitution," and government based on "the precepts of liberty, justice and peace taught by the Hebrew prophets; [that] will uphold the full social and political equality of all its citizens, without distinction of race, creed or sex."[3] By 1950 the Israeli parliament, the Knesset, legislated that drafting a constitution, which the declaration of independence stated would be written "not later than the first day of October, 1948," would be delayed indefinitely.[4] Instead of a constitution, Israel would have Basic Laws that established constitutive principles. At the time of this writing, there are thirteen Basic Laws, some of which grapple with the key questions of the meaning of a Jewish state and a Jewish democracy—including the most recent (and controversial) 2018 Basic Law: Israel as the Nation-State of the Jewish People.

The establishment and fulfilment of a Jewish state also had many practical implications for the Zionist movement. First, it meant that Jews worldwide—and particularly Jewish refugees—had a guaranteed right to citizenship and refuge in the new state. Incorporating these immigrants, a process known as the ingathering of exiles, involved monumental logistical and cultural challenges. A no less significant outcome of the state's establishment was the outbreak of war with both the Palestinians and neighboring Arab countries. This war and early Israeli policies led to the dispersion (both by expulsion and flight) of hundreds of thousands of Palestinians in Israel and the Arab world, with vast humanitarian, geopolitical, and military fallout. On a more existential level, questions about the relationships between religion and nation that had raged since Herzl founded the Zionist Organization now fueled conversations among political, cultural, religious, and intellectual figures about how religion would or would not function in the state. The 1967 War between Israel and its neighboring Arab countries also changed the political, geographical, and demographic contours of the state, and its outcomes rekindled debates about the scope and soul of Zionism itself.

# POPULATION MOVEMENT

The creation of the State of Israel, much like the creation of other new states in the twentieth century, prompted massive population movements. These had significant push-and-pull factors for both Jewish and Palestinian populations.

## Jewish Refugees and Immigrants

Zionism had achieved in Israel what even the British Mandate could not, which was legally unlimited Jewish immigration. In 1950 the Knesset passed the foundational Law of Return guaranteeing that "every Jew has the right to come to this country as an *oleh*."[5] *Oleh* literally means one "ascending"—it is the same word used for the Psalms of Ascents, which were originally for annual pilgrimages to Jerusalem—but is used as a colloquial term for "immigrant." The establishment of Israel thus brought a massive influx of Jews from Europe and the Middle East to house, feed, educate, employ, and attempt to unify. By the early 1950s, Israel had taken in as many immigrants as existing residents (as journalist Ari Shavit notes, this would be like if the United States absorbed 350 million immigrants in a few years!).[6] A period of austerity while weathering this challenge was tolerated due to a shared sense of desperation and national mission. In 1970 the Law of Return was expanded to include anyone with at least one

Jewish grandparent, in order to mirror the definition of Jewishness under the Nazi Nuremburg laws—if Jews and their families ever faced similar danger they would have a guaranteed refuge. This law and its amendment have been instrumental for later waves of immigration as well; after the fall of the Soviet Union in the early 1990s, around one million former Soviet citizens came to Israel under these qualifications. This wave increased the Jewish population of Israel by nearly 20 percent; the introduction of a large Russian-speaking population, many of whom had no background in Judaism or Zionism while living under communism, had a massive cultural impact.

Nearly all the first Jewish immigrants from Europe were survivors of the Holocaust. Preeminent Israeli historian Zeev Sternhell, who lost his family in the Holocaust and survived a spate of obstacles in fleeing genocide, reflected on his arrival to Israel as a youth: "I immigrated to Israel . . . on a boat with a large transport of children . . . In the State of Israel I no longer had to justify or explain. It was a great relief . . . I was alone, without possessions or protection. But I was filled with the amazing feeling that the long, excruciating journey had come to an end."[7] Many Ashkenazi refugees were settled in centralized, urban areas like Jaffa and Haifa, which had more employment and cultural opportunities. Approximately 150,000 of them were directly settled into the homes and villages of Palestinians who fled or had been expelled during the war of 1948–49. Thousands of others lived in temporary camps. By the end of the 1950s, Israel had built more permanent housing blocks and offered homebuying loans to accommodate these immigrants.

In Israel's early years, surviving the Holocaust had a social stigma, as Jews struggled to understand the enormity of the Holocaust's trauma. Some who had already been in Palestine before World War II insinuated that Holocaust survivors bore at least some of the blame for not heeding Zionist warnings of the dangers of exile or the need for national self-determination and self-defense. Even though there were steps taken to understand and memorialize the Holocaust (such as the 1954 establishment of Yad Vashem in Jerusalem, today serving as the World Holocaust Memorial Center), Israeli society exercised what historian Tom Segev called the "Great Silence" on what Holocaust survivors actually endured.[8] While individual survivors of course processed their trauma differently, many coped by trying to relegate their experiences to a forgotten past and to focus solely on a new future. It was only after the 1962 arrest of Nazi officer Adolf Eichmann in Argentina and his trial in Jerusalem that Israeli society collectively began to bring the experiences of Holocaust survivors into the open.

Along with European Jews, there was also a huge wave of Jews from Middle Eastern and North African countries. With the outbreak of the 1948 war, some Arab countries suspected their Jewish citizens to be a fifth column whose loyalties lay with Israel. This happened even in countries like Iraq, where Jews had millennia of history and political and cultural involvement (and where there was even a small but organized contingent of anti-Zionist Jews). Popular antisemitism and new government measures encouraged Jews to leave Iraq and to renounce their citizenship. Author Sasson Somekh reflected on this alienating process in his memoir *Baghdad, Yesterday*, and Iraqi Jewish Israeli Louise Aynachi recalled, "against everything they believed in, my parents boarded a plane in March 1951. Against everything we believed in, my husband and I and our three children boarded a plane in June 1951 . . . On the wooden bench of a Mossad Skymaster I sat crying, watching the Baghdad I loved fade away."[9] While many of these Jews from Arab countries, particularly those from Morocco and Yemen, were impoverished, others had comfortable and even prestigious lives in their home countries and faced a dramatic shift in social and economic status in their displacement.

Jews from Middle Eastern countries became known in Israeli society as Mizrahim (literally "Easterners"). These Mizrahi immigrants were very different from the old-guard Zionists and European immigrants: many were devoutly observant of Judaism (and practiced Sephardic traditions distinct from the European Ashkenazim), on average they had more children than European Jews, and they generally spoke Arabic as their mother tongue. Most were not as steeped in traditions of the Haskalah or modern Hebrew literature as their European counterparts, in fact many intellectual Mizrahi Jews were more influenced by the Arabic literary *Nahda* ("awakening"). The Israeli government settled most Mizrahi immigrants into transit camps in more peripheral areas of the country, where they were marginalized economically and socially from the Ashkenazi majority. Some Mizrahim organized to protest their unequal treatment, and in 1959 riots even erupted in Haifa in response to their poor living conditions and economic prospects. By the 1970s Moroccan Jewish activists had formed the Israeli Black Panthers to organize demonstrations and attempt to make inroads among Israeli policymakers. While these earlier activists were generally politically leftist, the marginalization Mizrahim experienced under left-leaning Labor administrations (and in many cases their negative experiences leaving Arab countries) in part steered Mizrahim toward more right-wing opposition parties and religious parties in Israeli elections. By the 1980s Mizrahim formed their own parties, which have come to play a major role in Israeli electoral politics and coalition building. Their cultural background has influenced mainstream Israeli culture, particularly in music and cuisine. Some scholars and activists, such as the Mizrahi Democratic Rainbow Coalition (formed in 1996) have noted the importance of recognizing these Israelis as "Arab Jews," who challenge the assumed binaries between these groups and stand to address social and economic inequalities in Israel in a unique way. Their heritage also challenges common Eurocentric assumptions about Jewish culture, since they draw from their own textual, cultural, and political traditions and experiences.

## Palestinian Refugees

The outbreak of war in Palestine had pushed around 750,000 Palestinian Arabs—85 percent of their population at the time—out of their homes. Many left on the assumption they were temporarily fleeing a warzone and would return when the threat passed, and others were forced to leave by Zionist military and paramilitary forces. This destruction and dispersion that came with the establishment of Israel is known among Palestinians as the *Nakba* (Arabic for *"catastrophe"*). After the 1948 war, the Israeli government enacted a series of laws and policies to prevent the return of Palestinians, essentially forcing them to stay in the various countries to which they fled. For those who left Palestine in 1948, and for their descendants, securing a right of return to their homeland remains one of the key national and humanitarian demands for any future peace agreement between Israel and the Palestinians.

Some Palestinians became what were known as present absentees, meaning they fled to other areas within the borders of the State of Israel and thus became Israeli citizens but were forbidden to return to their prewar homes. Until 1966 most of these Israeli Palestinians lived under military administration with martial law. This administration curtailed their movement (which limited their employment opportunities), significantly limited their property ownership, and in some cases utilized violence, such as the infamous killing of forty-six residents of Kfar Kassem returning to their village after a curfew they had not known was in place. Military rule also made political organization and resistance especially difficult, as schools and newspapers were censored and monitored.[10]

Some Israelis raised early objections to the laws preventing Palestinian return or limiting the freedoms of Israeli Palestinians under military administration. Critics like Martin Buber spoke out against land appropriation, martial law, and Prime Minister Ben Gurion's harsh posture toward the Arabs of Israel.[11] The Israeli Communist Party and furthest left-wing Zionist party were the marginal cases in terms of mixed Jewish–Arab party membership and mutual political vision, such as advocating for Israeli Palestinians to return to their villages. Despite the many equal rights that Arab Israelis now share with Jewish Israelis, they have in many ways lived as second-class citizens even since the military administration ended in 1966. Israel's 2001 Or Commission of Inquiry reported significant economic, social, legal, and political inequalities between Jewish and Arab citizens and municipalities.[12] These inequalities can include smaller budget allocations for infrastructure, schools, and health programs. The use of Arabic in public life has also been stifled and marginalized, such as by excluding or removing Arabic from public signage. Like Buber, many have continued to contest this as incompatible with the state's foundations; as writer Peter Beinart asserted, "being a Jewish state does not require Israel to pursue discriminatory land policies or to spend more on its Jewish citizens than on its Arab ones."[13]

## GOVERNMENT OF THE JEWISH STATE

Along with the massive impact of the population movements discussed above, another obvious consequence of the establishment of Israel was the creation of a new government, which aimed to institutionalize long-standing Zionist goals. The government of the State of Israel is based on a parliamentary democracy in which all citizens elect national and local representative governments. There is an elected Knesset serving as the legislature—120 members to hearken back to the number of the "Great Knesset during the Second Temple period."[14] The cabinet, comprised of the prime minister and his or her appointed ministers, exercises very strong executive powers, and an independent civil judicial branch is overseen by a Supreme Court. There is not a hard separation between church and state in Israel since religious courts receive state funding and exercise legal jurisdiction over most personal status law. This dual civic and religious legal structure is a holdover from the Ottoman and British administrations, and is considered a crucial compromise for shared autonomy between secular and religious leaders in Israel.

It is difficult to overstate the visionary and resolute role played by first prime minister Ben Gurion in the formation of Israel's government. Ben Gurion exercised a governing ethos best described as state-centrist, which was a continuation and perhaps intensification of the traditional Labor Zionist outlook that prioritized the community over the individual. He foregrounded the growth and security of the state, particularly through building a heavily state-led economy, a strong military, and, significantly, by avoiding and even stifling issues that could stoke culture clashes and dissention. Ben Gurion's clarion call in a speech just four years before the establishment of the state illustrated his leadership style: "The charge that has been laid upon your generation is—unconditional allegiance, for life and death."[15] "The Jewish revolution," as Ben Gurion called it, "is incomparably difficult, and, unless there is unity and co-operation, it will fail."[16] This need for unity in the state's infancy was perhaps the major reason a constitution was postponed, since finalizing contentious issues (especially the role of religion in the state) could foment major and disruptive social cleavages or even violence. In Ben Gurion's view, avoiding division was necessary to do the unprecedented work of establishing state institutions, protecting the country militarily at a vulnerable time, and absorbing hundreds of thousands of Jewish immigrants.

Through the first thirty years of Israel's existence, center-left parties—the biggest and most enduring one being the Labor Party, established in 1968—controlled the government, forming governing coalitions with smaller, usually religious parties that did not challenge Labor's economic or diplomatic policies as much as Revisionist Zionist parties. The Histadrut, the Labor Zionist umbrella organization established at the beginning of the Mandate period, continued to serve many functions, though many others were transferred to the state government. In 1977 the dominance of Labor ended with the election of the right-wing Likud Party, led by long-time Revisionist leader Menachem Begin. A variety of social, military, and economic factors led to the rightward shift in Israeli politics that has largely continued into the present. Even though Likud and other right-wing governments have prevailed in the last several decades, the Labor Party and Labor administrations of the early state have an undeniable and enduring legacy regarding the establishment, growth, and even character of the State of Israel. Coalition building with minority religious parties has also remained a regular feature of Knesset coalition and government cabinet-building, regardless of whether the majority party leans to the right or left.

## RELIGION AND THE STATE

With the establishment of Israel, perennial questions, debates, and visions in the Zionist movement regarding the relationships between religion and the Jewish nation shifted to consider relationships between religion and the Jewish state. One important juncture for "church–state relations" for the Zionist movement is known as the "status quo agreement" of 1947, when the main ultraorthodox party and the Zionist Organization agreed to retain rabbinic authority over personal status law and religious education in the eventual establishment of a Jewish state. Securing authority over personal status and education reassured ultraorthodox (known in Israel as Haredi) constituencies, who were otherwise hesitant to recognize the largely secular Zionist leadership. The 1953 Rabbinical Courts Jurisdiction law (also known as the Marriage and Divorce Law) was the most tangible expression of this early "status quo agreement." It requires all personal status or family law—including marriage, divorce, inheritance, and conversion—to be conducted by religious courts, and therefore enshrines religious status as a legal and bureaucratic pillar of the state. This arrangement is not only considered foundational for power sharing among different Jewish constituencies, but also a key concession for other groups in Israel who prefer the religious control of family law, such as some Muslim and Christian Palestinian Israeli communities.

Military service was another significant area of compromise and tension regarding religion and state. The 1949 Military Service Law required (and still requires) that all Jewish citizens serve in the Israel Defense Forces (IDF) or in national service—three years for men and two years for women (men also have mandatory reserves duty until age forty). This law exempted ultraorthodox men who study full time in religious institutions (*yeshivot*, singular *yeshiva*), as well as religious women. In 1952 Ben Gurion met, in what became a famous exchange in order to discuss *yeshiva* student conscription, with one of the foremost Haredi leaders in Israel, Rabbi Avraham Karelitz. Karelitz compared the religious and secular Jews of Israel to a Talmudic analogy in which two camels approach on a path, one with a heavy load and one without, and the camel without the load must yield to the one that is burdened.[17] Karelitz maintained that the religious Israeli Jews were the loaded camel, since they carried the burden of keeping the Torah. Ben Gurion accepted Karelitz's analogy, but insisted that the secular population of Israel shouldered the heavier commandments of settling the land and defending life. Karelitz remained uncompelled, arguing that "it is only thanks to the fact that we learn Torah that they [the soldiers] are able to exist."[18] This impasse regarding ultraorthodox military service had minor numerical impact at the time of this encounter, especially when contrasted to the possible opposition that could have arisen among Haredim at such a vulnerable and formative time for the state. But *yeshiva* students have since grown to account for a significant number in Israel; in 2008 they were around 11 percent of military exemptions.[19] Many Israelis share Ben Gurion's frustration at his early meeting with Karelitz, arguing that since the ultraorthodox benefit from state resources they should share the same responsibilities as other citizens.[20] Others worry that such a systematic exemption perpetuates secular–religious divides, since military service is not only considered a necessity for security, but creates a profound cultural and social bond and network by enveloping all socioeconomic and ethnic groups among Israeli Jews. The military has also made progressive accommodations for religiously observant soldiers, including a program that combines military service with Torah study. Even so, the continuing military exemption for ultraorthodox Israelis highlights the different ideologies, evident at the beginning of Zionism itself, regarding what or who actually sustains and protects the Jewish nation.

## WHO IS A JEW?

While the personal status law remained under religious authority, the ramifications of this authority have impacted other areas of government policy, perhaps most fundamentally in the way the state determines who is a Jew. The legal and bureaucratic implications of determining who is a Jew—seen for instance in the case of Brother Daniel—followed decades of Zionist debate and ambiguity about whether and to what extent religion does or should shape the boundaries and character of the Jewish nation. As Israeli legal scholar Gad Barzilai has put it, "the real struggles have not been about who is a Jew but about who [decides] who is a Jew."[21] Answering "who is a Jew?" according to *halakha* is straightforward: anyone born of a Jewish mother or who has converted to Judaism under an authorized *beit din* ("religious court"). Other streams within Judaism have adopted wider criteria; Reform Judaism affirms that anyone born to a Jewish mother *or father* is Jewish, and both Reform and Conservative Judaism have more lenient conversion requirements than Orthodox *halakha*.

How the state would register who is a Jew precipitated a crisis that nearly collapsed the government coalition in 1958. The minister of the interior stipulated that registration clerks should register the religion and nationality of an immigrant or citizen according to their self-identification, and specifically allowed for a couple comprised of a Jewish father and non-Jewish mother to register their children as Jews if they chose. It was not the prerogative of the registration clerk, the minister of the interior argued, to decide who was and was not a Jew, and therefore claims of Jewish identity must be taken in "good faith."[22] This was not a novel policy but reflected common practice throughout the state's first decade. Cabinet members debated the validity of these qualifications, with orthodox ministers insisting on halakhic criteria. In a gesture of compromise, the cabinet agreed to place stronger qualifications upon who may legitimately claim in "good faith" they were a Jew by stipulating that the individual could not be a convert to another religion. Since this did not resolve the policy's departure from *halakha*, two cabinet members still resigned from the government, and significant debate took place among Israeli policymakers and the public. In the aftermath of this controversy, the government formed a committee of inquiry to examine how to best register children of non-Jewish mothers whose parents wanted to register them as Jews. Ben Gurion, as head of this committee, solicited responses from nearly fifty of the most reputable religious and secular Jewish leaders in Israel and worldwide. The committee's ambitious goal was "to formulate registration guidelines 'that accord with the tradition accepted by all circles of Judaism, the Orthodox and liberals of all trends.'"[23] Over and above this, the guidelines had to comply with "the special circumstances of Israel as a sovereign Jewish nation ensuring freedom of conscience and religion and as the center for the ingathering of exiles."[24] In the absence of a decisive resolution to these ambitious requests, the cabinet ultimately decided to leave the definition of who is a Jew to the decision of the minister of the interior.

Status and identity do not always overlap neatly, and the diversity within Jewish history, and Zionist precedents for a wide range of interpretations of the Jewish nation, allow for individuals, families, and communities to identify as Jewish in myriad ways.[25] But the potential alignment between these identities and *status* in Israel is complicated by the persistence of religious jurisdiction for personal status alongside a civic jurisdiction for all other matters. Many Israelis contend that the persistence of dual statuses (regardless of how effectively they align with identity) creates practical inequalities based on religion, and that a democratic state is incompatible with religious requirements for marriage, divorce, and other areas of personal status.[26] Nitzan Horowitz has brought these arguments into his activism for the legalization of gay marriage in Israel, deeming "the separation of religion and state as central to our Zionist vision." For Horowitz and other LGBTQ+ activists, being a Jewish state does not mean having a religious administration: "the mixing of religious institutions in government and law violates the country's democratic character, without even strengthening its Jewish character."[27] Those who occupy different statuses under civil and religious jurisdictions can in fact face significant frustrations or obstacles. For instance, a woman with at least one Jewish grandparent (and who has not converted to another religion/does not constitute a danger to the state) can become a citizen of Israel under the Law of Return. She or any other female citizen of Israel is assured equality under the Israeli Declaration of Independence and the 1951 Women's Equal Rights Law, and thus cannot be discriminated against in government positions, voting rights, employment, or other civil rights. At the same time, she is subject to the gender requirements of her religion for family law. This has a host of practical implications; most notably, someone not considered Jewish by a religious court cannot legally marry in Israel, and/or if they divorce they can encounter significant legal problems in areas of child custody or remarriage. Marriages conducted abroad will be legally recognized, so Israeli couples often travel abroad to get married, or obtain civil unions instead. The maintenance of religious jurisdiction thus impacts many in Israel who legally and socially identify as Jewish by nationality, and continues to complicate the ongoing relationship between religion and nation evident in the start of the Zionist movement.

## WHAT IS A JEWISH (AND DEMOCRATIC) STATE?

Israel's Declaration of Independence pronounced itself as a Jewish state as well as one based on democratic values such as "complete equality of social and political rights to all its inhabitants" and "full and equal citizenship and due representation in all its provisional and permanent institutions."[28] In the absence of a constitution that specifies how these principles operate in different branches of government, some laws have been passed to formalize and strengthen what it means for Israel to be a Jewish state, a democratic state, and both a Jewish and a democratic state. In 1992 the Basic Law: Human Dignity and Liberty was legislated "to establish in a Basic Law the values of the State of Israel as a Jewish and democratic state."[29] The legal category of "Jewish and democratic state" had first been legislated in 1985 as an amendment to Basic Law: the Knesset. The amendment states that a political party list or candidate could not run for election "if the goals or actions of the list or the actions of the person, expressly or by implication, include . . . negation of the existence of the State of Israel as a Jewish and democratic state" (this amendment also deemed ineligible those who openly incite racism).[30] In 2003, Supreme Court Justice Aharon Barak issued a formal opinion on the meaning of this amendment, asserting that Zionism contributed to the "core characteristics" of what it means to be a Jewish state: the Law of Return, a Jewish demographic majority, Hebrew as "the official and principal language of the State," and holidays and national symbols centered in Jewish religious and cultural heritage.[31] Barak's minimum definition for democracy, to exist alongside these core characteristics, was "sovereignty of the people" through "free and egalitarian elections" and rights like "dignity and equality . . . separations of powers, the rule of law, and an independent judiciary system."[32] Despite the legal categorization of Israel as Jewish and democratic, the non-profit think tank Israel Democracy Institute (IDI) referred to the definition of the concept as "the big question," the answer to which varies across individuals.[33] This variation is to be expected given the a range of interpretations in Zionist history of how Jewish religious and cultural heritage—or what aspects of it—should be expressed in the context of a Jewish state.

While Israel operates a procedural democracy with processes like elections, checks and balances in government functions, and guarantees of individual liberties, the country could more accurately be described as an "ethnocracy" or "ethnic democracy," since its democratic process is limited by the requirement for the government to reflect the identity of an ethnic group.[34] Since Israel lacks other substantive features of democracies, such as a constitution and a separation between church and state, codifying the state as both Jewish and democratic further supports an ethnocratic model. The importance of a Jewish demographic majority in Israel in Israel's identity as a Jewish and democratic state is a frequent example of why the government could be termed more of an ethnocracy than democracy. Barak mentioned it in his legal ruling quoted above, and Amir Avramovitz, director in the generally centrist Israel Democracy Institute, explicitly identifies a Jewish majority as a condition for the "Zionist goal—democracy."[35] "Without such a majority," Avramovitz concludes, "it will be impossible to create a state which will be both a national Jewish state and a democracy."[36] If the democracy is at risk because of a demographic majority (or conversely if a demographic majority is at risk because of a democracy), it is reasonable to conclude that the system is an ethnocracy or some other kind of qualified democracy.

In 2018, the Knesset passed Basic Law: Israel as the Nation-State of the Jewish People (known as the Nation State Law) to specify and strengthen the Jewish character of the State of Israel. In 2011 members of the Knesset submitted a draft for this law in order to counterbalance what they saw as a disproportionate emphasis in the Supreme Court toward Israel's democratic nature, as well as growing scrutiny among different sectors of the legitimacy of the state's Jewish identity. The proposal became a fulcrum of debate in Israeli society, and the bill was considered over the next seven years until its ultimate passage in 2018. This law codified that Israel is a state for the Jewish nation, and that its state symbols, language, and policies regarding immigration and settlement prioritize and emphasize its Jewish character. As a Basic Law it essentially endows constitutional weight for the Zionist goal of creating and safeguarding a Jewish state. The prime minster at the time, Benjamin Netanyahu, hailed the law as "a pivotal moment in the annals of Zionism" and declared that "122 years after Herzl made his vision known, with this law we determined the founding principle of our existence."[37] Other members of the Knesset claimed it as "Zionism's flagship bill" and even "the most important law in the history of the state of Israel."[38] Supporters' fanfare over the significance of this bill indicated their confidence that the Basic Law concretized Zionist aims in the Israeli government; they hoped that it solidified the Jewish character of the state in the same way the Basic Law: Human Dignity and Liberty safeguarded Israel's democratic nature.

The law's proposal, as well as its passage, raised strong opposition and critique from different sectors of society who contested the need for such a law or the legitimacy of its content. Avner Inbar, a fellow for the center-left Israeli think tank Molad, asserted that "there is no need to counterbalance democracy with Jewishness when Jews enjoy a stable democratic majority, and no justification to do so if, someday, they won't."[39] The legal nonprofit Adalah asserted that the bill "create[d] various avenues for segregation in land and housing and incentives based on the principle of 'advancing Jewish settlement.'"[40] Critiques like these led to the most exclusionary components of the bill, such as the approval of Jewish-only communities, being removed from the final version. Members of the Israel Democracy Institute published many critiques of the law, and even drafted an alternative—Basic Law: The Character and Essence of the State of Israel—that would fortify both the democratic and Jewish character of the state instead of "just one aspect."[41] Other commentators, like members of Molad, echoed concerns about antidemocratic implications of the law while also questioning whether it does, in fact, guard Jewish identity. A Molad fellow warned that the law allows government imposition on the definition of Jewish identity and culture, since, he argued, "it is based on simplistic assumptions about the character of Jewish tradition."[42] Whereas articles of the law allow non-Jews to determine their own cultural contours, Jewish culture becomes constrained to official government interpretations.

Opposition to the Nation State Law raged even after its celebrated passage. After its vote, some members of the Knesset tore copies of the bill and were escorted out of the building. The Association for Civil Rights in Israel challenged the law in the Supreme Court, claiming it discriminated against the state's non-Jewish citizens and thus violated the Basic Law: Human Dignity and Liberty (discussed above). In 2021 the Supreme Court upheld the law with a majority of 10–1; the dissenter was the only Palestinian Israeli judge on the court. As the court discerned, the law codifying the character and symbols of the state is not unconstitutional because it does not in itself harm the civil rights of individual citizens. The conservative think tank Kohelet, which strives to "ensure that Jewish and Zionist values are an integral part of our legal system and civil society," celebrated the Supreme Court's decision and the law's potential to "rein in any trend which aims to redefine [Israel's] nationalism."[43] President of Israel at the time, Isaac Herzog, expressed more reservations, asserting that, "the question is whether the law will hurt or strengthen Israel. History will be the judge. I very much hope the delicate balance between [Israel's]

Jewish and democratic aspects will not be upset."[44] For Herzog and other skeptics, the Nation State Law, which was intended to end any ambiguity about the Jewish and democratic identity of the State of Israel, may have been controversial enough to only exacerbate the ambiguity of that dual identity further.

## CHANGES ON THE GROUND

Israel underwent watershed geographical, political, and social changes with the outbreak and outcomes of the 1967 War. The details of the causes of the war itself are complex, but in short, brinkmanship between Israel and the Egyptian president Gamal Abdel Nasser led to Israel's strike on the Egyptian air force, prompting a coordinated response by the militaries of Egypt, Jordan, Syria, and Iraq. Also known as the Six-Day War for its stunning brevity, Israel captured the Sinai Peninsula and Gaza Strip from Egypt, the Golan Heights from Syria, and the West Bank—including the Old City and East Jerusalem—from Jordan. Over 300,000 more Palestinians became refugees as a result of this war, fleeing mainly to Jordan.

The rightful arrangement of the territories and peoples affected by this war are hotly debated and fought over to this day. Israel, the Palestinians, the Arab countries, and the international community struggled with how to proceed after the war. The United Nations issued Resolution 242, which demanded the return of territories captured in war and maintenance of the prewar "Green Line" as the borders of Israel. Israeli officials initially seemed to anticipate relinquishing most of the land as part of a negotiated peace settlement. However, both Israeli and Arab contingents obstructed progress toward these ends. The Arab League Summit voted to refuse any negotiations for peace. Among Israelis, the potential benefits of the territories for national security and growth seemed too numerous to resist. Israeli journalist and historian Gershom Gorenberg referred to the continued Israeli control of these former Arab countries' territories as an "accidental empire," in which the inertia of the Labor administrations in Israel after the war created an environment where small military outposts and small exceptional religious settlements grew into "facts on the ground" that physically altered the social and political landscape.[45] When the Likud Party assumed the majority in 1977, infrastructure was already in place for the government to enact and facilitate its more overtly expansionist aims.

East Jerusalem was an exception to almost all discussions of land relinquishment, and Israel moved quickly to preserve it from any possibilities of return in a peace settlement. Its capture had major emotional resonance for Israelis and for Jews, Christians, and Muslims the world over, as it included Mount Zion, ancient churches, ancient synagogues, and perhaps most significantly, the Temple Mount, also the site of the Al-Aqsa Mosque and the Dome of the Rock. The neighborhood surrounding the Wailing Wall was quickly demolished to make room for a large plaza to accommodate worshipers and tourists, and to establish the new identity of the Old City. Most Palestinian East Jerusalemites consequently obtained Israeli permanent resident status but did not acquire citizenship (or voting rights). By 1980 Israel passed a Basic Law enshrining the whole of Jerusalem as the "complete and united" capital of Israel in order to prevent any policies that would divide the city into separate Jewish and Palestinian municipalities, and to affirm the legitimacy of the entire city's territory—not just the West Jerusalem area it controlled before the Six-Day War—as Israel's capital. Since 1967, the Old City of Jerusalem has become fairly seamlessly integrated with Western Jerusalem; a luxury mall now covers the area that had been the so-called "no-man's land" separating Jordan and Israel after 1949. Since both Palestinians and Israelis claim Jerusalem as their national capital, Jerusalem remains an especially contentious part of any negotiations regarding Israel and Palestine.

Israeli control of the territories captured in the 1967 War is generally referred to as occupation among the international community, since Israel entered in wartime conditions and continues to have a military, administrative, and growing civilian presence in these territories despite having not formally annexed them into the state. The United Nations Security Council resolved that Israeli control of the territories captured in the 1967 War is a violation of Article 49 of the Fourth Geneva Convention, which prohibits forced movement of civilians, and of UN Resolution 2625, which asserts "every State has the duty to refrain . . . from the threat or use of force against the territorial integrity or political independence of any State . . . Such a threat or use of force constitutes a violation of international law."[46] However, Israeli officials and Zionist supporters have argued that since the armistice lines from 1949 were not permanent borders but rather negotiated demarcations of control and ceasefire, and since Jordan's annexation of the West Bank after 1949 had not been universally recognized by the international community, Israel did not technically come to control another state's sovereign territory but rather a disputed territory.[47] Many Israeli officials have further maintained that the outbreak of war between Israel, Egypt, and Jordan annulled the agreed-upon armistice lines and thus expansion of control beyond them should not be considered illegal. Additionally, the official Israeli position on Israeli settlements is that since the Jewish Israelis who move to settlements in the disputed territory do so on a voluntary rather than forced basis, and since these Jewish communities do not explicitly "[intend] to displace Arab inhabitants," their movement does not violate the Geneva Convention's prohibition of forced relocation of civilians. Instead, the Israeli Ministry of Foreign Affairs considers the Jewish Israelis who move to these territories to be returning "to towns and villages from which they or their ancestors had been ousted."[48] In short, not only are the territories Israel has controlled since 1967 themselves disputed, but the classification of these territories as "occupied" is itself oftentimes disputed.

Regardless of whether Israeli settlement activity is intended to displace the Arab inhabitants or not, decades of policies in these territories have resulted in the creation of stark inequalities between its Jewish and Palestinian residents. While many smaller religious Jewish settlements have proliferated in these territories, most of the largest and most developed settlements are cities with both secular and religious Jews who have no religious or political agenda but are attracted by lower housing costs. This continued growth of Israeli Jewish settlement has resulted in increasing demands for land and military presence, and has also harbored vigilantism among more extremist Jewish settlers. While Palestinians in Gaza and the West Bank have no political representation in Israel, they are subject to Israeli policies and have served as an economic pillar of the Israeli labor market. This employment trend has reversed over the years; while in the early 1980s 70 percent of Palestinians in the territories worked within Israel, only 11 percent were able to by the early 1990s.

The political, military, and social status of the territories Israel acquired in 1967 continues to provoke a constant tide of resistance among Palestinians in the territories, Jewish and Palestinian Israelis, and people worldwide. In 1985 the Israeli cabinet adopted what they called an "iron fist policy" to manage the Palestinian population in the Occupied Territories, using widespread administrative detention, household raids, town curfews, and deportations to inhibit Palestinian dissent. By 2003 Israel had begun the construction of a separation barrier between the West Bank and Israel, the route of which went significantly further than the 1967 Green Line and is therefore considered by many, including the UN International Court of Justice, to be an illegitimate land grab. More military checkpoints were established throughout the West Bank to control or obstruct movement (ostensibly for security reasons, but some argue for political reasons as well). In 2005, Israel unilaterally withdrew all Israeli civilian settlements from the Gaza Strip and removed its military presence, but still has significant control over imports and exports from Gaza, its coastline and airspace, and population movement. Israel's withdrawal of civilian and military populations from the Gaza Strip has given Israel plausible deniability of Gaza's military occupation while simultaneously maintaining significant aspects of geographic, political, and economic sovereignty.[49]

## OCCUPATION AND THE SOUL OF ZIONISM

The changes that came about in 1967 reignited old debates about the goals and identity of the Zionist movement. Not long after the war, the Israeli finance minister worried that "if we keep holding the territories, in the end the territories will hold us."[50] By this he meant the policies that were followed in the territories would impact on and reflect the character of the state as a whole. As many commentators have noted, Israel cannot be Jewish, democratic, and in all territory of the biblical Land of Israel—any two of these will necessarily compromise the third. Israelis have thus grappled with how these characteristics represent the soul of Zionism and its place in the State of Israel, and what the implications are of prioritizing one aspect—Jewish, democratic, the whole Land of Israel—over another.

One of the most significant outcomes of the 1967 War was a revolutionary political mobilization of religious Zionists. Just weeks before the war religious Zionist leader Rabbi Zvi Yehuda Kook (son of eminent religious Zionist Rabbi Avraham Yitzhak Kook, discussed in Chapter 2) delivered an Israeli Independence Day speech that many of his followers later considered prophetic. Attendees described his voice as adopting an emotional pitch as he dismissed the significance of the establishment of Israel in 1948, insisting that without the whole territory of Israel they were still not victorious. "They divided our land! . . . Where is every meter of the land which [God] bequeathed to us alone?! Have we forgotten that all of the land is ours?! . . . Have we the right to give up even one grain of the Land of God? . . . But our prophets, our sages and those who followed them, said: 'The seed of Abraham, Isaac, and Jacob will return and will reestablish settlement and independent political rule in the Land.'"[51] The rapid wartime acquisition of these territories—the general area of ancient Judea and Samaria—seemed to religious Zionists like an act of God for a new stage of redemption. In the 1970s Zvi Yehuda Kook's students formed the influential network Gush Emunim (*Bloc of the Faithful*), which became the vehicle for expanding religious Jewish settlement into the West Bank. Gush Emunim forged ties between the Israeli government and leaders of the settlement movement and resisted possible attempts to exchange or surrender land in any peace deals. At times Gush Emunim leaders and members controversially used or condoned the use of terror to achieve its means, most famously with several plots to blow up the Dome of the Rock to force Israel's hand to acquire the Temple Mount. The organization fragmented by the mid-1980s but its leaders and supporters established political parties and formed the Yesha Council, a representative and administrative body of leaders in the West Bank that operates under the Israeli Ministry of the Interior. The 1967 War thus motivated religious Zionists to expand their involvement in the Israeli government beyond some of its earlier priorities of personal status law or state Sabbath and kosher observance. As a result, since 1967 religious Zionism has become salient in other areas of Israeli government as well, influencing and creating political parties and governing bodies (like Yesha) that help solidify the territories of the whole Land of Israel into the cultural and political landscape of the state.

The prospect of territorial expansion did not only propel Zionists inspired by biblical promises, but those with deep roots in the secular center-left Labor Party. Jewish American author Peter Beinart noted that the Labor Zionist history of pioneering, agricultural settlement and expansion, and romanticizing the landscape and legacy of the Hebrew Bible had imbued territorial expansion into "the Zionist

DNA."[52] Israel's military success revived earlier secular Zionist aspirations to settle what they termed "Greater Israel"—all territory west of the Jordan River. After the war secular cultural figures like renowned poet Haim Gauri formed the Movement for the Whole Land of Israel and supported expansion into the territories on a nationalist rather than religious basis. The Labor administrations after the war opted to allow small settlements not only to monitor security but also to honor the concerns of these supporters and ideologues. The support among both left and right, secular and religious for Israeli control and/or settlement of these territories remains one of the most consequential, contentious, violent, and yet also celebrated developments of the Zionist movement.

While segments across the political spectrum mobilized to retain and develop the territories after the 1967 War as a continuation or fulfilment of the Zionist movement, many Jewish Israelis mobilized opposition to this occupation and even insisted it threatened the character of Israel as a Jewish and democratic state. Peace Now was one of the earliest and most significant antioccupation organizations, forming in 1978 in response to Prime Minister Begin's openly expansionist aims. Peace Now warned in an open letter that "a policy that will lead to a continuation of our rule over a million Arabs will harm the Jewish-democratic character of the state, and will make it difficult for us to identify with the path of the State of Israel."[53] In 1989, organizers formed B'Tselem: the Israeli Information Center for Human Rights in the Occupied Territories (*B'Tselem* is Hebrew for *in the image*, alluding to the biblical account of humans created "in the image of God"). B'Tselem initially aimed to simply document human rights violations in the Occupied Territories, but the ongoing nature of the occupation led the organization to expand its goals, "to expose the injustice, violence and dispossession inherent to the regime of occupation, to deconstruct the apparatuses that enable it, and challenge its legitimacy in Israel and internationally."[54] Jewish Israelis

further left-leaning than those for Peace Now established Gush Shalom (*Peace Bloc*) in 1992 "to influence Israeli public opinion and lead
it towards peace and reconciliation with the Palestinian people," not
just by ending the occupation but by supporting a Palestinian right of
return and establishment of a Palestinian state.[55] At times, members
of these groups met with Palestinian leaders even when their respective governments refused to do so. Many other Israeli groups are specifically devoted to legal, humanitarian, and political concerns related
to the occupation; in 2004 former Israeli soldiers who served in the
Occupied Territories formed Breaking the Silence to "stimulate public debate about the price paid for a reality in which young soldiers
face a civilian population on a daily basis, and are engaged in the
control of that population's everyday life."[56] It aims "to bring an end
to the occupation" with the belief that "military rule enforced over
another nation necessarily violates basic rights of the civilian population and is impossible without the use of constant violence."[57]

Some of these criticisms of Israel's policies in the state and with the
Palestinians have been classed under the notion of "Post-Zionism"—
a term describing a "de-mythologizing attitude when examining
the Israeli and Zionist experience."[58] Initially the term referred to a
cohort of Jewish Israeli scholars in the 1980s and 1990s who placed
the Palestinian refugee crisis and its ramifications at the center of the
history of Zionism. They had access to newly declassified sources that
revealed the various intentional and unintentional ways that Palestinians were "cleansed" from the new State of Israel. These scholars
were part of the first generation to grow up in an era in which
Israel was an established fact, unlike its more precarious position
between the 1940s and 1960s; some have argued they therefore had
fewer compunctions about leveling criticism at their state. These
"New Historians" (one of these, Tom Segev, prefers the provocative
term "First Historians") challenged the wider narrative and identity
of Israeli history; instead of a beleaguered nation of immigrants

struggling to survive, Israel was culpable of crimes at its very founda-tion, and the influence of Zionism upon its government should be scrutinized thoroughly.[59] In post-Zionist critiques, therefore, criticism of the occupation of the Palestinian Territories is folded into broader critiques about the role of Zionism in the state.

## CONCLUSION

Theodor Herzl's exhortation that "if you will it, it is no dream" has now gone down in history, and can be found on T-shirts, mugs, and other paraphernalia around the world. Indeed, the State of Israel was Zionism's dream come true. But as Israeli author Amos Oz reflected, "the only way to keep any dream or fantasy intact and rosy and per-fect and flawless is never to try to live it out."[60] Living out the Zionist dream has both amplified old questions and raised new: What a Jew-ish state means in the context of democracy, family law, population movement, and war is a question that both supporters and critics—and critical supporters—continue to answer today.

# 5 | CHRISTIAN ZIONISM

## INTRODUCTION

In his diaries, Theodor Herzl recalled a visit from "a sympathetic and sensitive man, with the long grey beard of a prophet" in Vienna on March 10, 1896. This man was William Hechler, an Anglican priest and author of the tract *The Restoration of the Jews to Palestine* (1883). He was ready to use his connections with German royalty and nobility to propagate Herzl's plan for a Jewish state. Hechler mourned the persecution Jews were facing, especially in eastern Europe, and his reading (and elaborate calculations) of the Bible led him to believe that Jewish settlement in the Holy Land was a critical component of God's redemptive plan. Herzl recorded in his diary, quite matter-of-factly, that Hechler predicted Jewish sovereignty in Palestine in the year 1897–98. "Hechler declares my movement to be a 'Biblical' one," Herzl noted, "even though I go about it rationally."[1] Herzl and Hechler, both visionaries (and arguably eccentrics) in their own right, soon became friends and allies. Herzl's diary is peppered with endearing details and anecdotes about Hechler; on Herzl's first visit to Hechler's home, Hechler "sang and played for me on the organ a Zionist song of his own composition," and when the two met over a drink, "I drank Bavarian beer, Hechler milk."[2] "My good Hechler," as Herzl would refer to him, was a regular presence at the Zionist Congress, he accompanied Herzl when he met the German kaiser while touring Ottoman Palestine in 1898, and visited Herzl on his death bed in 1904. As it turned out, Hechler's interest and investment in the Zionist movement was just an early episode in the significant and ongoing involvement of Christians with Zionism that continues through the present day.[3]

Various Christian understandings of the relationships between Christianity, Judaism, the Bible, and the Land of Israel have materialized since the church was formed. New Testament scholar W. D. Davies, whose 1974 book *The Gospel and the Land* remains influential, posited that Christians have tended to approach the physical land of Israel in four major ways: "Rejection, spiritualization, historical concern, [and] sacramental concentration."[4] The reasons for this expansive range, from outright rejection to divine sacrament, are manifold. The New Testament is comparatively quiet about the issue of the land in contrast to its prominent role and setting in the Hebrew Bible, and the early church does not seem to have viewed the Roman destruction of Jerusalem or expulsion of the Jews as a unique threat to its own mission. Some early church leaders even welcomed the end of Jewish sovereignty in the land, such as second-century Church Father Justin Martyr who deemed the church as the "True Israel," a moniker that took on a destructive life of its own as church leaders embraced the concept in subsequent centuries. Teachings by Justin Martyr, John Chrysostom, and other Church Fathers regarding Jewish expulsion from the land cultivated major antisemitic tropes and misconceptions, most notably the belief that Jews were exiled as divine judgment for their rejection (and even crucifixion) of Christ and that this was a sign of their cursed status. The corollary to this belief was the teaching that the church superseded or replaced Israel by becoming the new and favored object of its ancient promises. This doctrine, known as supersessionism or replacement theology, discouraged any question of whether Christians needed to support the idea of a Jewish political presence in the land promised in the Hebrew Bible. Any Scripture regarding the land was generally viewed as either nullified or reca-pitulated as spiritual rather than physical blessings. Christians did not view the land itself negatively, however, and maintained a connection to it as a pilgrimage site (or, in the medieval Crusades, as an object of conquest).

The Reformation ushered a significant shift in Christian thinking about the Land of Israel. The Reformers' emphasis on close study of Scripture—and particularly the Old Testament—invigorated Protestants' interest in the people, territory, and prophecies of the Bible. The physical movement and resettlement of Protestant commu-nities, at times as a result of religio-political persecution, was evocative of biblical narratives of exodus, settlement, exile, and return. The significance of Jerusalem in the Gospels and in the book of Revelation stoked interest in its role in God's plan for fulfilling promises for the Second Coming and Last Judgment. Protestant writers penned books and tracts about the restoration of the Jews to the Holy Land; thus the belief in and support for this return is known as restorationism. Seismic political shifts led Christians to contemplate seismic spiritual shifts, and by the time of the French Revolution, Napoleonic Wars, and rise of industrialization, people anticipated and even mobilized for new developments in God's providential plans. When the political Zionist movement emerged at the end of the nineteenth century, res-torationists reasoned that the expected return of the Jewish Diaspora to the Land of Israel—and therefore, more importantly, the Second Coming of Christ—could be imminent.

There is no single, official definition of Christian Zionism. Defini-tions of Christian Zionism can include Christians who support Zion-ism as well as Christians who support Zionism for specifically Christian and theological reasons, which can augment or even replace elements of "regular" Zionism. Within these broad definitions there are gener-ally four main types of Christian Zionism: dispensationalist, biblical/ Hebraic, humanitarian, and political/civilizational. These types are by no means mutually exclusive—there are certainly individuals and organizations who would share some if not all features of them (and conversely, there are some who would oppose tenets of other types, even while supporting the same aims). These types of Christian Zionism generally have distinctive historical backgrounds and scriptural emphases, and also garner distinctive critiques.

## DISPENSATIONALIST CHRISTIAN ZIONISM
### Background

One of the most influential, and arguably most controversial, forms of Christian Zionism emerged from a theology known as dispensationalism. This theology asserts that God deals with humanity differently in different periods of human history, called dispensations, which are constituted by unique promises, tests, and fulfilments. According to this framework, the Covenant Age of Abraham and the patriarchs, for instance, was distinct from the Age of Law, which constituted the time from Moses through the establishment of the Church Age, beginning at Pentecost. While dispensationalists differ on the correct number of dispensations, they all agree that dispensations circumscribe different plans for Israel and the church. Dispensationalists maintain that while Christ's death and resurrection are the basis for salvation for both Jews and Christians, the two groups are not recipients of the same promises or destinies, and the Bible must be read and interpreted accordingly. This ideology thus provides a template for biblical teaching: Scriptures that relate to the people of Israel—and particularly related to land promises—are not to be extrapolated or reinterpreted as applying to the church in any way; Scripture that establishes or instructs the church is similarly distinct from Israel's mission.[5] Most notably, dispensationalism maintains that God's ultimate redemption will manifest differently for these two groups: Israel will receive an earthly kingdom, located in the geography specified in the Hebrew Bible, and the church will reign with Christ from heaven.

Dispensationalist theology emerged in the mid-nineteenth century, attained wider prominence in the early twentieth century, and was popularized by the end of the twentieth century. In the 1840s Anglican Irishman John Nelson Darby taught that when the Jews rejected Jesus's first coming, God established the church among Gentiles with the promise of spiritual salvation in heaven. According to Darby, the Jews had an outstanding promise of earthly restoration in Israel that will occur when the church is fully built up and taken by Christ before his millennial reign. American pastor William Blackstone expanded upon dispensationalist teaching in his 1878 book *Jesus Is Coming*. This book analyzed and cross-referenced biblical themes, passages, and details concerning the end times, and emphasized the role of a contemporary return of Jews to the Holy Land. Blackstone created various diagrams illustrating the different dispensations and the unfolding of the rapture, tribulation, second coming, millennium, and final judgment. Blackstone laid a detailed foundation for dispensationalism that appealed to ministers like Dwight Moody and R. A. Torrey, though his teachings did not yet widely influence laypeople.

Cyrus Scofield brought dispensationalism to a much wider audience. His 1909 Scofield Reference Bible was the first Bible massproduced with commentary on the same pages as Scripture. Scofield's reference notes were meant to facilitate what he viewed as the most literal interpretation of the Bible, so that readers would not read additional meaning into passages—and specifically that readers of the Prophetic books would not attribute to the church what was meant for the people of Israel.[6] Scofield's study Bible had great commercial success and Oxford University Press issued new editions in 1917 and 1967. It is still in print in many languages today.

Darby, Blackstone, and Scofield taught that the tribulation was a pivotal event in God's plan and the last stage of the church dispensation of grace. They believed Christ will come secretly to bring the church into heaven—by resurrection for Christians who have already died and by rapture for Christians contemporary to the event. During the seven-year tribulation a figure called the antichrist will forge a false worldwide peace that will culminate in terrible persecution and an international military invasion of Israel. The nation of Israel will realize on a mass scale that Jesus had been the Messiah, and many Jews will evangelize the world at this time. At the close of the tribulation Christ will return to Earth and establish a thousand-year reign from his seat in Jerusalem. At the end of this millennium, he will execute the Final Judgment, destroy Satan, and establish the New Heavens and New Earth. Darby, Blackstone, and Scofield all predicted that the physical gathering of Jews in Israel and the rebuilding of the Temple would take place after the rapture and during the tribulation. But regardless of the timeline, they taught that the Jews in Israel would feature centrally in the end of days.

The Zionist movement and the establishment of Israel in 1948 struck a key change for proponents of dispensationalism. The 1967 War that resulted in Israel's control of East Jerusalem and the biblical territory of Judea and Samaria seemed even more portentous as the potential dawn of the Kingdom Age. Dispensationalism made its way out of study Bibles and onto best-seller lists. Hal Lindsey's *Late Great Planet Earth* (1970) vividly linked dispensationalist interpretations of biblical prophecy with contemporary geopolitics. Lindsey made some modifications and unique contributions to his dispensationalist predecessors; he placed the establishment of Israel *before* the tribulation instead of during, and he confidently detailed how Russia is the force referred to as the "king of the North" (Daniel 11:40 and Joel 2:20) and will spearhead the multinational war against Israel.[7] Lindsey's narrative captured the imagination of millions, and he still maintains a significant television and internet presence. Tim LaHaye and Jerry B. Jenkins fictionalized the dispensationalist schema in the *Left Behind* action novel series. The series of sixteen novels, the first of which was released in 1995, has sold tens of millions of copies and has been adapted into at least four films. Dispensationalist theology has been espoused in major Christian institutes of higher education such as Dallas Theological Seminary, Moody Bible College, and Liberty University. Dispensationalist theology thus continues to influence the leadership and culture of a wide number of Christians.

## Scriptural Basis

Scriptural passages that are especially foundational for dispensationalism and dispensationalist Christian Zionism are those that highlight the geography of end times prophecies. Passages that refer to Jerusalem and the Temple in any multinational conflict are particularly important. Dispensationalists do not generally interpret these passages to refer to the destruction of the First Temple by the Babylonians in 586 BCE or the Second Temple by Rome in 70 CE, but rather to foretell the events of Christ's return and the end of the age. The finality of certain pronouncements, like those in Zechariah 14 and Joel 3:17–21, support a dispensationalist view of a battle in the Holy Land that, unlike that in 70 CE, ends with decisive victory for Israel. Zechariah says "Jerusalem will remain aloft on its site . . . It shall be inhabited; for never again will it be doomed to destruction. Jerusalem shall abide in security" (Zechariah 14:10–11). Ezekiel prophesizes that multinational forces "shall go against a land restored from war, a land where people were gathered from many nations on the mountains of Israel, which had long lain waste; its people were brought out from the nations and now are living in safety" (Ezekiel 38:8), and dispensationalists believe this illustrates the Jews' return "from many nations" with the establishment of Israel in 1948, and the recovery from wars that took place there since its establishment.

New Testament Scripture like Jesus's statements in Luke 21:20 and Matthew 24:16 are regarded as further proof of this end-times conflict: "When you see Jerusalem surrounded by armies, then know that its desolation has come near" (Luke 21:20). The dispensationalists regard 2 Thessalonians 2:1–12 as a crucial text describing the antichrist, in which Paul describes the "man of lawlessness" or "man of sin" who will "[set] himself up in God's temple, proclaiming himself to be God" (2 Thessalonians 2:4). Dispensationalists attribute these passages to end-time prophecy rather than the 70 CE destruction of the Temple. The references to Har Megiddo (Armageddon) in Revelation 16 are perhaps the most famous of these predicted multinational battles in the end of times, and dispensationalists interpret this to mean that Israel would be present in Galilee for a final battle. Dispensational Christian Zionists interpret these passages' specific geographical markers in the Land of Israel as proof for the inevitability of conflict in the region during God's final stages of world redemption.

Dispensationalists also highlight passages that support a dispensationalist distinction between Israel and the church. Paul's writings in Romans 9–11 are one commonly cited example. Paul points to Israel's role in world redemption, juxtaposing Israel and the Gentiles: "Now if their stumbling means riches for the world, and if their defeat means riches for Gentiles, how much more will their full inclusion mean!" (Romans 11:11–12). This passage is interpreted to imply that despite Israel's rejection of Jesus as the Messiah and the consequent creation of the church, the promises made to Israel as a nation throughout the Hebrew Bible still apply to Israel, which retains its own redemptive trajectory that will ultimately complement rather than compete with that of the church. Similarly, in 11:28–31 Paul's contrast between the Gentile Christians and Israel overall is interpreted by dispensationalists to mean a broader, fixed contrast between the roles of each of them, yet to be fully realized. Finally, dispensationalists make an argument from the silence in the Hebrew Bible on any *explicit* reference to an entity called the church. Its absence in the Hebrew Bible is for dispensationalists an indication that the church was not relevant to Israel's own trajectory.

## Critique

Dispensationalist Christian Zionism has its critics both from within the church and in other sectors of society. Some Christians oppose dispensationalism for theological and/or hermeneutical reasons.[8] For instance, despite its claims to be the most literal reading of Scripture by refusing to transmute promises to Israel into promises for the church, dispensationalism is criticized as a form of eisegesis (reading interpretations into Scripture rather than exegeting meaning from the text). It does so by dividing God's relationship to humanity in overly schematic ways that ignore or twist the meaning of scriptural passages and themes. In particular it fails to account for both Old and New Testaments as a totality in which Jesus Christ is the ultimate promise and revelation of God's Word, as well as the many explicit passages regarding the unity of the people of God (such as John 17:20–26, Acts 15:6–11, Romans 11:13–24, and Ephesians 2–3). Reformed theology has especially taken issue with dispensational hermeneutics; the Presbyterian Church of America deemed dispensationalism outside the Westminster Standards (its summary statement of faith), and Israeli Reformed pastor Baruch Maoz has critiqued it as an "atomization" of Scripture.[9] This atomization lends itself to its own use of figurative interpretations in the name of literalism. For instance, attempting to declare direct correlations between Scripture and current events—like citing the north as Russia or the formation of the European Union as the precursor to the antichrist—could be at best hermeneutical overreach or at worst an abuse of Scripture.

Dispensationalism has also drawn criticism for its occasional expressions of antisemitism. At first glance this seems contradictory, since a system of thought that emphasizes the Jews' unique and enduring blessing from God runs counter to antisemitic beliefs about the Jews' accursed status. Indeed, some arguments against dispensationalism can recall latent forms of Marcionism—a heresy from the second century CE that denied any divine inspiration of the Old Testament or the covenants with Israel. Nevertheless, proponents of dispensationalism have succumbed to antisemitic claims. Dispensationalist figurehead William Blackstone accused Jews of "blindness, and hard, stony hearts" that led to their rejection and crucifixion of Jesus, and referred to the Jews' "guilt of innocent blood"—rhetoric mirroring the long-standing antisemitic charge against all Jews for deicide and echoing other antisemitic tropes like the blood libel.[10] Many dispensationalists predict the antichrist will be Jewish and explain this in very problematic ways. Prominent dispensationalist pastor and political lobbyist Jerry Falwell explained that the antichrist was predicted to be Jewish because a false messiah would need to be Jewish in the same way Jesus was. But dispensationalist author Hal Lindsey and pastor Pat Robertson have given descriptions of this Jewish antichrist that echo antisemitic tropes like Jewish control over banking and Jewish propagation of communism. Lindsey writes of the antichrist's false prophet that "this person, who is called the second beast, is going to be a Jew . . . he will be given control over the economics of the world system and cause everyone who will not swear allegiance to the Dictator [antichrist] to be put to death or to be in a situation where they cannot buy or sell or hold a job."[11] David Brog, a Jewish leader who works closely with Christian Zionists, conceded that while they may not harbor animosity against Jews, dispensationalist Christian Zionism does seem to propagate a binary worldview in which everything is a battle between good and evil, and in which conspiracy theories—many of which borrow from historic antisemitic claims—are deployed for explaining complex processes.[12] Both Christian and Jewish critics of dispensationalism also accuse dispensationalists of using Jews and Israel as a means to an end (and one that would not go well for many of them, no less). This not only objectifies Jews but could even be construed as wishing harm for them, as those bearing the full brunt of the anticipated events. Dispensationalists forcefully deny these accusations, instead pointing at their enduring value of the Jewish people, and in the ultimate benefit of God's final redemption.

Some Christians, including some dispensationalists themselves, also take issue with how dispensationalism gets applied in Zionist politics. Historian Judith Mendelsohn Rood, who embraces dispensationalist theology, argues that dispensationalism is only meant to prevent misinterpretation of Scripture by dismissing its context, and does not have direct policy implications with respect to Zionism.[13] Other critics of dispensationalism in Zionist politics emphasize that belief in a special role for Israel in the end times or even the enduring promise of the Land of Israel to the Jews should not amount to uncritical support of any policies by the Israeli government, especially those that may persecute or discriminate against Palestinians. Dispensationalist Mark Bailey, a Bible scholar and administrator at Dallas Theological Seminary, noted for example that Ezekiel 47:21–22 refers to non-Jews in the restored Israel, whom Israel is to consider "as citizens of Israel; with you they shall be allotted an inheritance among the tribes of Israel."[14] Bailey thus situates Palestinian inclusion in Israel as part of a dispensationalist framework. Dispensationalist John S. Feinberg also asserts that "we can say unequivocally that Scripture forbids social and political oppression and injustice," and therefore there is no biblical mandate for "unwavering support" of Israeli policies if they promote injustice.[15] Dispensationalist emphasis on Jewish inheritance of the Land of Israel or on end-times strife should not, critics say, promote obstructionist, belligerent, or exclusionary policies in Israel/Palestine, and can even coexist with criticism of these policies.

## BIBLICAL/HEBRAIC CHRISTIAN ZIONISM
### Background
While dispensationalism has been particularly influential for Christian Zionism, not all Christian Zionists are dispensationalists, and many prefer to use the term "Biblical Zionism." This term is

both meant to distance "Christian Zionism" from dispensationalist connotations, and to serve as a succinct claim to biblical authority. Biblical Zionists argue that one need not use a dispensationalist "template" for Scripture to conclude that the covenant God made with Abraham and his descendants, and the land that it entailed, is permanent. Consequently, Biblical Zionists are especially conscious of hermeneutical attempts to allegorize or spiritualize promises of the Land of Israel to apply to the church as God's people. Celebrating and supporting the presence of Jews in the Land of Israel as a natural fulfilment of biblical promises is thus the foundation of Biblical Zionism. Biblical Zionism often shares many commonalities with dispensationalism, such as premillennialism (the doctrine of a literal thousand-year reign of Christ inaugurated at his second coming). But Biblical Zionism does not stress different redemptive trajectories for Jews and Gentiles, and it tends to emphasize the ways that the establishment of Israel has *already* fulfilled biblical prophecy, rather than its end times implications.[16]

Related to "Biblical Zionism" is what could be termed "Hebraic Christian Zionism," which underscores the Jewish character of the Bible itself (both the Old and New Testaments). These Christian Zionists identify with Israel as an expression of Jewish culture, themes, and traditions that have influenced Christian faith but have been denied or obscured under centuries of church tradition and Christian antisemitism. One Christian Zionist newsletter lamented that, "Paul instructs Gentiles to learn from the nation of Israel. Sadly, later Church leaders led our heritage out of the illuminating Hebrew olive grove down the darkening tunnel of Greek philosophy, Roman polity and Western conformity."[17] Another Christian Zionist organization urges Christians to support Zionism as a debt owed to Jews for being the source of their faith. Hebraic Christian Zionism is thus viewed as a corrective for replacement theology, as it recognizes Israel's blessing and distinct identity within God's plan (without making it so distinct as to be separate, as can be the case in dispensationalist thought). This emphasis on "recovery" of Hebrew customs has led Christian Zionists to embrace the Feast of Tabernacles and Feast of Weeks, citing Zechariah 14:16–19, which prophesizes the Gentiles will observe the Feast of Tabernacles, and Acts 2 in which the Spirit is given to both Jews and Gentiles who had gathered for the Feast of Weeks (Pentecost). The centrality of Jerusalem for the celebration of these festivals encourages Christian sympathies with Zionism and Israeli control of territory where the Temple once stood.

## Scriptural Basis

Biblical Zionism generally emphasizes passages about the permanence of God's covenant with Abraham and his descendants, and of the Kingdom of David. Verses like Psalm 105:7–11 declare that God "is mindful of his covenant forever . . . which he confirmed to Jacob as a statute, to Israel as an everlasting covenant, saying, 'to you I will give the land of Canaan as your portion for an inheritance.'" Other passages refer to an eternal dwelling, such as Amos 9:15 in which God promises that "I will plant [Israel] upon their land, and they shall *never again* be plucked up out of the land that I have given them," and Joel 3:20, which declares that "Judah shall be inhabited *forever*, and Jerusalem to *all generations*" (emphases added).

Biblical Zionists also cite passages depicting a physical ingathering of the tribes of Israel to the land promised to the patriarchs, as these passages are interpreted to be fulfilled with Jewish immigration to the Holy Land during the Zionist movement and after the State of Israel was established. While many of these prophecies are certainly about the return of Judah from Babylon under King Cyrus in the sixth century BCE, other verses stand out for their more universal character. For example, Ezekiel 36:24 states, "I will take you from *the nations*, and gather you from *all the countries*, and bring you into your own land" (Ezekiel 36:24, emphasis added). Isaiah 11:12 promises that God will "gather the dispersed from the *four corners of the earth*" (emphasis added;

see also Jeremiah 23:7–8). Jeremiah specifically says that "in those days the house of Judah shall join the house of Israel, and together they shall come from the *land of the north* to the land that I gave your ancestors for a heritage" (Jeremiah 3:18, emphasis added). Since the ten tribes of Israel are traditionally deemed as lost, having not returned *en masse* from Assyrian exile, this passage of Israel's reunion with Judah is particularly compelling for Biblical Zionists because Israel's return had not been fulfilled during biblical history the way Judah's had been. Biblical Zionists thus point to the Jewish ingathering that began with the Zionist movement and continued after the establishment of Israel as fulfilment of the Bible's prophecies of Israel returning to the land from the nations and the north, and even more foundationally, the fulfilment of God's faithfulness to his people.

## Critique

Like dispensationalist Zionism, Biblical Zionism has invited critiques on both practical and hermeneutical grounds. A key hermeneutical argument is that Biblical Zionism tends to conflate Old Testament promises with each other, so that promises made to the Patriarchs, Moses, Joshua, the united Kingdom of Israel and Judah, the tribe of Judah, the tribes of Israel, the exiles in Assyria or Babylon are not only interchangeable with each other, but are also "transferred from the biblical text to the state of Israel."[18] Anthropologist Aron Engberg demonstrates how this is done with the foundational passage, Genesis 12:3, when God promises Abram "I will bless those who bless you, and whoever curses you I will curse." "To interpret [this] as referring to a religious obligation to express political, moral and financial support for a contemporary state, and the ways in which divine blessings (and curses) are tied to these practices, is, hermeneutically speaking, very far from a literal interpretation," Engberg writes.[19] The most literal interpretation of the passage would instead yield an almost opposite reading, that the promise would apply only to individuals in contact with the person of Abraham, and not to subsequent generations of Abraham's descendants. Critics thus allege that Biblical Zionists who apply passages like Genesis 12:3 to the modern State of Israel apply the same type of allegorizing they claim to resist.

Furthermore, commentators have underscored that the Bible is not conclusive on specific geographical outcomes for God's people. The scope of the promised land in the Old Testament itself is ambiguous, with different boundaries specified in different parts of the Hebrew Bible. Numbers 34:1–12 is one of the few detailed demarcations and is significantly different than the scope stated in other passages (compare, for instance, with the other land descriptions in Joshua 15:1–12 or Ezekiel 47:15–20). Some biblical scholars argue that God's expansive land promises are meant to convey "size, scale, and quality" of the promise rather than specific borders.[20] When a passage says the promised land will reach "from the Red Sea to the [Mediterranean Sea], and from the wilderness to the Euphrates" (Exodus 23:31), or from "the Wadi of Egypt to the great river, the Euphrates" (Genesis 15:18; see also Deuteronomy 1:7 and 11:24, and Joshua 1:4), it actually expresses a reach of God's promise to the "inhabited world," rather than determining geographic limits.[21] As Palestinian scholar and pastor Yohanna Katanacho explains it, "God's intentions were not to formulate fixed borders but to unite the ends of the world under the Abrahamic banner."[22]

The relative silence about the land in the New Testament could further support the perspective that the Bible is ambiguous about the geography and demographic makeup of God's land promises. Bible scholars have noted Paul's letters as an indication of this; in Romans 4:13 he writes that Abraham received a promise that he "would be heir of the *world*," instead of the land, which is the word used in the original promise to which Paul refers—possibly implying that God's original promise of the Land was part of a wider promise for the world.[23] In Ephesians Paul rewords the promise for the Fifth Commandment with a similar conflation of the Land with the

Earth. While Exodus 20:12 and Deuteronomy 5:16 command honor for father and mother, "so that you may live long in the land that the Lord your God is giving you," Paul writes that this command is the first to come with the promise that "you may live long *on the earth*" (Ephesians 6:2–3, emphasis added). Paul is evidently not fastidious about the actual territory of the promise to Abraham or in the Fifth Commandment. Jesus himself also had much to say about the Gospel's scope beyond the Land of Israel. He assures the woman at the well that God desires worshipers in Spirit and truth, not in Jerusalem or Gerizim (John 4:21). When the disciples ask the resurrected Jesus if he is finally going to restore the kingdom to Israel, Jesus essentially redirects their target boundary: "It is not for you to know the times or periods that the Father has set by his own authority. But . . . you will be my witnesses in Jerusalem, in all Judea and Samaria, and to the ends of the earth" (Acts 1:6–8).

Scholars and ministers who oppose the concept of Biblical Zionism prioritize verses and scriptural themes that assert God's covenants have been fulfilled in Christ. What it means to be fulfilled in Christ is debated; passages that directly compare Israel and Christ could suggest that it is Christ, and not a specific nation (or the church for that matter), who is the ultimate *recipient* of the promise of the land. Fulfilment in Christ could also mean that promise of land was in fact a promise of a Messiah born from that land, and therefore that he was the ultimate inheritance of the covenant. Jesus's comparison of the destruction and rebuilding of the Temple to his own body is perhaps the most vivid example of himself equating or superseding a geographic location (John 2:19–21, Matthew 26:59–64; Jesus also refers to himself as "greater than the Temple" in Matthew 12:6). But scholars have also noted how the New Testament drew other comparisons between Jesus and key prophecies about the restoration of the Land. For instance, Jesus's claim to be the "living water" (John 7:30–39) could allude to Ezekiel 47:1–12 and Revelation 22:1–2, which depict a river of life flowing from the Temple through Jerusalem—a passage some-times cited by Biblical and Dispensationalist Zionists as proof of a future literal Temple instead of an illustration of Christ. In Acts 15:16 James seems to interpret Amos 9:11–12, promising the rebuilding of David's tent, as having been achieved with the resurrection of Christ, thereby equating the restoration of Israel with Jesus's resurrection.[24] If the Bible teaches that Christ's appearance, resurrection, and/or sec-ond appearance were in fact fulfilment of the promises that included the Land of Israel, then the Bible would not then directly support a stance of Biblical Christian Zionism.

Critics of Biblical Zionism also note that the New Testament has much to say about the expansion of the inheritors of the promise to include anyone in Christ, both Jew and Gentile. Prophesies, psalms, and commandments include non-Israelites in the recipients of the Land (Psalm 87, Isaiah 19:23–25) or at least permanent equal resi-dents (i.e., Exodus 22:21, Leviticus 19:33 and 23:22, Joshua 8:32–35). Even more explicitly, Paul instructs the Galatians that "those who believe are descendants of Abraham . . . If you belong to Christ, then you are Abraham's offspring, heirs according to the promise" (Galatians 3:7, 29). In Romans Paul calls all believers co-heirs with Christ (Romans 8:17), and to the Ephesians he writes that Gentiles who were "aliens from the commonwealth Israel and strangers to the covenants of promise" have been included, since God has "made both groups into one" and created "one new humanity in place of the two," so that both Jews and Gentiles are "citizens with the saints," "members of God's household," and "built together spiritually into a dwelling place for God" (Ephesians 2:11–22). These interpretations are not to be confused with supersessionism, since Gentile believers do not replace Israel but are rather added to it.

Critics also raise practical objections to Biblical Zionism, asserting that it can fail to uphold biblical requirements of justice, a prerequi-site for anything that would profess to be biblical. Wheaton College

New Testament scholar Gary Burge argues that the biblical promises to inhabit the Land are contingent upon Israel meeting the biblical conditions given by God to Moses on Mt. Sinai. According to this perspective, Biblical Zionism is only legitimate if the modern State of Israel can or does uphold these biblical commandments, particularly in the treatment of the foreigner—in the contemporary context, the Palestinians.[25] Some self-professing Biblical Zionist scholars, pastors, and activists readily concede this point, insisting that blessing Israel and blessing Palestinians can happen simultaneously. Israeli Messianic Jew Philip Ben-Shmuel argues for a "Christ-like Zionism" that blesses Jews and Palestinians with equal rights in the same land.[26] These critiques share a concern that "biblical" must be a standard that applies the teachings of scripture in a holistic way, and warn that Biblical Zionism can focus on a limited set of passages and themes (like the restoration of the Jews to the promised land) at the exclusion of others like justice toward the foreigner.

## HUMANITARIAN CHRISTIAN ZIONISM
### Background

Another main type of Christian Zionism has been driven by humanitarian motivations to alleviate or prevent Jewish suffering from antisemitism. Early Christian Zionists expressed this in their motley efforts; William Hechler viewed Herzl's Zionist project as a solution to the poverty and discrimination that eastern European Jews faced, and William Blackstone made humanitarian concerns the cornerstone of his early campaigns to "consider the condition of the Israelites and their claims to Palestine as their ancient home, and to promote, in all other just and proper ways, the alleviation of their suffering condition."[27] Blackstone argued that the situation of the Russian Jews was intolerable, and therefore the two million Russian Jews must relocate, "but where shall . . . such poor people go? Europe is crowded . . .

Shall they come to America? That will be a tremendous expense, and require years. Why not give Palestine back to them again?"[28]

Antisemitism had been worsening during the latter part of the nineteenth century and reached genocidal proportions by the 1930s and 1940s. Protestant Christian groups campaigned against British restrictions on Jewish immigration to Palestine as it limited their possibilities for escape from Europe. In the aftermath of World War II, Christian groups urged the establishment of a state both to accommodate displaced Holocaust survivors and to prevent the recurrence of institutionalized antisemitic persecution. Mainline (Episcopal, Methodist, Presbyterian) Protestant denominations were the vanguard for this type of Christian Zionism. Reinhold Niebuhr, perhaps the most influential mainline pastor and thinker of the twentieth century, campaigned for Zionism on almost entirely humanitarian grounds, remaining "curiously inattentive" to any other theological connotations of the movement.[29] "The Jews require a homeland," Niebuhr wrote in 1942, "if for no other reason, because even the most generous immigration laws of the Western democracies will not permit all the dispossessed Jews of Europe to find a haven in which they may look forward to a tolerable future."[30] Niebuhr warned that the Nazi persecution of Jews across Europe did not arise in a vacuum and therefore it would still be a dangerous place for Jews even in a Nazi defeat.

Even after the establishment of Israel, Christians continued to advocate for Zionism on humanitarian grounds. Martin Luther King Jr. visited Jerusalem in 1959, and in 1967 signed a letter against Egypt's saber-rattling rhetoric against Israel that ultimately spurred the Six-Day War. In 1968 King asserted that "peace for Israel means security, and we must stand with all of our might to protect its right to exist, its territorial integrity."[31] Niebuhr also wrote of Israel's need for defense as the "David" against the "Goliath" of the Arab world ("a population of 20 to 40 million people"), which "never accepted Israel's existence as a nation or granted it the right of survival."[32] He therefore considered supporting Israel in the wake of the 1967 War as an existential need. Calls for Christian Zionism on humanitarian grounds often cited the Holocaust; in 1975 the Ecumenical Theological Research Fraternity in Israel issued a statement urging Christians to "be aware that Zionism . . . was for most Jews the only viable answer to anti-Jewish racism culminating in the destruction of European Jewry during the Nazi Holocaust."[33] Jewish Zionist author and activist David Brog even compares later Christian Zionists with the Righteous Gentiles who risked their well-being to rescue Jews from the Holocaust.[34] More recent literature from a major Christian Zionist organization frames support of Zionism as a way to "help combat the growing darkness of anti-Semitism," comparing Christian Zionism to the action of Rahab "who . . . was blessed because she protected two Jewish men from death."[35] Christian support of Zionism on humanitarian grounds has thus endured well beyond the earlier Christian Zionist organizing on behalf of creating a state for Jews.

Christians have also framed support for Zionism as rectification for centuries of antisemitism and replacement theology. Zionism is cited as a remedy against what Jewish philosopher Jules Isaac has termed the church's "teaching of contempt," and, as Niebuhr claimed, could serve as a "partial expiation" for the fruits of this teaching.[36] Supporting the creation or maintenance of a state specifically for Jews is understood as an "act of restorative justice" for Jewish marginalization and persecution.[37] Influential Christian scholars Roy and Alice Eckardt, who worked closely with Niebuhr, linked support for Israel with mending Christian–Jewish relations, such as in their book *Encounter with Israel: Challenge to Conscience* (1970). Another more recent writer confessed in a circular for a prominent Christian Zionist organization, "after centuries of wounding curses inflicted upon the Jewish people by my Christian forebears, I realized that I was being given the opportunity to be a vessel of God's mercy for the healing of Jewish hearts."[38] This perspective underscores a belief that Christians, despite their culpability in Jewish suffering in the past, can help rectify the harm of this suffering by contributing material and moral support to the State of Israel.

## Scriptural Basis

Humanitarian Christian Zionism is generally galvanized more by circumstances than by specific scriptural interpretations. Of course, the Bible is replete with commands and exhortations to care for those in need generally. But there are some verses that humanitarian-based Christians Zionists have cited for their stance. A very common example of this is Psalm 122:6–9, exhorting the reader to "Pray for the peace of Jerusalem." Another verse is Romans 15:26–7, in which Paul tells the Romans that the Gentile churches in Macedonia and Achaia were "pleased to make a contribution for the poor among the Lord's people in Jerusalem." Paul adds with this example the general observation that "for if the Gentiles have shared in the Jews' spiritual blessings, they owe it to the Jews to share with them their material blessings." This verse has been interpreted by humanitarian Christian Zionists to encourage material support for the Zionist movement and State of Israel.[39]

## Critique

Christian Zionism based on humanitarian concerns is subject to several critiques, the most significant being the humanitarian impact Zionism has had on Palestinians and the Arab world. In 1956, the World Council of Churches stated that, in response to Israel, "we cannot say an absolute *no*, for we must sympathize with the sufferings of the Jewish people and rejoice whenever by God's grace they are delivered from them. Yet we cannot say an absolute *yes*, for the setting up of the State of Israel . . . has involved great suffering to many Arabs who have lost their land and their homes."[40] One critic told Niebuhr that "until I am otherwise persuaded I shall have to agree with the Arab who said to me in effect: 'You Christians and

Westerners, not we, persecuted the Jews and you make us pay the price."[41] In the same aforementioned speech in which Martin Luther King Jr. called for Israel's security, he also emphasized the need for Arabs to be granted economic security. Historian Clayborne Carson, who has written and overseen many projects on Dr. King, confirmed "King's heartfelt concern for the economic and racial injustices that plague the Palestinian people."[42] These critics stress that any support of Zionism must therefore consider the whole picture of humanitarian concerns. The destruction of Palestinian villages in 1948, refusal to readmit refugees after the war, military occupation of land acquired in 1967, and unequal resources or representation of Israeli Palestinians in Israel, must also inform Christian pursuits of humanitarian interests in the region.

## POLITICAL/CIVILIZATIONAL CHRISTIAN ZIONISM
### Background

The final major motivation for Christian Zionist support is bolstering and defending strategic political and/or civilizational aims. The category "Judeo-Christian," situating Christians and Jews as social and spiritual allies, started to crystallize in the early to mid-twentieth century. Nineteenth-century biblical studies had led to a growing awareness among Jewish and Christian scholars of the Jewishness of Jesus himself and of the Bible as a text. While Jesus's Jewish identity may seem obvious today, centuries of antisemitism promoted ignorance or denial of that reality. The stark social, political, and religious differences that existed between Christians and Jews, particularly in Europe, prevented an easy hyphenation of "Judeo-Christian." By the 1920s and 1930s, there was growing awareness and cultivation of this shared identity in the United States, with groups forming to foster relationships between the communities.

Two major phenomena led mid-twentieth-century Christians to think of themselves as part of the same tradition as Jews. First was the outcome of the Holocaust, which prompted Christians both in Europe and worldwide to reckon with how they were implicated in the genocide of European Jews, and thus what Christians owed to Jews both historically and morally. Second was the rise of the Cold War and the fight against communism. Many Christians and Jews in the United States increasingly saw themselves as fellow believers in God struggling against the atheistic basis of communism. Jewish American author (and former communist activist) Will Herberg was a noteworthy proponent of this idea; his seminal book *Protestant-Catholic-Jew* (1955) helped popularize the concept of Judeo-Christianity in America, which he suggested was based on shared faith in "the American Way of Life." This American Way of Life encompassed the historically unlikely communion of Catholics, Protestants, and Jews, and did not and could not include those from other religions, who, according to Herberg, would always be foreign to American culture. Herberg speaks fairly parenthetically about Zionism, but the notion of a shared Judeo-Christian culture eventually became foundational for Christian support of a Jewish state. Espousal of a Judeo-Christian way of life has persisted beyond the Cold War competition between communism and capitalism; by 2006, Zionist activist David Brog objected to the media's use of the term "strange bedfellows" to describe Christian–Jewish cooperation for Zionism, since, he argued "there is at the heart of this alliance a shared passion for a shared moral code that transcends differences" between the two religions.[43]

Another common political motivation for Christian support of Zionism is as a force in a civilizational struggle against Islamic terror or domination. Niebuhr warned that "Israel is the only sure strategic anchor of the democratic world, particularly since Khrushchev and Nasser have proved that Islam is not as immune to Communism as had been supposed."[44] Niebuhr's analysis was factually wrong—Nasser was vehemently opposed to Islamic political influence during his rule and persecuted the Egyptian Islamic Brotherhood—but

UNDERSTANDING ZIONISM

the sentiment about the twin threats of communism and Islam is illustrative of Christian motivations for strengthening Zionist causes. The 1979 Revolution in Iran, deposing the US- and Israel-allied Muhammad Reza Shah and installing a government under Shia Muslim clerics, mobilized American Christians to support Israel militarily and ideologically against Iranian threats. As pastor John Hagee stated in a 2007 speech, "it is 1938; Iran is Germany and Ahmadinejad is the new Hitler." This statement was arguably over-stepping the boundaries of historical analogy, but was met with a standing ovation, indicating the resounding acceptance among Christian Zionists that Israel faced against Islamic Iran the same existential threat as that of European Jews against Nazism on the eve of World War II.[45]

The terrorist attacks by al-Qaeda against the United States on September 11, 2001, provoked new urgency among Christian Zionists. These attacks took place at the same time as the Second Intifada, during which terror by Palestinian Islamic groups Hamas and Islamic Jihad were rampant in Israel. Many Christian Zionists therefore adopted and supported policies that approached attacks or threats from any Muslims—whether Iranians, al-Qaeda, or Palestinian militants—as battles in the same war. Mike Evans, one of the more openly right-wing Christian Zionist leaders, deemed Israel "the last firewall between Islamic terrorists and America."[46] Christian Zionists sent a letter to President George W. Bush imploring him to defend Israel as they "attempt to defeat the *same forces* of terrorism that we [America] have been battling since [9/11]" (emphasis added).[47] Pastor and Republican political activist Pat Robertson warned that Islam was the force that wanted to "give East Jerusalem to [Palestinian leader] Yasser Arafat" and in so doing was no less than part of "Satan's plan to prevent the return of Jesus Christ."[48] These views imply a fear that if Israel were to fall, the US would lose its only strong ally in the region and there would be no one to keep the majority-Muslim countries of the Middle East from uniting to coordinate a

132

catastrophic war against the United States and the creation of an Islamic world order.

Some Christian Zionists view Zionism not only as a defense against geopolitical collapse but also as a lever for divine favor or punishment. This position indicates what historian Daniel Hummel has called a "nation-based prosperity theology," where supporting Israel is a necessary component of inviting God's favor on a national level.[49] In this paradigm, weak support of Israel as a Jewish state in possession of territory promised in the Bible does not just pose a political or military threat but a spiritual and existential one. For instance, a Chick Publishers tract entitled "Love the Jewish People" lists African countries that cut diplomatic ties to Israel and subsequently suffered famine. The tract also lamented that while "God blessed England" when it supported the Jews' demand for a national homeland during the British Mandate, its abandonment of Zionism meant "God has CURSED Britain! She is finished as a major power . . . because she crossed the Jews!"[50] This cause-and-effect relationship is frequently touted by other Christian Zionists. Jerry Falwell preached that "If this nation wants her fields to remain white with grain, her scientific achievements to remain notable, and her freedom to remain intact, America must continue to stand with Israel."[51] Some prominent American Christian Zionists also surmised that tragedies like the assassination of Israeli prime minister Yitzhak Rabin in 1995, Hurricane Katrina in 2005, and the stroke and coma of Israeli prime minister Ariel Sharon were consequences of Israeli willingness to return biblical land to Palestinians and the United States' support of land-for-peace plans.[52]

## Scriptural Basis

Christian Zionism based on political and civilizational motivations is not typically reliant on scriptural arguments (or when it is, it generally marshals many of the same Scriptures and interpretations as those that undergird other types of Christian Zionism). Genesis 12:1–3 is common verse for a transactional political Christian Zionism, in which God promises Abraham that "I will bless those who bless you, and the one who curses you I will curse." Aside from this foundational passage, political/civilizational Christian Zionists quote passages in Genesis about the destiny of other nations, specifically those who descend from Noah's cursed son Ham and from Ishmael, Abraham's first-born son through Sarah's handmaiden Hagar. Christian Zionist leaders have reasoned that Ishmael would never have been born if Abraham and Sarah had been patient and had faith in God's original promise for their child. Influential leaders like Hal Lindsey, Jerry Falwell, and Franklin Graham have taught that Ishmael and his descendants, the Arabs, live in a perennial unresolved rivalry because of this disobedience. Some translations of Genesis 16:12 say Ishmael "will be a wild donkey of a man; his hand will be against everyone and everyone's hand against him, and he will live in hostility toward all his brothers," and this is sometimes cited as proof of a wider civilizational rivalry. Despite the fact that other translations have interpreted this passage to be that Ishmael will "live in proximity to all his brothers," translations of Genesis 16:12 are still used to suggest a permanent animosity between the Arabs as the descendants of Ishmael and the Jews as the descendants of Isaac.[53]

The influential Scofield Reference Bible also perpetuates ideas of essential civilizational differences based on the account of Noah and his sons Shem, Japhet, and Ham in Genesis 9:18–27. Genesis 9:19 states that from Noah's three sons "came the people who were scattered over the whole earth." Ham dishonored Noah and thus Noah pronounced a curse on Ham's son Canaan, that "the lowest of slaves will he be to his brothers." In his note for Genesis 9:1 Scofield identifies this curse as the source of a decisive civilizational rift, stating that "government, science, and art, speaking broadly, are and have been Japhetic, so that history is the indisputable record of the exact fulfilment of these declarations."[54] In the same note Scofield also concludes that, "a prophetic declaration is made that from Ham will descend an inferior and servile posterity." The use of Genesis 8 and

9 as prooftexts to extrapolate a timeless conflict between descendants of Shem and Japhet (the creators of civilization), and descendants of Ham and Canaan (subject to servitude), can frame Zionism and the State of Israel as representatives of the "right side" of prophetic history. Those who resist them—specifically Palestinians or more broadly, Muslims—therefore represent an accursed people on a futile mission.

## Critique

Many Christians believe that the civilizational conflicts invoked regarding Zionism are not substantiated either historically or theologically. Arguments that Jews, Muslims, and Christians will inevitably clash ignore the many rich legacies of shared society (albeit imperfect, like any society) between these religious groups in both the Middle East and various parts of the world. Furthermore, historical method demands attention to change over time and the influence of various contexts and their contingencies, rather than essentializing entire groups of people and their histories.[55]

Beyond historical discrepancies, there are also theological and hermeneutical critiques. Many Christians object to the prosperity gospel model that dominates in this type of Christian Zionism, in which diplomatic, financial, and theological support for the State of Israel is treated like currency in God's providential economy. Furthermore, Bible scholar Tony Maalouf argues that there is a biblical basis for the Arabs' inclusion, rather than rejection, in God's plan.[56] Ishmael received his own blessing and role in redemptive history, and is not meant to be considered an accursed figure. God promised to bless Ishmael and to make him into a nation as well, and even the meaning of his name testifies that "God hears" (Genesis 17:20, 21:13). God's description of Ishmael as a "wild donkey of a man" (Genesis 16:12) was meant to imply freedom and to reassure a weeping Hagar that her son would experience a stark contrast to her own enslaved state. The Bible reports cooperation between the two brothers and their descendants;

Ishmael and Isaac buried their father together, and members of the Hagarite and Ishmaelite tribes are listed as leaders in King David's government (1 Chronicles 27:30, 1 Samuel 27:8, 1 Chronicles 2:7). Arabs are also depicted in the Bible as playing positive roles: Arabian traders rescued Joseph from death, Moses's father-in-law Jethro was Arabian and had descendants that served as Temple scribes, and young Jesus and his family are sheltered in Egypt as refugees from Herod. The "biblical history yields no evidence of a sustained pattern of enmity between the line of Ishmael (and the biblical Arabs associated with him) and that of Israel."[57] As a result, "uninformed Christians should stop spreading the idea that this conflict is unavoidable since it is deeply rooted in biblical history and prophecy."[58] Christians should focus on ministry and evangelism, rather than on holy wars with religions or their adherents. Ultimately, creating civilizational dichotomies does not support the overall message of Jesus's ministry and Great Commission to make disciples of all nations.

## ORGANIZED CHRISTIAN ZIONISM

The varying motivations for Christian support of Zionism—Dispensationalist, Biblical, Humanitarian, and Political—have propelled a robust Christian Zionist movement made up of a variety of organizations with wide-ranging agendas. Many of the earliest Christian efforts on behalf of Zionism were individual initiatives, such as those by William Hechler who worked alongside Herzl. Another example was William Blackstone, who organized one of the earliest campaigns for Jewish settlement of Palestine; in 1891 he undertook a newspaper advertising campaign to encourage President Benjamin Harrison to support Jewish settlement in Palestine. He also organized a petition of signatures, known as the Blackstone Memorial, among hundreds of prominent American pastors, businesspeople, and elected officials. His projects did not ultimately propel concrete policy changes, though they did spur American leaders to consider their role in the issue, and later Supreme Court Justice Louis Brandeis even urged Blackstone to reissue the petition to President Woodrow Wilson during the geopolitical upheaval of World War I.

Initially, larger-scale Christian organizing on behalf of Zionism was primarily led by mainline Protestant Christians. The Federal Council of Churches (precursor to the contemporary National Council of Churches) launched a fundraising effort for Zionism as early as 1928, and by the mid-1940s the American Christian Palestine Committee formed under the leadership of prominent ministers like Reinhold Niebuhr to advocate for American and international support for a Jewish state in Palestine. Once Israel was established in 1948, evangelical Christian Zionist organizing gradually coalesced, rising in prominence between the 1980s and the turn of the twenty-first century. Organized Christian Zionist efforts have exercised a few main and often interconnected emphases: political advocacy, humanitarian aid, education, and tourism. These activities have been international in scope, and despite its largely American origins, they have gained increasing traction among Christians in the Global South as well.

## Zionist Partnerships with Christians

Some of the cooperation between Christians and Zionism has been welcomed and cultivated by Zionist leaders. The early Israeli Ministry of Religion established an office for Christian Affairs, and circulated the periodical *Christian News from Israel* to promote awareness of Christian activities and freedoms in Israel. In 1961 Israel hosted the World Conference of Pentecostal Churches, which received a written address by Prime Minister David Ben Gurion and during which all attendees received a state medal. Furthermore, the prominent Zionist Israeli archaeologist Yohanan Aharoni taught at a Christian educational institute in Jerusalem. These gestures demonstrated Israeli appreciation and encouragement of formal Christian support of the Jewish state.

This gradual cultivation made way for more concerted efforts at Israeli–Christian cooperation after the 1967 War. World opinion was divided on Israel's wartime acquisition of Jerusalem and the areas of what was in the Bible called Judea and Samaria. In 1971 the Israeli government provided facilities for the Jerusalem Conference on Biblical Prophecy and the retired David Ben Gurion addressed this major gathering in person.[59] Subsequent conferences and summits have boasted prominent Israeli officials, from ambassadors to prime ministers, as speakers and participants. Israeli prime ministers have enjoyed close relationships with prominent Christian Zionist leaders, perhaps most famous being the friendship between Menachem Begin and Jerry Falwell, on whom the Israeli government conferred the prestigious Jabotinsky Award (named after the Revisionist Zionist founder). Former Israeli prime minister Shimon Peres and former IDF chiefs of staff have also served as chairmen and on the board of governors for a Christian Zionist museum in Jerusalem. In 2004 members of the Israeli Knesset formed the Knesset Allies Caucus, which hosts regular meetings with Christian Zionists. The partnerships between Christians and Zionist causes have thus been mutually reinforcing over the years.

## Political Advocacy

Some of the largest and most active Christian Zionist organizations have made political advocacy for Zionism central to their aims. The abovementioned 1891 Blackstone Memorial is an early individual case (and a strategy he renewed with a petition to President Woodrow Wilson in 1917 to support the British Balfour Declaration). In the wake of World War II, the American Christian Palestine Committee lobbied Congress to pass a pro-Zionist resolution. By the end of the 1970s one of the most significant conservative Christian advocacy groups, Jerry Falwell's Moral Majority, deemed support of Israel a key part of its platform. Another significant organization, the International Christian Embassy in Jerusalem (ICEJ), formed in direct response to Israel's 1980 Jerusalem Law, which enshrined Israel's possession of both West and East Jerusalem as a united capital of Israel. As this law formalized annexation of East Jerusalem, most countries that had embassies in West Jerusalem (which had been part of Israel since its founding) relocated embassies to Tel Aviv in protest. The creation of a "Christian Embassy" in Jerusalem was thus a physical statement to support Israel's law and its claim to both West and East Jerusalem. Among other objectives, the ICEJ maintains branches internationally to organize "pro-Israel marches and petitions, aimed toward governments and people of influence."[60]

Other prominent organizations and organizational branches have formed to facilitate Christian Zionist political advocacy. The International Fellowship of Christians and Jews founded in 1983 is not itself a Christian organization but it mobilizes Christian Zionists through its Stand for Israel program, "providing [Christians] with the facts they need to advocate for the Jewish state and fight anti-Israel bias in the media," and to undertake political lobbying and "informal advocacy" at the grassroots level.[61] Christians United for Israel (CUFI), founded in 2006 and currently boasting ten million members, hosts an annual summit in Washington DC that includes a lobbying blitz at the Capitol. Its stated mission is "to act as a defensive shield against . . . political threats that seek to delegitimize Israel's existence and weaken the close relationship between Israel and the US."[62] The longest-serving Israeli prime minister, Benjamin Netanyahu, even claimed he considered CUFI "a vital part of Israel's national security" due to their successful mobilization of support.[63] Groups like CUFI have lobbied for concrete policies, such as relocating the United States embassy from Tel Aviv back to Jerusalem (undertaken by the Trump administration in 2018), withdrawing funding from UN agencies due to claims that they are biased toward Palestinians or enable terrorist activities, and calling for sanctions or even a preemptive strike on

Iran. These political advocacy groups thus strive for grassroots influence among Christians, as well as diplomatic influence among elected
officials.

One of the most contentious policies Christian Zionists have
supported is for continued Israeli control of all territory con-
quered during the 1967 War. In 1995, the Christian Friends of
Israeli Communities formed as a "Christian response to the Oslo
Peace Accords," which was a then-historic agreement to establish a
Palestinian government in Gaza and the West Bank in exchange for
normalized relations with Israel. This group raises around a million
dollars annually from Christians, who aim to materially and morally strengthen Jewish settlements (oftentimes called "communities"
by those who reject the more pejorative term "settlements") in the
land already negotiated to Palestinians. The grassroots appeal of
Christian support for Jewish settlement in the territories was highlighted in a cover story for a "Christian Edition" of the *Jerusalem
Post* magazine, featuring Christian contributions to the major West
Bank Jewish city Ariel. "Its expansion is a sore point for Palestinians
and left-wing activists," the article notes, but it "owes much of its
success to the city's special connection to Evangelical Christians,"
cultivated by the city's mayor.[64] Individual church congregations
and organizations provided Ariel with volunteers for work projects and funds for everything from a mini-golf course to medical
equipment.[65]

The Temple Mount, especially sacred in both Judaism and
Islam, has been a flashpoint in Israeli politics and Israeli–Palestinian
violence, and is another piece of contested land that Christian
Zionists have campaigned to belong to Israel. After Israel's capture
of East Jerusalem in 1967, Israel maintained its policy of status-quo
agreements for administration of religious properties and jurisdictions, and thus Muslim custodianship of the Temple Mount continues per the status quo under the prior Jordanian, British, and
Ottoman governments. Despite these agreements, some nationalist

religious Jewish groups have partnered with some Christian Zionists to pursue building the Third Temple on this spot.[66] The Temple Institute in Jerusalem, established by Jewish Israeli proponents for the Third Temple, oversees research and advocacy about the Temple construction and operation, and Christian Zionist leaders such as Calvary Chapel founder Chuck Smith have contributed finances, publicity, and other efforts for this cause. Mississippi pastor Clyde Lott and his organization Canaan Land Restoration of Israel Inc. launched agricultural collaborations between groups in the US and Israel to breed a red heifer needed for the Temple's consecration and maintenance ("The common denominator between us is cows," Lott said of Christians and Jews).[67] Individual pastors and ministries are donors to the Temple Institute and frequent its museum in Jerusalem, which displays replicas and "Temple-ready sacred vessels."[68] These practical partnerships advance a distinct political trajectory that rejects current international agreements and negotiations.

## Humanitarian Aid and Outreach

Some Christian Zionist organizations undertake large-scale humanitarian aid projects for Israelis and Jewish immigrants to Israel. Christian Zionists view these efforts as serving a dual purpose of comforting those in need while also fulfilling redemptive prophecy. The Christian Zionist organization Bridges for Peace, founded in 1967, celebrates that its volunteers and supporters "put our faith into action with 50.8 tons of kosher food provided monthly . . . across the land of Israel. That means 26,000 people are fed monthly, 390 hungry school children receive hot lunches daily, and hundreds of other precious Jewish lives are strengthened in their call to build up Zion. Bridges has repaired over 1,050 homes, [and] stockpiled 318 tons of wartime readiness supplies."[69] The International Christian Embassy in Jerusalem runs programs for immigrant support and social assistance, including "food, dental care, computer equipment, hearing aids, oxygen tanks, furniture, sheets, shoes, coats, an ambulance, a medical clinic, playground equipment, [and] heaters."[70] Bridges for Peace, along with the International Fellowship of Christians and Jews, also provide funding and resources to aid Jewish immigration to Israel, such as paying for immigrants' airfares or chartering flights. The Christian organization HaYovel (Hebrew for "Jubilee") organizes Christian volunteers to aid farmers in West Bank settlements, especially during harvest seasons.[71]

The issue of evangelistic outreach has been a hotly contentious question in the development of Christian Zionism. Proselytization has been a sore spot in Jewish–Christian relations broadly, including in Israel. After centuries of forced conversion, forced assimilation, and religious persecution and marginalization, many Jews and Christians have concluded that any efforts to bring Jews into the church are painfully fraught and should be avoided. While some Israeli ultraorthodox groups and politicians have put forth antimissionary legislation in Israel, it has not passed, but there has still been a tacit agreement between Christian Zionists and Israelis who work with them that evangelism would not be part of their efforts.[72] The Knesset Christian Allies Caucus is explicitly opposed to missions targeting Jews, and the founder of Christian Friends of Israeli Communities shared that her "relationship with her Christian partners and donors has long been based on their willingness 'to set aside any evangelizing agenda.'"[73] While there are certainly evangelism efforts taking place in Israel, many if not most openly Zionist Christian organizations emphasize acts of service rather than explicit evangelism. Spiritual outreach thus mainly takes the form of organized prayer efforts. The annual International Day of Prayer for the Peace of Jerusalem is a major example of this, bringing as many as 200,000 congregations together in simultaneous prayer for Israel. Mike Evans's Jerusalem Prayer Team has as many as seventy-seven million members.[74] Turning to God in prayer on behalf of Israel, rather than trying to evangelize Israelis directly, is thus less socially and politically disruptive and, for believers, possibly even more spiritually potent.

## Educational Efforts and Institutions

Many Christian Zionist organizations have prioritized education, both for the purpose of spiritual edification and for public advocacy. The early American Christian Palestine Committee "carried on a comprehensive educational program into the late 1950s and early 1960s to inform the American public concerning the new Israel," organizing seminars and conferences, maintaining a speakers' bureau for regular lectures, and publishing literature.[75] In the aftermath of the 1967 War, Reinhold Niebuhr's student Franklin Littell, who would go on to be perhaps the foremost Christian scholar of Holocaust studies and Jewish–Christian relations, collaborated with other mainline ministers and academics to establish the advocacy group Christians Concerned for Israel. Later Christian Zionist organizations prioritized education and information, and the largest Christian organizations, like CUFI, Bridges for Peace, and ICEJ, publish a prolific number of books, blogs, pamphlets, magazines, newsletters, and videos. CUFI states "our mission and vision is foremost to educate our members before motivating and activating them," and it circulates a daily newsletter, Israel365, to a quarter of a million subscribers.[76] CUFI even has materials for children, from YouTube channels to Sunday school curriculum. Bridges for Peace also touts its "long heritage of biblical Zionist scholars [who] have shaped our education ministry so that today we offer invaluable resources like . . . the news magazine Dispatch from Jerusalem, the monthly Hebraic-rooted Israel Teaching Letter, and a weekly email update from Jerusalem."[77] The Friends of Zion Museum in Jerusalem was established in 2015 with the purpose of educating Christians about their own history of Christian–Zionist cooperation. Providing regular and detailed information about the relationships between Israel, Zionism, and Christianity through a wide variety of media is a significant way

Christian Zionist organizations can deepen individuals' knowledge of and engagement with Zionism, while also widening the number of individuals in their spheres of influence.

## Study Programs

Along with a steady volume of publications and media, many Christian Zionist organizations facilitate study programs and leadership seminars in or about Israel and Zionism. The Institute of Holy Land Studies, now called Jerusalem University College, was founded in 1957 by American Christian Zionist Douglas Young to educate Christians on biblical history and geography. The college maintains long- and short-term study programs both in-person and online, with courses transferrable to a wide number of prominent Christian colleges and universities internationally. Rabbi Shlomo Riskin established the Center for Jewish Christian Understanding and Cooperation in the West Bank settlement city of Efrat, gaining significant participation among Christian Zionists. HaYovel frames its volunteer program as an educational experience through meeting Israeli Jewish communities in action.

Tourism is another major facet of Christian Zionist activity and often plays a key role in educational initiatives. There are different types of Christian tourism to Israel with different emphases. Many tour programs underscore the spiritual growth and identity that the first-hand experience of travel to the Holy Land can bring, and church congregations worldwide organize their own trips for this purpose. The Israeli Ministry of Tourism has focused attention on Christian tourism, creating a "Christian Leader's Toolkit" for planning tours.[78] The ICEJ Feast of Tabernacles is a major annual event for Christian Zionist tourism. Christian Zionist organizations offer other themed tours; the tour program Passages promotes tourism for Christian young adults on the basis that "a trip to Israel should be a rite of passage for every Christian."[79] Bridges for Peace also orchestrates year-long programs for young adults to volunteer in Israel in their "Zealous 8:2" program.

The proliferation of these study programs and tours have led other Christian groups to sponsor programs that do not have as explicit a Zionist emphasis, or are even critical of Zionism as a whole and aim to counterweight Christian Zionist programming.[80]

Other Christian Zionist tours promote a deeper understanding of Israel as a Jewish state and key Middle Eastern ally. One tour program asserts that "although the itinerary . . . emphasizes the spiritual aspect of this marvelous country, our guides are also experts in and passionate about the miracle of the return of the Jews and the restoration of the state of Israel. This fact, along with many modern day topics (military, politics, education, and other cultural aspects), will be woven into the commentary in order to give you well rounded information."[81] Christian tour groups that utilize official Israeli itineraries will include what the Israeli Ministry of Tourism has mandated as part of official tours, which are Masada (the fortress of the second-century battle between the Romans and Jews), the Western Wall, and Yad Vashem (the Holocaust memorial). These sites provide more background on and immersion in the Jewish history of the land alongside Christian devotional or biblical sites.

## CONCLUSION

The many organizational efforts by Christians in support of Zionism—political advocacy, education, humanitarian aid—can and do overlap and reinforce each other. Enrollment in an educational course in the settlement city of Efrat, for example, is more than education, it simultaneously develops knowledge of the Bible and Jewish traditions while also bolstering moral and financial support of a continued Israeli presence in the West Bank. Aiding Jewish immigration to Israel may place individuals struggling in one country in another perhaps more equipped to provide them services, while at the same time impacting the ongoing demographic question in Israel regarding the size and implications of the Jewish and Arab populations.

These multilayered motivations and outcomes were evident as early as Hechler's energetic campaign for Herzl's Zionist vision—both for the sake of the persecuted and impoverished east European Jews, and for the participation in the unfolding of prophecy. Navigating the roles of biblical interpretation and changing political realities remains the source of extensive mobilization, disagreement, and discipleship for many Christians engaging Zionism.

# 6 | ANTI-ZIONISM

In 2018, Israeli American actress Natalie Portman announced her refusal to attend a ceremony in Jerusalem where she was meant to be awarded the "Genesis Prize," known as the "Jewish Nobel Prize." "Recent events in Israel have been extremely distressing to her," a spokesperson noted in reference to violence between Israel and Palestinians the Gaza Strip, "and she does not feel comfortable participating in any public events in Israel."[1] Moreover, she opposed sharing a stage with right-wing Israeli prime minister Benjamin Netanyahu, who was slated to speak at the ceremony. Right-wing Israeli officials were quick to condemn Portman, who had a history of public support for Israel, including working as a research assistant for the outspoken supporter of Israel Alan Dershowitz at Harvard University, and writing and directing a film adaptation of the preeminent Israeli author Amos Oz's fictionalized autobiography, *A Tale of Love and Darkness*. One member of the Knesset even wanted to revoke her Israeli citizenship, which he claimed was used as a "tool for the haters of Israel."[2] The Israeli minister of energy claimed Portman's statement "borders on anti-semitism," and speculated that Portman would not have boycotted other countries with alleged human rights abuses.[3] Gilad Erdan, the minister of internal security and senior affairs, even appealed to Portman's role in the *Star Wars* movies, warning her that she was making the same mistake as Anakin Skywalker who "began to believe that the Jedi Knights were evil, and that the forces of the Dark Side were the protectors of democracy . . . I call upon you not to let the Dark Side win," urged Erdan.[4] The minister of culture Miri Regev meanwhile lamented that Portman "fell into the hands of BDS [Boycott, Divestment, and Sanctions] supporters."[5]

Natalie Portman clarified that she did not support the BDS movement to which the minister of culture referred. "Like many Israelis and Jews around the world, I can be critical of the leadership in Israel without wanting to boycott the entire nation."[6] She insisted, "I treasure my Israeli friends and family, Israeli food, books, art, cinema, and dance," and stated that she took the stand she did "because I care about Israel."[7] Analysts hailed Portman's decision as a herald for strained American support for Zionism. A columnist for *Business Insider* criticized Portman's statements for misunderstanding the history and nature of Zionism altogether.[8] Alternatively, the organization Peace Now released an ad campaign supporting Portman. Palestinian activist Yousef Munayyer published a piece in the American Jewish periodical *Forward*, with the headline, "Actually, Natalie Portman, You ARE Practicing BDS."[9] The controversy over Portman's decision highlights a convergence of critical issues in wider and ongoing debates about Zionism and its place in the State of Israel. For some, like Portman, dissent over Israeli policies expresses a loving stand against "violence, corruption, inequality, and abuse of power," while others warn that public criticism of Israel acts as a cover for antisemitic attitudes and policies. This range between patriotic critique and outright antisemitism has led policymakers to debate and delineate differences between anti-Zionism and antisemitism. Other commentators and activists ponder at what point criticism of Israeli policies crosses into criticism of Israel's Zionist foundations as a whole.

Opposition to Zionism entails a wide range of positions that is arguably as diverse, misunderstood, and at times even contradictory as Zionism itself. The left-leaning (some would say radical) organization

Jewish Voice for Peace defines anti-Zionism as "a loose term referring to criticism of the current policies of the Israeli state, and/or moral, ethical, or religious criticism of the idea of a Jewish nation-state," whereas the center-right-leaning Anti-Defamation League (ADL) defines anti-Zionism as "a prejudice against the Jewish movement for self-determination and the right of the Jewish people to a homeland in the State of Israel," which "can include threats to destroy the State of Israel (or otherwise eliminate its Jewish character), unfounded and inaccurate characterizations of Israel's power in the world, and language or actions that hold Israel to a different standard than other countries."[10] Anti-Zionism is thus understood as opposition against *actions by Israel* as well as opposition to or criticism of *the idea of a Jewish state itself*. Because these various spheres or expressions of opposition to Zionism can be so disparate, the term "anti-Zionism" is not actually a helpful concept, because it does not itself specify *what aspect* of Zionism is being opposed, or *what form* of opposition is being employed. Therefore, instead of trying to create a definition of anti-Zionism, it is more productive to inquire how different types of opposition to Zionism emerged, diverged, and evolved. Understanding the differences and contingencies between various types of opposition to Zionism is also necessary to better understand the divisive and important issue of the relationships between anti-Zionism and antisemitism.

## OPPOSITION TO ZIONISM AFTER THE ESTABLISHMENT OF ISRAEL

After Israel was established in 1948 and the war between Israel and Arab countries cooled with armistice agreements in 1949, military tensions and diplomatic ostracization became the norm between Israel and the Arab world. Many Arabs viewed Israel as an imposition of European imperialism—indirect political, cultural, and/or economic control of one government over another (as compared to colonialism, which entails direct administrative control). From the perspective of Arab countries, Israel was a continuation of the

British-sponsored Zionist movement that prevented the creation of an independent Arab state after the fall of the Ottoman Empire. The joint attack by Israel, Britain, and France on Egypt to prevent the nationalization of the Suez Canal in 1956 further cemented the view that Israel was an extension of the West. Against this background Egyptian president Gamal Abdel Nasser became the celebrated icon of a wider pan-Arab and anti-imperialist political identity, and his popular rhetoric about destroying Israel was one of the factors that led Israel to strike the Egyptian air force, initiating the 1967 War. Not all Arab countries shared Nasser's pan-Arab vision, however. King Abdullah of Jordan showed willingness to tolerate the Zionist cause if it meant strengthening his control of the West Bank, which Jordan annexed after the 1948 Arab–Israeli war, and Lebanon had anti-Muslim political factions that favored alliances with Israel. Nevertheless, all Arab countries raised concern over the plight of the Palestinians, even though they had no unified vision or plan to overcome it. Many Arab countries refused (or still refuse) to acknowledge Israel as a legitimate political entity, referring to Israel instead as the Zionist state, occupied Palestine, or "the '48 territories."

Internationally, many countries that had recent or ongoing struggles against colonialism sympathized with the Palestinian viewpoint of the establishment of Israel as a form of colonialist control over an indigenous population. In the 1970s Palestinian American scholar Edward Said penned his seminal essay "Zionism from the Standpoint of Its Victims," arguing that Zionism "can only be studied genealogically in the framework provided by imperialism."[11] Said claimed that from its beginnings Zionism relied on European division of "overseas territories and natives into various uneven classes"; he thus concluded "that is why . . . every single state or movement in the formerly colonized territories of Africa and Asia today fully supports and understands the Palestinian struggle."[12] Said's sweeping claim that "every" movement supported Palestine may be impossible to substantiate, but indeed many international diplomatic and political gatherings in Asia and Africa regularly issued statements in support of the Palestinians and critical of Zionism.

## PALESTINIAN OPPOSITION TO ZIONISM

Palestinian resistance to the existence and policies of the State of Israel gradually coalesced, both among Palestinian citizens of Israel and the Palestinian Diaspora, despite the initial chaos of refugee conditions, the limitations of movement and communication the military administration imposed upon Palestinian citizens of Israel, and divisions among Arab countries. Palestinian refugees increasingly believed that the liberation of Palestine had to precede regional Arab unity and that Palestinians must fight for themselves rather than rely on other Arab countries. In the late 1950s the Palestinian Liberation Movement, known by its Arabic acronym Fatah, formed among Palestinian refugees in Kuwait under the leadership of Yasser Arafat. It remained small and esoteric in its first several years but by the end of the 1960s had become the dominant Palestinian organization. In 1964, the Palestinian Liberation Organization (PLO) formed, with a charter declaring "Zionism is a colonialist movement in its inception, aggressive and expansionist in its goals, racist and segregationist in its configurations and fascist in its means and aims."[13] It denied the validity of the Balfour Declaration and of Israel as a country and therefore demanded "liberation" from this illegal entity. The PLO also insisted on "armed revolution" to achieve this liberation and framed armed resistance as a "defensive act" against attacks on the Palestinian right to self-determination. Other Palestinian organizations formed around this time as well; the Popular Front for the Liberation of Palestine (PFLP) advocated for a more pan-Arab orientation of the Palestinian struggle, and the Democratic Popular Front for the Liberation of Palestine (DPFLP) stressed a pro-Marxist approach to Palestinian liberation. Later groups insisted upon an

Islamic umbrella for Palestinian aims. Palestinian nationalism has thus undergone some intense factionalism, especially as it has shifted ideologically and politically over the decades.

The defeat of Arab countries by Israel during the 1967 War galvanized resistance both among Palestinians and the rest of the Arab world. The Arab League met in Khartoum, Sudan and passed a resolution known as the "3 No's": no peace with Israel, no recognition of Israel, and no negotiation with Israel. In 1969 Fatah, Egypt, and Lebanon signed the Cairo Agreement, authorizing PLO militants to operate from Lebanon. Fatah continued to rise to prominence through its guerilla and terrorist attacks against Israel. Arafat became the iconic chairman of the PLO, a position he held until his death in 2004, and under his leadership Fatah and the PLO became effectively intertwined. The PLO National Charter was revised and placed heavier emphasis on Palestinian (as compared to pan-Arab) national identity and vowed "the elimination of Zionism in Palestine."[14] By 1973, Palestinians entered discourse in Israel, Arab countries, and internationally as a national group in their own right and not just as a set of refugees. The Arab League recognized the PLO as the sole legitimate representatives of the Palestinian people (at that time, Israel only recognized Jordan as representative for the Palestinians). Still, Arab unity on the issue of Palestine remained elusive; in 1977 Egyptian president Anwar Sadat initiated direct negotiations with Israel, which was a shock especially in light of Egypt's prior leadership against its neighbor. In 1970, civil war (known as "Black September") broke out between Palestinian Fatah operatives and the Jordanian military, after which the PLO was expelled from Jordan and forced to relocate to Lebanon, where the PLO presence became a significant factor in the devastating Lebanese civil war (1975–90). The Palestinian resistance to Israel thus took place on an increasingly international stage.

Armed resistance has been a key tenet of Palestinian resistance to Zionism. A focus on violent resistance was consonant with other contemporary movements that saw themselves in an anticolonialist struggle, such as the famous case of Algeria, whose influential ideologue Frantz Fanon declared that the process of decolonization will always be violent.[15] Armed conflict took place both through international wars (such as the 1973 Yom Kippur War with Syria and Egypt launching a surprise attack), and through Palestinian guerilla attacks from Gaza, the West Bank, and Lebanon. Terrorism against civilians also became a militant strategy both in Israel and abroad; militants captured hostages and hijacked airplanes, and, in 1972, the group Black September shocked the world when it attacked the Israeli team at the Munich Olympics. Terror tactics like these increased worldwide awareness (though not exactly sympathy) of the situation of the Palestinian people's statelessness and conflict with Israel.

Palestinian acceptance of the use of violence and terror tactics has shifted both over time and within Palestinian factions. In 1988 Arafat officially renounced terrorism but not "the armed struggle against the Zionist entity"—presumably still condoning attacks on military targets or the use of weapons for defense.[16] By 1993, Arafat officially declared the sections of the PLO charter for armed struggle "now inoperative and no longer valid."[17] Despite these revised positions, other "rejectionist" Palestinian groups refused to relinquish violent tactics. In 1992, Hamas widened its target from Israeli soldiers to "every Zionist in Palestine."[18] Suicide bombings were introduced by Islamic factions in 1994 and were eventually adopted by Fatah-affiliated operatives as well. The militant al-Aqsa Martyrs Brigade was later formed by Fatah sympathizers, though is formally not claimed by the PLO, and analysts debate the extent to which Arafat had the power or the desire to discourage or intercept their attacks (some also note the fact that even after the PLO renounced terror, it still extended stipends to families of people who had been killed or imprisoned for armed struggle against Israel, de facto supporting violence done by third-party actors). However, there are many Palestinians and supporters of Palestinian causes who oppose the use of violence and especially of terror; in 2002, over 300 prominent Palestinian leaders circulated an open letter calling for an end to suicide bombings, and, in 2004, the Arab League called for an end to violence against civilians.[19] Indiscriminate violence against civilians has invited unequivocal criticism even among organizations opposing Israeli policies, such as Jewish Voice for Peace, which demands the end of suicide bombing, and Amnesty International, which classifies Hamas's use of indiscriminate violence as a war crime.

## First Intifada

Perhaps the most iconic and sustained expression of resistance to Israel's occupation of Palestinian Territories was the Intifada between 1987 and the early 1990s. In 1987 the First Intifada (Arabic for *"uprising,"* and sometimes more precisely translated as *"shaking off"*) was sparked after an Israeli military vehicle crashed into cars in Gaza, killing and injuring several Palestinians. This event triggered an uprising among a population frustrated by Israel's presence in the territories occupied in 1967, the "iron fist" policies Israeli forces used to quell opposition in these territories, and an increase in civilian Israeli settlements and land confiscations. A nucleus of Palestinian leaders soon formed to steer the unrest toward specific aims and methods by circulating anonymous communiques. They demanded the end of the "policy of repression, represented in policy of deportation, mass arrests, curfews, and the demolition of houses," rallying under the general slogan "Down with occupation; long live Palestine as a free and Arab country."[20] They famously rejected the use of any weapons other than stones as an attempt to highlight the disparity between Palestinian and Israeli military power. Instead, they promoted a civil disobedience campaign consisting of a general strike and mass demonstrations. Not all Palestinian groups agreed to spurn the use of weapons, remaining committed to terror and guerilla-style attacks. Many other Palestinians struggled economically in the face of a general strike and continued to work inside Israel and for Israeli enterprises in the West Bank, despite elaborate mobilization efforts to supply funds, essentials, or mutual aid to striking families (as well as considerable intimidation and even violence against strike breakers). Even so, the strike harmed the Israeli economy and created a crisis in Israeli society about the practicality and morality of suppressing popular opposition. The Intifada continued for around three years, but became an enduring cultural touchstone and set a precedent of popular uprising outside the control of both Israel and the PLO.

## Second Intifada

The Second Intifada erupted in the wake of several years of failed Palestinian–Israeli negotiations and the dramatically increasing Israeli civilian and military presence in the West Bank and Gaza. In 2000, longtime Israeli politician and leader of the right-wing Likud Party, Ariel Sharon, staged a police presence at the al-Aqsa complex on the Temple Mount in Jerusalem, and when riots predictably erupted against this encroachment on the Muslim-administered holy site, Israeli police responded with live ammunition. The humiliation and violence of these confrontations sparked what became the Second Intifada (2000–5). The Second Intifada had key differences from the first. For one, it did not develop the same level of leadership coordination as the First Intifada, and Yasser Arafat, as well as Palestinian police and security forces, were alternatingly unwilling or unable to control many of the violent operations. Groups outside the PLO increasingly gained popular legitimacy for their combative initiative that contrasted with PLO political stagnation (and as became increasingly known, systems of corruption). Unlike with the coordinated nonviolence and "stones" of the First Intifada, many Palestinians supported violence and acts of terrorism against both the Israeli military and civilian population. Furthermore, whereas most of the unrest in the First Intifada took place primarily against military or settler targets in the Occupied Territories, the Second Intifada targeted any Israelis, both in the territories and inside Israel. Palestinian citizens of Israel also staged protests in solidarity and shared frustration. The widespread strikes and violence of the Intifadas, along with the demonstrations and violence that Palestinians in Gaza and the West Bank continue to utilize to the present, are subject to contesting interpretations: for some the violence is proof of unchecked hostility and even fanaticism against Israel, for others it is a sign of increasing social, political, and/or economic desperation.

## RELIGION AND ANTI-ZIONISM

Despite the fact that much of the early Arab opposition to Zionism was among both Arab Christians and Muslims due to shared political and economic objections, opposition to Zionism became increasingly fused with Islamic principles. Earlier Palestinian resistance groups were nominally respectful of religion (particularly Islam and Christianity, the dominant religions among Palestinians), but generally espoused a Palestinian state based on "secular" principles. It was for this reason that Israel encouraged Islamic social institutions, especially in Gaza, in the 1970s and early 1980s as a way of redirecting, dividing, and dampening nationalist resistance movements. However, by the mid-1980s, Palestinian Muslim leaders increasingly viewed Israel as a threat to Palestinian physical, social, and spiritual well-being. The group Islamic Jihad formed to carry out armed struggle against Israel and promote the creation of an Islamic state. Hamas (the Arabic acronym for "Islamic Resistance Movement") also formed in 1987 to promote Islamic principles in the Palestinian national struggle. Hamas's 1988 charter opens with a quote from the founder of the Egyptian Muslim Brotherhood, who stated that "Israel will exist and will continue to exist until Islam will obliterate it, just as it obliterated others before it."[21] According to Hamas, the original Muslim conquests of Palestine in the seventh century CE made Palestine "an Islamic Waqf consecrated for future Moslem generations until Judgement Day. It, or any part of it, should not be squandered: it, or any part of it, should not be given up."[22] Hamas formed the Izz al-Din al-Qassam Brigades, a military wing named after the Mandate-era Palestinian guerilla leader whose union of Islam and resistance they espouse (likewise, the Qassam rockets Hamas shoots from Gaza into Israel carry his name). Despite their specifically Islamic causes, Hamas shares many of the objections to Zionism of other Palestinian organizations. For instance, the Hamas charter lamented Israel's use of collective punishment in the form of house demolitions and mass incarceration of young people, and another of its early leaflets condemns torture, travel restrictions, heavy taxes, and humiliation—all similar objections raised by secular groups.[23] Still, the Islamic inflection of Palestinian resistance to Zionism has grown significantly from the 1980s until the present.

The opposition among ultraorthodox Jewish circles that rose against Zionism in the formation of the movement has also persisted into the establishment of Israel. These anti-Zionist ultraorthodox Jews consider the establishment of a Jewish State a sinful attempt to circumvent the punishment of Exile and the timeline of messianic redemption, and reject its secular legal system, liberal popular culture, and use of the Hebrew language in secular life. The group Neturei Karta (Aramaic for "Guardians of the City Gates"), originally founded during the British Mandate period, is a particularly iconoclastic anti-Zionist ultraorthodox group. Neturei Karta's primary motivation is religious purity, insisting on differentiating between Zionism and Judaism; its anthem for instance asserts, "the holy Torah is our Law/We are loyal to it./We do not recognize the Heretic Zionist Regime/Its laws do not apply to us."[24] But their opposition to Israel as a Jewish State on religious grounds has also led them to oppose many of Israel's policies and actions regarding the Palestinians, and they thus share and publicize many of the objections and criticisms made against Israel by other political groups and figures, even some of whom have made demonstrably antisemitic claims.[25]

Some Palestinian Christians have developed opposition to Zionism that is rooted not only in wider Palestinian interests but specifically in the tradition of liberation theology. This theological trend emerged in South America in the 1960s in the midst of antidemocratic violence and economic exploitation, and it borrowed heavily from Marxist terminology and ideology prominent in Latin American antifascist movements of the time. The foundational 1971 text, *A Theology of Liberation: History, Politics, Salvation* by Peruvian priest Gustavo Gutiérrez, outlined God's "preferential option for the poor."[26] Gutierrez wrote of the poor that their plight is "a compelling obligation to fashion an entirely different social order" and advocated fellowship "with all the members of a particular social class who are fighting valiantly for their most basic rights and for an altered society in which they can live as human beings."[27] By the late 1980s some Palestinian Christians adopted this theology; Palestinian Anglican priest Naim Ateek established Sabeel: "an ecumenical grassroots liberation theology movement among the Palestinian Christians . . . to deepen the faith of Palestinian Christians, to promote unity among them and lead them to act for justice and peace."[28] Sabeel's adaptation of liberation theology in the context of Palestine has since grown a wide following, with international chapters, regular conferences and tours, literature in both Arabic and English, and partnerships with prominent Christian leaders in Israel, Palestine, and worldwide, such as South African archbishop the late Desmond Tutu, and the former Anglican priest Stephen Sizer who has written prolifically (and controversially) against Christian Zionist theology and policy.[29]

In 2009 Palestinian Christians (from various denominational backgrounds) issued the Kairos Document, echoing the influential antiapartheid Kairos Document (1985) by churches in South Africa speaking at a "critical hour" (*kairos* in Greek). The document addresses various groups: for Palestinian Christians to pursue hope, unity, and nonviolence; to Palestinian society at large to eschew extremism and violence; to Israel to end its military occupation and institutional discrimination of Palestinians in both Israel and the Occupied Territories; and to the international Christian community to recognize the suffering of the Palestinians and to hold Israel accountable. The signatories reject religious nationalism, whether "Jewish or Islamic," on the basis that it "suffocates the state, confines it within narrow limits, and transforms it into a state that practices discrimination and exclusion, preferring one citizen over another."[30] The document asserts that Christians are compelled to be involved, since "the problem is not just a political one, it is a policy in which human beings are destroyed, and this must be of concern to the Church." "If [the church] does take sides," it insists, "it is with the oppressed, to stand alongside them, just as Christ our Lord stood by the side of each poor person and each sinner."[31] While the document rejects the use of violence to resist Israel, it also claims that if Israel enacted just policies there would be no Palestinian violence.

Christians have also joined other international efforts to oppose Israeli occupation of the Palestinians and in some cases Zionism more broadly. The ecumenical and largely mainline World Council of Churches issued the "Amman Call" in 2007 protesting the Israeli treatment of Palestinians. The Bethlehem Bible College in the West Bank (which professes the statement of faith of the World Evangelical Alliance) has become a flagship for international evangelical criticism of Zionism through its biannual conference, "Christ at the Checkpoint," launched in 2010. Its 2012 Conference issued "Seven Affirmations," one of which defined Zionism as "ethnocentric, privileging one people at the expense of the others."[32] The US-based Churches for Middle East Peace (CMEP) "condemns all violence, regardless of the perpetrator."[33] CMEP openly affirms "a secure state of Israel," while also explicitly demanding "an end to the Israeli occupation of East Jerusalem, the West Bank, and the Gaza Strip," including more specific policies against the "existence and the expansion of Israeli settlements," roads for exclusive use by settlers, and the blockade and closures of Gaza.[34] Christian engagement with causes opposing aspects of Zionism or Israeli policies thus includes a wide theological and social background, from liberation theology to evangelicalism.

## INTERNATIONAL OPPOSITION

Opposition to Zionism, or to broader Israeli policies, is not limited to Palestinians and the Arab world but has been voiced in the international community as well. The most contested—and later retracted— indication of opposition to Zionism was the 1975 UN Resolution 3379 that stated, "Zionism is a form of racism and racial discrimination" and passed with a vote of 72 to 35 (with 32 abstentions). The resolution itself did not specify why Zionism was to be considered racist, but rather upheld various statements made at assemblies in Latin America and Africa that condemned Zionism alongside imperialism and apartheid. The United States vociferously opposed the decision, with then-US ambassador to the UN Daniel Moynihan calling it "obscene" and declaring that the US "does not acknowledge, it will not abide by, it will never acquiesce in this infamous act."[35] In 1991, the UN voted to repeal this resolution, but its passage cast a shadow on Israel and further established a mutually suspicious attitude between the UN and Israel. International debate on Zionism and racism continued, particularly with regard to whether the Zionist tenet of a Jewish state was a racially exclusionary one. In 2001 the UN hosted the Durban World Conference against Racism at which participants argued whether to include Zionism in a declaration against racism. The United States and Israel withdrew from the conference as a result, even though explicit condemnations of Zionism were ultimately removed from the final version of the declaration. A parallel international conference against racism was concurrently held by NGOs in Durban, which did issue a scathing and controversial declaration against Israel as a "racist, apartheid state."[36] This ongoing allegation that Zionism is itself racism is a deeply problematic bone of contention in wider conversations about Israeli policies and/or antisemitism.

Some of the most active American and international groups are more accurately opposed to the Israeli occupation of the territories captured in the 1967 War than to Zionism itself. These antioccupation groups attempt to bring an end to military occupation of Palestinians through various social, legal, and economic avenues. In 1996 Jewish Voice for Peace was founded as a "diverse and democratic community of activists inspired by Jewish tradition to work together for peace, social justice, and human rights."[37] The American lobbying group J Street (founded in 2007) identifies itself as "pro-Israel" while openly campaigning against Israeli control of Palestinian Territories. In 2014 progressive American Jews formed IfNotNow, "to end American Jewish support for the occupation" and to pressure United States policymakers to "use every tool in their toolbox, including American assistance, to push for an end to the occupation."[38] These international antioccupation groups have joined the efforts of older antioccupation groups formed in Israel, such as Gush Shalom and Peace Now.

One of the most controversial criticisms raised against Israel is the charge that it commits the crime of apartheid. While apartheid is commonly known for its institution in twentieth-century South Africa, in 1965 the International Convention on the Elimination of All Forms of Racial Discrimination categorized the practice of apartheid as a crime regardless of where it is implemented or whether the term "apartheid" is used in policy. The PLO accused Israel of apartheid against Palestinians as early as 1965, based on the fact that most Arabs inside Israel were governed under a separate military administration.[39] Edward Said was using the term apartheid for Israel and

Palestinians in the 1970s.[40] Jimmy Carter recalls that his security advisor warned Prime Minister Begin in the late 1970s that "a Palestinian 'Basutoland' (later Lesotho, the autonomous Black 'homeland' in apartheid South Africa) would not be an acceptable outcome" to the United States.[41] While these early allegations of apartheid have existed in particularly critical circles, even Zionists such as Yitzhak Rabin, Ehud Barak, Ehud Olmert, and other Israeli officials have warned over the years that temporary measures if made permanent would essentially constitute apartheid. Israel's ongoing control of the territories, increasingly desperate resistance by Palestinians, and the erection of the security barrier (known interchangeably as the security fence, security wall, "the wall," or the "apartheid wall") emboldened and expanded charges of apartheid, including increasing statements by Israeli, Palestinian, and international organizations.[42]

While the charge of apartheid has fueled heated rhetoric and organized campaigns, it also moved into legal realms. In March 2021 the International Criminal Court (ICC) opened investigations as to whether Israel can be charged with apartheid under the 1973 International Convention on the Suppression and Punishment of the Crime of Apartheid. The 1973 International Convention defined apartheid as a crime against humanity in which "inhuman acts [are] committed for the purpose of establishing and maintaining domination by one racial group of persons over any other racial group of persons and systematically oppressing them."[43] Maintaining military administration over the Palestinian Territories has resulted in many instances of examples specified as "inhuman acts" in the Convention, including "serious bodily or mental harm," "arbitrary arrest or illegal imprisonment"—which are regular outcomes of military raids—as well as "any measures, including legislative measures, designed to divide the population along racial lines by the creation of separate reserves and ghettos" or through expropriation of land of a certain group.[44] The division of population in the Occupied Palestinian Territories occurs with cities and towns in which Palestinians may not reside, roads they may not use or checkpoints they must pass, home demolitions, and refusals for building permits. The Apartheid Convention also includes as an example of inhuman acts "any legislative measures and other measures calculated to prevent a racial group or groups from participation in the political, social, economic and cultural life of the country," and the ongoing separate legal and political status existing between Palestinian Arabs and Israeli Jews in the Occupied Palestinian Territories could constitute this exclusion.[45] Despite the fact that the actions listed as examples of inhumane acts may occur in the military control of the Palestinian Territories, politicians and legal experts dispute whether the actions are in fact a result of intentional racial or ethnic discrimination. Those who oppose the possible designation of Israel's government of the Palestinian Territories as apartheid contest that differences in treatment of Palestinians and Jews are a result of national conflict and not ethnic discrimination. Determination of guilt or administration of sentences is therefore very unclear, but would likely involve international sanctions and demand for some kind of compensation or reparation. As Human Rights Watch noted, there is not yet a precedent in the ICC for prosecuting apartheid, since the ICC can only prosecute crimes committed since 2002 when the court was founded. While these legal and political arguments accuse Israel of committing apartheid, others argue that the accusation itself is a form of persecution by demonizing Israel for actions taken for the purpose of security and defense.

Opposition to the occupation is not inherently opposition to Zionism, though the two can go together or can often be muddled. The various types of opposition to the Israeli occupation of Palestinian Territories do not always have the same stance toward the Zionist tenet of a Jewish nation-state. Some groups are opposed to the notion of a Jewish state, regardless of the military or settler presence in the Palestinian Territories. IfNotNow does not explicitly reject or promote Zionism but also allows and welcomes members from either perspective. In 2014 Jewish Voice for Peace revised its position on Zionism, noting that "at its founding, JVP made a conscious choice as an organization to abstain from taking a position on Zionism," but later felt the need to stake a position that "Palestinian partners had long theorized Zionism as a root cause of the Palestinian condition, and more and more of our members not only agreed, but understood Zionism as damaging to Jewish identity and spiritual life."[46] Other antioccupation groups, on the other hand, are still openly supportive of Israel as a Jewish state within the "Green Line"; Peace Now was founded, for instance, to save rather than abolish the notion of a Jewish state, and the New Israel Fund "supports an end to the occupation of Palestinian territories as a central principle of the strategic framework in which we operate," but is also opposed to initiatives that "seek to undermine the existence of the state of Israel as a Jewish homeland."[47] The mobilization against Israeli policies in the West Bank and Gaza therefore vary in both ends and means, and many of them do not oppose (and some even openly defend) Israel as a state or even as an explicitly Jewish state. As the Palestinian scholar and political leader Sari Nusseibeh wrote, "one day the Israelis may realise that the reason for the never-ending turmoil disrupting their lives has nothing to do with our opposition to the Jewish state but is rooted in the more mundane fact that human beings are not constituted to accept injustice."[48]

## BOYCOTT, DIVESTMENT, AND SANCTIONS (BDS) CAMPAIGNS

One of the most controversial forms of opposition to Zionism and/ or the Israeli occupation has been through economic measures like boycott, divestment, and sanctions. These efforts were inspired by multinational boycott, divestment, and sanction campaigns against the apartheid government of South Africa, which eventually ended in the early 1990s after significant domestic and international pressure. Various forms of boycott and economic pressure against Israel have been promoted by certain groups over the years even before the formation of BDS. The Arab Revolt of 1936–39 included a widespread Palestinian boycott of Jewish industry in Palestine, and when the Arab League formed in 1945 its members committed to this boycott as well, which some Arab states maintain to this day. The above-mentioned case of the general strikes of the First Intifada is another noteworthy example of Palestinian boycott. In 1997 the antioccupation group Gush Shalom tried to launch a "National Boycott of Settlement Products," which was controversial but gained support from "sixty-eight prominent Israeli personalities."[49] Thus by the time the BDS movement officially coalesced in 2004, there had been some precedent of economic pressure as a form of resistance.

An official organized boycott movement launched with the 2004 Palestinian Campaign for the Academic and Cultural Boycott of Israel and the 2005 Palestinian Call for Boycott, Divestment and Sanctions against Israel (BDS). These calls were issued by 170 Palestinian organizations in the face of failing peace negotiations and the accelerating construction of the security barrier in 2004, and mobilized the formation of the Palestinian BDS National Convention (BNC) in 2007. This organization maintains a series of expansive demands: *boycott* of "complicit Israeli sporting, cultural, and academic institutions, and . . . all Israeli and international companies engaged in violations of Palestinian human rights," *divestment* from "the State of Israel and all Israeli and international companies that sustain Israeli apartheid," and *sanctions* enacted by governments "to end Israeli apartheid, and not aid or assist its maintenance, by banning business with illegal Israeli settlements, ending military trade and free trade agreements, as well as suspending Israel's membership in international forums such as UN bodies and FIFA."[50] They call for these to continue "until Israel meets its obligation to recognize the Palestinian people's inalienable right to determination," "[ends] its occupation and colonization of all Arab lands," dismantles the security wall, recognizes full equality for Palestinian citizens of Israel (in the 1948 borders), and allows a right of return for Palestinian refugees (including their descendants) to their original homes.[51] The designation of "all Arab lands" has lent itself to varying and contesting interpretations, with some arguing this means Israel must relinquish control of all of historic Palestine, and others considering it just the territories occupied from Jordan, Syria, and Egypt after the 1967 War. The BDS National Convention calls for boycott not only against institutions operating within the Occupied Territories, but against Israel as a whole. This scope includes individuals or organizations that aim to operate in both Israel and the Palestinian Territories, which the BNC claims "[sell] the illusion of peace to Palestinians—and the world—and [bribes] Palestinians into submission to Israeli dictates and its perpetual colonial hegemony."[52] The BNC maintains that, regardless of the political position of individual Israelis or Israeli institutions, they are complicit in the policies of their government, and cooperation with them "normalizes" the existence of Israel and its institutionalized discrimination of Palestinians, whether in Israel or the West Bank.

Aside from the official and maximalist BDS campaigns, there are various boycott, divestment, or sanctions campaigns that target specific Israeli policies and businesses that support or profit from Israeli control of the West Bank and Gaza. The European Union, as well as a number of European countries, have initiated various forms of divestment and sanctions.[53] After several years of controversial deliberation, the Presbyterian Church (USA) voted in 2014 to divest from Caterpillar, Motorola, and Hewlett Packard, after monitoring them through the Mission Responsibility Through Investment Committee established in 2004. Other Christian denominations like the Church of England, United Methodist Church, and United Church of Christ have all publicly supported some form of boycott of or divestment from Israel, and Churches for Middle East Peace has affirmed that this type of organized protest has "precedence among churches in the

U.S. Civil Rights Movement and in many other times and locations."[54] Jewish Voice for Peace urges the US to enforce the Leahy Law, which limits military aid to serve only defensive purposes and prohibits aid in the case of human rights violations, and argues that the occupation disqualifies Israel from US aid on both counts.[55] Along with these organizations, university campuses have been significant sites for various BDS campaigns, especially through student government resolutions for university divestment from businesses supporting the Israeli occupation, or boycotts of study abroad programs in Israel.

Zionist critics of the BDS movement argue its tactics are both unjust and ineffective. They contend that BDS singles Israel out while ignoring abuses and terror carried out by Palestinian militants and officials. Other Zionist critics argue that any boycott ends up also economically harming Palestinians employed by Israeli enterprises targeted by BDS. Critics further argue that by insisting on full ostracization until demands are met, BDS disrupts ongoing attempts at negotiations of a peaceful settlement for a two-state solution, and promotes widening social cleavages that could also promote antisemitism.[56]

These concerns over BDS have led Israeli and United States government officials to draft and pass legislation against BDS or even against support of the movement. In 2017 Israel passed a controversial amendment (which is sporadically enforced) allowing Israel to refuse entry to anyone who publicly supports BDS. Between 2014 and the present as many as 32 US states have passed various laws or restrictions against BDS.[57] In 2018 Republican and Democrat senators jointly proposed a federal bill against BDS, but it did not pass. Some of this legislation has since been overturned by courts on the basis of the 1982 Supreme Court decision that politically motivated boycotts are protected by the First Amendment. And significantly, not all opponents of BDS support going to the extent of anti-BDS legislation. Deborah Lipstadt, a preeminent historian of antisemitism and President Joseph Biden's 2022 appointee for Special Envoy to Monitor and Combat Anti-Semitism, opposes BDS but opposes legislation against it as well. The Anti-Defamation League (ADL) has also been divided over the desirability or utility of legislation against BDS.[58] The attempts to legislate against BDS, and the ensuing debate over such legislation, indicates the extent of opposition to the aims and methods of BDS against Israel.

Between the poles of the maximalist BNC positions on BDS on the one hand, and attempts to outlaw BDS on the other, there are many individuals and organizations who support a diverse spectrum of boycott, divestment, or sanction initiatives. While the PCUSA divested from companies operating in the Occupied Palestinian Territories, they also rejected the official BDS campaign since it targets Israel and not just the Israeli occupation.[59] The cultural boycott is especially divisive. Natalie Portman, in her refusal of the Genesis Prize in Jerusalem, clarified that her actions do not condone the umbrella BDS movement (even though both her critics and supporters claimed otherwise). In 2013 Jewish American journalist Peter Beinart proposed the term "Zionist BDS" to describe efforts that target industries and initiatives in the Occupied Territories while simultaneously strengthening industries and initiatives within the Green Line.[60] Longtime Palestinian activist and scholar Sari Nusseibeh opposes cultural and academic boycotts, as does vocal critic of Israel Noam Chomsky, who argues that academic boycott is too "hypocritical" since "US institutions . . . are implicated in far worse activities."[61] Christian advocacy groups like Sabeel, Christ at the Checkpoint, and Churches for Middle East Peace, who support economic boycott and divestment, still cultivate intercultural engagement between various Israeli and Palestinian groups or initiatives. Ultimately, the wide range of boycott, divestment, and sanction initiatives, under either the official Palestinian BDS National Committee or by other institutions, proves that BDS is not a unified or unanimous movement and should not be construed as such.

## ANTI-ZIONISM AND ANTISEMITISM

Connections between anti-Zionism and antisemitism have been the subject of considerable public debate, scholarly discussion, and even violence. There have been and continue to be many cases in which anti-Zionism is a cover for, if not an open expression of, antisemitism. The earliest and most devastating cases of this were in Arab governments that forced or intimidated their Jewish citizens to leave after the establishment of Israel, questioning Jews' national loyalties or scapegoating Jewish citizens to detract from their own more specific problems. Jews in Morocco, Iraq, Egypt, and Syria faced regular episodes of popular violence during the 1948 war in Palestine and in the subsequent wars with Israel. Jews in Iraq and other Arab countries faced expulsion from their jobs, had assets frozen, and in many cases when permitted to emigrate were forced to relinquish their citizenship and have their property confiscated by the state. In these cases, opposition to the establishment and policies of a Jewish state in Israel/Palestine manifested in state-sponsored persecution of Jewish communities and individuals.

International opposition of Israeli actions and against Zionism has also unfortunately continued to often go hand in hand with popular violence and violent rhetoric against Jews, regardless of their connection to Israel. Periods of combat between Israel and Gaza have coincided with significant violent acts against Jews and Jewish institutions worldwide. Scholars from Yale found in 2006 that in Europe "anti-Israel sentiment consistently predicts the probability that an individual is anti-Semitic, with the likelihood of measured anti-Semitism increasing with the extent of anti-Israel sentiment observed."[62] Some anti-Israel rallies in Europe have raised chants of "death to the Jews" or "Jews, Jews, cowardly swine," and some pro-Israel counterdemonstrators have been attacked.[63] Opposition to Israel as the Jewish state unfortunately has led and can lead to antisemitism against Jews in general.

What should alarm Christians is that long-standing Christian and European antisemitic tropes and prejudices are also regularly evoked in criticism of Israel as a Jewish state. One of the most significant examples of this is the continued publication and circulation of the nineteenth-century forgery *The Protocols of the Elders of Zion* in Middle Eastern countries. Egyptian president Gamal Abdel Nasser recommended *The Protocols*, and the original Hamas charter actually refers to it as a factual source (it is not, however, referenced in its 2017 revision). The antisemitic texts and worldviews developed in Europe and in the history of Christianity have also influenced growing Islamic antisemitism and/or political opposition to Zionism. There are many political cartoons that utilize European antisemitic imagery and tropes, depicting Israelis or Jews with exaggerated and grotesque features, or as vermin or pests.[64] There are also frequent references to Jews as Christ-killers. As early as 1947 a Palestinian leader dismissed Zionist criticism by asking "does this properly come from the mouth of a people who have crucified the founder of Christianity?"[65] A later political cartoon depicts a Palestinian girl crucified on the cross, surrounded by Jews, obviously evoking the charge of deicide. Israeli Messianic Jewish historian Gershon Nerel argues that Arab Christians of various denominations "adopt, revive and revise the anti-Israel heritage of Christianity," blending it with "the Islamic theology concerning Judaism."[66] Associations between Israel and the crucifixion recur in Palestinian Christian discourse, such as a Sabeel booklet framing Palestine as walking through Jesus's "Via Dolorosa" in Jerusalem.[67] Rabbi Walter Raskow—a vocal critic of Israel—insightfully differentiated the way a crucifixion image is used in the Palestinian–Israeli context from the way it was used in Latin American contexts in which liberation theology emerged. Raskow argues that when Latin American liberation theologians highlighted the power of the Roman Empire and its crucifixion of Christ, "it's clear the empire you're talking about is America."[68] However, this invocation of imperial execution of the

Lord lands differently in the context of the Israeli–Palestinian context, and his reasoning is worth quoting at length:

> to talk about the crucifixion of Jesus seems on the surface like that's the same thing, but when you are doing it in the context of a Jewish state, when you're doing it in the context of 2000 years of Jewish suffering from the Christian dogma of deicide that the Jews killed God and the violence that has been visited on the Jewish community by people upholding that theology, to hear that strikes a nerve that has 2000 years of pain behind it and that has to be heard . . . there needs to be a different metaphor a different language a different way of drawing on Christian liberation theology.[69]

The fusion of Islam and opposition to Zionism that began in the British Mandate and intensified in the 1980s has also bred antisemitism twisted from Quranic and Islamic traditions about Jews in the history of Islam. Despite Islam's reverence for Jews as "People of the Book," some passages from the Qur'an and the Hadith depict Jews in hateful or combative language. One frequently quoted verse warns, "Khaybar, Khaybar, O Jews, Muhammad's army will return," referring to an attack on the Jews in the city of Khaybar where they were suspected of plotting rebellion against the Islamic capital of Medina in 628 CE. The British organization Muslims Against Antisemitism has formed to combat Islamic antisemitism as it appears in discourse against Zionism. According to this group "anti-Semitism doesn't owe itself necessarily to Islamism but a mutation of activism for Palestinian justice," where a verse like "Khaybar, Khaybar O Jews" is taken from its seventh-century context to fuel "social demonstrations against the State of Israel."[70] One example of a fusion of antisemitism, Islam, and anti-Zionism is Nation of Islam leader Louis Farrakhan, who regularly and publicly preached open antisemitism in his criticism of Israel. While the Nation of Islam subscribes to race-based views considered reprehensible to "mainstream Muslims" and is considered a hate group by the Southern Poverty Law Center, it still propagates its views in the name of Islam. Farrakhan claimed that "the Zionists have pushed Obama to do their bidding," have "been working for years to control your representatives in Congress," and that "Zionists dominate the government of the United States of America and her banking system."[71] Farrakhan's language against Zionists echoes antisemitic accusations that Jews are manipulating government leaders and international finance, and thus disseminates antisemitic sentiment in the guise of criticism of Zionism.

The combination of antisemitism with Islamic criticism of Zionism is especially pronounced in the ideology espoused by Hamas. The original 1988 Hamas charter lifted incendiary Quranic prooftexts and employed antisemitic language, referring to "warmongering Jews," and asserting that "Israel, Judaism and Jews challenge Islam and the Moslem people."[72] Hamas updated its covenant in 2017, and it now seems to distinguish between Zionism and Judaism by claiming that "its conflict is with the Zionist project not with the Jews because of their religion."[73] "Hamas does not wage a struggle against the Jews because they are Jewish," asserts the document, "but wages a struggle against the Zionists who occupy Palestine."[74] The document does not claim responsibility for antisemitism expressed in Hamas's history, but instead asserts that "anti-Semitism and the persecution of the Jews are phenomena fundamentally linked to European history and not to the history of the Arabs and the Muslims or to their heritage."[75] Nevertheless in 2019 senior Hamas official Fathi Hamad repeatedly called for mass violence against "every Jew on the globe," a clearly antisemitic appeal.[76] The 2017 charter's attempt to distance antisemitism or anti-Judaism from Hamas ideology has not erased the group's role in disseminating antisemitic stereotypes and prejudices or in promoting violence based upon them.

Antisemitism in criticism of Zionism and Israel can manifest on both the political right and left, particularly in the United States.

The generally conservative *Jerusalem Post* observed this in its analysis of the massacres at synagogues in Pittsburgh, Pennsylvania (2018), and Poway, California (2019), both committed by avowed right-wing assailants: "Anti-Israel and anti-Zionist views are [common] in this far-right antisemitic circle, sometimes overlapping or dovetailing with far-left antisemitic views, which are difficult to distinguish."[77] Right-wing American groups and publications will frequently express antisemitic rhetoric and ideology, and they equate Zionists and Jews as guilty of the same machinations. The "alt-right" regularly refers to Western political and economic systems as the Zionist Occupied Government (ZOG) and contends that it is systematically puppeteering Western governments toward its own world domination and the destruction of the white race. The use of the term "Zionist" here is not in direct reference to the Zionist movement, but is synonymous in these right-wing circles as "Jewish."

Left-wing antisemitism in anti-Zionism is often—though not always—more subtle than its right-wing counterparts. Certainly there are cases of explicit antisemitism in anti-Zionist discourse; in 2015 for instance a university in Durban voted to demand "that Jewish students, especially those who do not support the Palestinian struggle, should deregister."[78] Left-wing anti-Zionism is perhaps more susceptible to what Deborah Lipstadt terms "antisemitic enablers": those who amplify leaders or groups despite their record of antisemitic speech or action, or who advance antisemitic stereotypes without intending to express antisemitism. Jeremy Corbyn's leadership of the UK Labour Party is a particularly illustrative case of this, as he repeatedly consorted with or praised Palestinians with records of violence against Israeli civilians, and regularly downplayed any charges of antisemitism against his party as simply pro-Israel fear-mongering. Similarly, US Women's March cofounder Tamika Mallory attended a Louis Farrakhan rally in 2018 and not only refused to condemn his history of antisemitism but defended her support of the Nation of Islam leader by echoing tropes of deicide, stating, "if your leader does not have the same enemies as Jesus, they may not be THE leader."[79] Alongside "antisemitic enabling" that takes place in criticism of Zionism, there is also significant denial of antisemitism in anti-Zionist discourse; one scholar wrote relatively dismissively of the relationship between antisemitism and anti-Zionism, stating "there have been attempts by agents provocateurs to encourage and bait people so that the charge of antisemitism could be used to discredit our movement."[80] This implies that anti-Zionist antisemitism would only come from outside provocation and not from within the movement itself, further implicating that any caution against antisemitism need only be taken against pro-Zionist, not anti-Zionist entities. But Amnesty International and Human Rights Watch—both of which have accused Israel with the crimes of apartheid and persecution—also condemned the 2001 Durban NGO conference statement against Israel, citing antisemitism in the document as well as in the discourse leading up to its final draft.[81] Another scholar generally critical of Zionist policies warns her fellow critics against "[reducing] Jewish attachments to the land of Israel/Palestine to a colonial act," because this rhetoric "echoes cultural memories of anti-Semitism and a willingness to accept Jews as individuals but not as a group."[82] Left-leaning criticism that automatically conflates anything related to Israel and Zionism with colonialism alienates Jews by viewing any connections to Zionism and Israel with suspicion or condemnation, despite the fact Zionist and Israeli history is deeply complex and variegated and intersects with Jewish history in a number of ways.

The reality of antisemitism in anti-Zionism has led to deliberation and debate regarding the equation of the two in popular discourse and public policies. There were some early precedents of explicitly distinguishing between anti-Zionism and antisemitism; in 1944 a joint statement by Arab countries wrote that they were "second to none in regretting the woes that have been inflicted upon the Jews of Europe

. . . but the question of these Jews should not be confused with Zionism."[83] A Palestinian response to the UNSCOP committee in 1947 also insisted that Arab opposition to Zionism in Palestine had "nothing in common with anti-Semitism."[84] And prominent American journalist Dorothy Thompson challenged the allegations that opposing Zionist policies or parties is equated to antisemitism as early as 1949.[85] But just as there is no official, unanimous definition of anti-Zionism, official definitions of antisemitism are also contested. The International Holocaust Remembrance Alliance (IHRA) issued a "non-legally binding working definition" of antisemitism in 2016, asserting that "Antisemitism is a certain perception of Jews, which may be expressed as hatred toward Jews. Rhetorical and physical manifestations of antisemitism are directed toward Jewish or non-Jewish individuals and/ or their property, toward Jewish community institutions and religious facilities."[86] The IHRA noted that "manifestations [of this definition] might include the targeting of the State of Israel, conceived as a Jewish collectivity." The definition cites among "contemporary examples of antisemitism" different expressions of anti-Zionism, such as "denying the Jewish people their right to self-determination, e.g., by claiming that the existence of a State of Israel is a racist endeavor," or by "applying double standards by requiring of it a behavior not expected or demanded of any other democratic nation."[87] The definition also cites the use of antisemitic imagery and incendiary language in criticism of Israel, as well rhetoric that implicates all Jews as culpable for Israel's actions. The IHRA definition has since been adopted by dozens of countries and organizations worldwide, including the European Union, United States, individual US states, and institutions of higher education.

The widespread acceptance of the IHRA definition has been contested by a number of organizations, scholars, and policymakers who take issue with the definition's equation of antisemitism with certain types of criticism of Israel. Jewish Voice for Peace issued a response cosigned by thirty other Jewish organizations worldwide, stating that the IHRA definition "is worded in such a way as to be easily adopted or considered by western governments to intentionally equate legitimate criticisms of Israel and advocacy for Palestinian rights with antisemitism, as a means to suppress the former."[88] A group of Palestinian academics and journalists also issued an open letter detailing their critique of the IHRA definition. "The fight against antisemitism should not be turned into a stratagem to delegitimise the fight against the oppression of the Palestinians, the denial of their rights and the occupation of their land," warns the letter.[89] These groups warn that the type of criticism that may be necessary to address injustices regarding Israel and the Palestinians could be reclassified under the IHRA definition of antisemitism, leading this necessary criticism to be dismissed or even penalized.

In 2021 a wide coalition of scholars in the fields of Jewish Studies, Israel Studies, Genocide Studies, Middle East Studies, and related fields issued the Jerusalem Declaration on Antisemitism (JDA) as an alternative or supplement to the IHRA definition. The JDA defines antisemitism as "discrimination, prejudice, hostility or violence against Jews as Jews (or Jewish institutions as Jewish)."[90] It includes general guidelines for identifying antisemitism according to this definition, and specifically addresses the "widely-felt need for clarity on the limits of legitimate political speech and action concerning Zionism, Israel, and Palestine."[91] The signatories do not share a political agenda or perspective and emphasize that "determining that a controversial view or action is not antisemitic implies neither that we endorse it nor that we do not."[92] The JDA maintains that antisemitism and anti-Zionism are "categorically different," and since the two are not equal, it clarifies the conditions in which anti-Zionism can utilize, promote, or condone antisemitism. Some examples are similar to those in the IHRA definition, such as applying "classical antisemitism" (such as tropes or stereotypes) to the State of Israel, assuming non-Israeli Jews are more loyal to Israel than their countries of citizenship or residence, and "holding Jews collectively responsible" for Israel's actions. The JDA even adds the example of "requiring people, because they are Jewish, publicly to condemn Israel or Zionism (for example, at a political meeting)."[93] But the JDA diverges from the IHRA definition by highlighting examples of anti-Zionism that are not in themselves examples of antisemitism, including advocating "full grant of political, national, civil and human rights" for Palestinians, "evidence-based criticism of Israel as a state" including "its institutions and founding principles," and "criticizing or opposing Zionism as a form of nationalism."[94] The JDA also disagrees with IHRA in that it explicitly asserts that "criticism . . . reflecting a 'double standard,' is not, in and of itself, antisemitic."[95] "In general, the same norms of debate that apply to other states and to other conflicts over national self-determination apply in the case of Israel and Palestine," concludes the JDA.[96] The JDA therefore denies that criticism of Israel or Zionism is a form of antisemitism in itself, but instead clarifies how to identify when criticisms of Israel are antisemitic.

Concern and controversy over anti-Zionism and antisemitism are also frequently raised in discourse regarding BDS. The BDS movement explicitly claims it is "opposed on principle to all forms of discrimination, including antisemitism" but it is common for advocacy groups to identify BDS as an expression of "new anti-Semitism that targets the Jewish state instead of the Jewish people" or at least acts as "fuel to those whose motives are truly antisemitic."[97] Even longtime left-wing Israeli politician and activist Uri Avnery observed in 2007 that "it is enough for Israelis to point out that the first step on the way to Auschwitz was the Nazi slogan: 'Don't buy from Jews' . . . an international boycott would arouse in many Jews around the world the deepest fears of anti-Semitism."[98] Other critics argue that if it is not antisemitism itself, BDS movements create an environment to demonize Israel and Jews. Many other organizations both internationally and in Israel have disagreed, and the JDA specifically absolves BDS, arguing that since boycott, divestment, and sanctions are "commonplace, non-violent forms of political protest against states," the movement is not inherently antisemitic.[99] The open letter issued by Palestinian scholars on the IHRA definition of antisemitism also specifically condemns that its "portrayal of the BDS campaign as antisemitic is a gross distortion of what is fundamentally a legitimate non-violent means of struggle for Palestinian rights."[100] One of the signatories of this statement was Sari Nusseibeh, who, as discussed above, openly opposes the academic boycott, but still defends BDS against charges of essential antisemitism.

Finally, the overall criticism of Zionism as an ideology—supporting a Jewish state as a form of Jewish national self-determination—is also a live wire in the contentious debates over anti-Zionism and antisemitism. The IHRA definition seems to imply that criticism of the notion of a Jewish state is an example of antisemitism. Alternatively, the JDA definition describes "denying the right of Jews in the State of Israel to exist and flourish, collectively and individually, as Jews, in accordance with the principles of equality" as an example of antisemitism. The JDA Frequently Asked Questions clarify that this example applies "to Jewish inhabitants of the state, whatever its constitution or name."[101] In other words, the Jews who now live in the State of Israel would be victims of antisemitism if they could not exist and flourish as Jewish individuals or in association as Jewish communities. It does not therefore mean, according to JDA signatories, that "to propose a different set of political or constitutional arrangements" for Israel, to criticize or oppose Zionism overall, to "[condemn] Israel's settler-colonialism or apartheid," or to criticize "Israel's foundation and its racist institutions or policies" is antisemitic.

Ultimately, "Anti-Zionist" is not a clear term, and thus should be parsed into ends, means, and degrees. Organized military resistance against Israel as a state or against its citizens is very different from joint statements issued by academic or religious figureheads; economic or publicity campaigns to end specific policies in the Palestinian Territories are very different from countries' categorical refusal to negotiate with Israel. At times opposition to Zionism harbors antisemitism, but other times resistance to Zionism and its policies are not antisemitic and even come from sectors within the State of Israel itself. This intermixture of anti-Zionism and antisemitism creates a volatile and oftentimes zero-sum context for grappling with criticism of Zionism. While Zionism has not been a fixed and static movement or ideology, neither have the opposition movements to Zionism, and any comprehensive or honest historical and political treatment of these subjects must therefore contend with this contingency.

# 7 | FUTURE DIRECTIONS

Envisioning a future for Zionism has been part of conceptualizing the Zionist movement since its beginning. Theodor Herzl depicted this in his utopian *Altneuland*, and today different projects like "Israel 2048," "Palestine +100," and "Herzl's Vision 2.0" hypothesize, hope, or fear for how Zionism will unfold in future decades.[1] Israelis and Palestinians use creative media to envision and critique the direction of their nationalist aspirations. One of the more comical of these creations is Palestinian Israeli Sayed Kashua's show *Arab Labor* (based on his semi-autobiographical novel *Dancing Arabs*). The episode "Independence Day" satirizes what Zionism means in the context of lived reality, both now and for future generations. The show's Israeli Palestinian protagonist Amjad Alian and his family arrive at the hospital with his wife in labor on the eve of Israeli Independence Day. At the same time arrives a Jewish Israeli couple with the wife in labor (and they walk straight through the entrance as the Alian family gets their bags screened). Meanwhile, a right-wing Russian Jewish Israeli politician is devising a publicity stunt, and he and his aides decide that since all Israelis would love money, they will win favor by donating one million shekels to the first baby born in Israel on its Independence Day. The politician appears on national television—broadcast in the delivery ward—to read this pledge, in which his Russian assistant had mistyped "the first baby born c'Israel" (which would mean "as Israel") instead of "b'Israel" (in Israel) (the letters c' and b' can not only look similar if written unclearly but are also vertically adjacent on the Hebrew keyboard). The news anchor is momentarily confused and corrects his pledge to clarify the prize goes to the first baby *in* Israel. This announcement triggers slapstick competition between Amjad (along with his father) and the Jewish Israeli husband to get their wives to deliver their millionaire baby first. Alas, Amjad's child is born first, and the Jewish couple sulks that the fecund Arab Israelis come ahead of them. The right-wing politician fumes that his stunt backfired by awarding an Arab couple, until he realizes his aide's typo provided an out; he apologizes to the Alian family that the precise text of the pledge states the million-shekel prize goes to the first baby born *as* (in other words, *named*) Israel on Independence Day. Amjad faces an immediate choice: does he really name his Palestinian Israeli son "Israel" to obtain a small fortune? Amjad's father insists they will "fight for their right" to get the prize, even if they name the baby Israel (dramatically adding "we will name the baby Herzl if we have to!"). Amjad's wife, on the other hand, does not even view it as a choice (and the Israeli couple, watching breathlessly from the next bed over at the chance to nab the prize, cheer "Good for you!" for her willingness to forfeit the money for her cultural ideals). She even threatens to leave Amjad if he were to do such a thing, and she not only refuses to name the baby Israel, but changes her preference for their "universal" name Adam in favor of her father-in-law's original insistence on the name Ismail (Ishmael in Arabic).

The politician offers Amjad an hour to decide, during which Amjad and his father hatch a plan; Amjad horrifies his family by dramatically announcing he will name the baby Israel, and after storming off to the registry his father pleads with the Jewish couple to "save his family from destruction" by making a deal to share the prize money—the Jewish couple names *their* baby Israel to claim the money on the Alians' behalf, in exchange for a percentage of the prize ("no more than 10%!" he insists to Amjad). Amjad eventually agrees to a 50/50 split with the Jewish couple, and he registers his son as Ismail. The writers of *Arab Labor* masterfully posit here what national identity means in the State of Israel and its next generations: these couples are both eligible for the same "prize," but it comes at a different cost for each. For the Alians to win the prize they must shun their national identity while already inhabiting a lower status (experiencing a security check during labor, stoking the bitterness of their Jewish compatriots, prompting politicians to scramble for loopholes to avoid including them in their largesse). When their politically active Palestinian friend Amal scolds Amjad for considering the name Israel she emphasizes it was "on the anniversary of the Nakba of all days," to which Amjad blurts out "why do you always bring the Nakba into things?!"[2] This question, and Amjad's dilemma over the money, suggests that basic issues of personal security can overshadow nationalist ideals even in a society of such stark divisions. Yet the outcome of both babies getting their own national names, and the Jewish and Palestinian families splitting the money in half (all the while spurning the politician's grandstanding with the Independence Day prize itself) playfully but incisively presents the complexities of national identity in Israel, now and for the next generations. What kind of country would Ismail and Israel grow up in?

Scholars, politicians, religious leaders, and artists seem to agree the future direction of Zionism is dynamic, with possibilities worth envisioning, anticipating, or in some cases, avoiding. Historian Gil Troy uses the word "torchbearers" to describe current Zionist leaders across the political and religious spectrum, a term evocative of unknown paths.[3] The 2005 establishment of the Institute for Zionist Strategies suggests the idea warrants, well, strategies; and the 2006–7 publication of the Vision Documents for Arab Israelis in Israel also invokes new horizons in the title. Political platforms and visions that aim to protect, dissect, or contest Israel's Zionist character are still evolving, and continue to shape foundational yet unresolved components of Israel's government structure. These foundational components include the constitution of Israel, still yet to be promulgated since its 1950 deferral, and the Israeli–Palestinian conflict and peace negotiations, which tend to hinge on whether there should or will be one or two states for Jews and Palestinians in the land between the Jordan River and the Mediterranean Sea, and the type(s) of state(s) these visions would entail.

## ZIONISM IN A FUTURE CONSTITUTION

Many discussions about the future of Zionism mull the ways in which the Jewish character of Israel will shape the content of a future constitution enshrining the relationship between different government branches and the rights and responsibilities of citizens. In 1950 Israel chose to defer a constitution and instead enact a series of Basic Laws, which have constitutional weight and theoretically serve as sections of the future constitution. The Basic Laws guarantee Israel's character as both a Jewish and democratic state but have not specified how this is implemented across government branches. Promulgating a constitution would force drafters to finalize the role of religion in these government functions, and this daunting and potentially divisive prospect has led to what one Israeli political scientist called the "decision not to decide" on this matter.[4] However, various political and scholarly groups in Israel have emphasized the need ultimately to promulgate a constitution, and have even crafted draft proposals to stimulate its progress. These proposals have weighted the role of religion in general, and the Jewish character of the state in particular, in different ways.

The Israel Democracy Institute (IDI) mobilized perhaps the most thorough attempt to date to advance a constitution, gathering in 1998 over one hundred politically, religiously, and ethnically diverse Israeli leaders "to debate the fundamental issues underlying a prospective constitution."[5] The fellows of the IDI believed that the lack of a constitution posed a social and political threat in Israel. One of the drafters, former government staffer Uri Dromi, insisted that such a document was important because, "in the absence of an embracing super-framework, some set of rules of the game approved by all, Israeli society might fall apart."[6] Dromi thus considered his participation in the drafting of the constitution the most important thing he has done in service of his country, including his former role as a military pilot. The associates at the IDI reasoned it was unrealistic to wait to resolve societal divisions before promulgating a constitution, and that if anything the divisions were likely to worsen without the "binding norms" of a constitution to moderate these divisions.[7] The IDI associates observed worsening divisions, particularly "regarding the Jewish characteristics of the collective identity [and regarding] the ability to balance between democratic and Jewish in defining the character of the State."[8] After five years of writing and incorporating solicited feedback, the IDI presented a draft constitution to the Knesset. Their title, "Constitution by Consensus," was chosen because almost no major constituency would consider a final draft exactly what they want, but almost all would agree it creates a necessary safeguard of basic rights.[9]

The IDI draft constitution has the Israeli Declaration of Independence as its preamble, and its drafters emphasized that despite the many disagreements between the drafters, "the unifying needlework which has made these compromises possible is the belief that the State of Israel is the realization of the Zionist dream—the rebirth of the Jewish people's aspirations throughout the generations. The force driving this rebirth is the Zionist movement."[10] The drafters thus agreed that they "have strived to interweave both values, Judaism and democracy, into one constitutional tapestry."[11] In so doing they leave room to accommodate the fact that "the Jewish supporting pillar for the draft Constitution is not monolithic; a look into its centrality as a factor in shaping the identity of the Israeli collective is open to many reactions and observations."[12] They include in the draft a Bill of Rights to exemplify "the juncture where democracy merges with Judaism: human rights and minority rights are derived from the values of Jewish culture as well as from the set of humanistic, universal values."[13] Despite the inclusion of Israeli Palestinians in the initial Public Council, none were drafters for the final document. It is perhaps not uncoincidental that, a year later, the legal center Adalah proposed a draft constitution with a decidedly less Zionist character than that proposed by the IDI. The IDI draft does however include more explicit protections for Arabs in Israel than are in the Declaration of Independence alone, for instance it expands the prohibition of discrimination to include the basis of nationality, it includes sections acknowledging the state's Arabs and their group rights (including the use of Arabic), and removes the candidacy requirement of affirming the Jewish and democratic nature of the state (instead, limiting Knesset participation from those who threaten the existence of the state altogether).

Another project aiming to clarify and solidify the relationship between religion and nation is the 2003 Gavison–Medan Covenant (also released under the auspices of the IDI). Over a three-year period, secular Zionist and respected legal scholar Ruth Gavison and eminent *yeshiva* scholar Yaacov Medan drafted an outline for compromise between the various Jewish groups in Israel—primarily between Orthodox and secular, but also addressing salient issues for other Jewish denominations.[14] The report on this covenant insists that "a stable arrangement is needed to order the totality of relations between Torah and state and among the diverse groups that call Israel home: the religiously observant, the traditional and the free thinkers in all their diversity."[15] The covenant report emphasizes the instrumentality of such a covenant for safeguarding a Zionist future, ominously asserting that cooperative approaches between religious and secular sectors was more necessary than ever, "in light of our existential distress and the growing concern that the powers of discord will over-come the defenders of the common interest and unity among the Jew-ish people as a whole and within the State of Israel in particular."[16] Gavison and Medan concede that their proposed covenant would prove difficult for themselves and their communities. One of the most difficult compromises for both groups would be the covenant's proposal on marriage, which would allow the institution of civil het-erosexual marriage but still require religious jurisdiction over divorce (which, in not uncommon cases, would then prohibit the possibil-ity of civil remarriage). While many secular Israelis would welcome the huge step of instituting civil marriage, they would bristle against the limitation to heterosexual couples and the religious requirements for divorce (and therefore remarriage). Religious Israelis (and in the context of the Gavison–Medan Covenant, specifically religious Jew-ish Israelis) would lament the institution of civil marriage and what they perceive as the illegitimate marriages that it could propagate, but would value the retention of religious jurisdiction over divorce and remarriage as well as keeping marriage a heterosexual institution in Israel. Medan expressed that, even with certain religious protections under a covenant, religious Zionists like himself fear "a future erosion of the remaining link between the state and the Torah command-ments."[17] Gavison, on the other hand, admits that while agreeing to retain religious jurisdiction over divorce is difficult and distasteful to her, the "cultural-national" benefits would still outweigh this cost, reflecting the principle that "society is allowed to limit the freedom of those of its members who benefit from the fact that they live in a soci-ety in which their community exercises national self-determination."[18] In other words, infringements on some freedoms are worth the greater freedom of a nation-state, and without Jewish autonomy over an area like marriage the Jewish character of the state overall would be more difficult to maintain. While the Gavison–Medan Covenant is nonbinding, it stands out as an example of prominent religious and cultural leaders who, like the IDI's draft constitution, have diagnosed a need for institutionalizing a balance between religion and state in a way that strengthens a Jewish and democratic identity for Israel.

# BETWEEN STATE BORDERS AND NATIONAL BOUNDARIES: PROPOSALS FOR ARRANGEMENTS OF A FUTURE ISRAEL/PALESTINE

## Two States for Two Nations

Perhaps one reason why the future of Zionism in the State of Israel appears to many to be in flux is because Israel's physical borders and geopolitical horizons are still in flux or in dispute. Historic diplomatic efforts have ostensibly already determined the desired outcome of these fluctuations and disputes; since the early 1990s, the aim of the creation of a Palestinian state in part of historic (British Mandate) Palestine alongside Israel in its Green Line border has become official policy for Israel, the Palestinian Liberation Organization (PLO), the United States, the European Union, and the United Nations. This "two-state solution," as it is popularly known, had precedents in the 1937 Peel Commission Partition Plan, which was not implemented, and the 1947 United Nations resolution to endorse and create separate Jewish and Palestinian states at the end of the British Mandate. These two separate states did not come to pass—the outbreak and outcomes of the 1948 war rendered serious consideration of a two-state arrangement largely obsolete, since Israel secured different and more expansive borders than those proposed in the plan, and the territory allotted for a Palestinian state was absorbed by Jordan and Egypt. Member of the Knesset Uri Avnery, on the extreme Left fringe of the 1960s political scene, proposed the creation of a Palestinian state, but his views were marginal and criticized.[19] After the 1967 War, Jordanian and Israeli officials together considered creating a Palestinian autonomous region in the West Bank in federation with the Kingdom of Jordan, but this never materialized and by 1988 Jordan officially renounced any claim or oversight to the West Bank. Several Palestinian intellectuals had broached what Walid Khalidi in 1978 called "the unthinkable"—creating an independent Palestinian state alongside Israel.[20] But the two-state solution only became a real diplomatic possibility for the first time in 1988, after PLO chairman Yasser Arafat ceremonially declared Palestinian independence in the territory specified in UN Resolution 242.

Arafat's acknowledgment of Israel's 1967 borders opened a way for significant negotiation efforts to take place, the most momentous of which were secret direct talks between Israelis and PLO members held in Oslo, Norway, that created the basis for the 1993 Oslo Accords. The details of this pivotal agreement continue to receive wide scholarly, journalistic, and political attention. In an optimal outcome of these accords, Israel and Palestine would each have mutually recognized sovereign states with secure borders. The two states would serve as cultural centers for their respective national diasporas, members of which also would gain and/or retain the ability to become citizens of their respective countries. For most proponents of a two-state solution, Israel would remain a Jewish nation-state with equal civil rights for all citizens. Israel might allow a token number of Palestinian refugees to return to homes or villages within Israel, but most Palestinian refugees would only be permitted to obtain citizenship in the State of Palestine, whether or not they were originally from those areas. Palestinian Israeli citizens would be allowed to move freely between the two states, and would have their civil (individual) rights protected under Israeli law, but claims to national rights would be exercised exclusively in Palestine. This outcome would follow the phased withdrawal of Israeli military and/or civilian presence in territories Israel controlled since the 1967 War, with possibilities for "territorial swaps." The process toward implementing these agreements has involved a gradual establishment of autonomous Palestinian governing institutions, most notably the administration known as the

Palestinian National Authority, including a National Council and a police force.

Despite the initial celebration of such unprecedented agreements, actualizing the agreements from Oslo has met with overwhelming obstacles. Strong elements on both sides have opposed movement toward the full establishment of both states. The right-wing Jewish Israeli sectors protested vehemently, and tragically in 1994 Prime Minister Yitzhak Rabin was assassinated by an ultraorthodox extremist as both a punishment and to prevent agreements to relinquish territory. Conversely, Hamas maintains popular support among Palestinians but does not subscribe to the Oslo agreements (or subsequent agreements), insisting on the Palestinians' right to all of historic Palestine (however, some argue that Article 20 of their revised 2017 charter implies the possibility of conceding to the 1967 borders in what would be considered a permanent truce).[21] Along with this popular resistance from both nations, Israeli and Palestinian politicians have failed to meet necessary benchmarks for progress. Agreements on the issues most sensitive to both sides—such as refugees, Jerusalem, and Jewish settlements in the West Bank—are also still deferred to "final status" negotiations after benchmarks have been met, further delaying progress. The ongoing delay of the Oslo Accords has prompted similar proposals by various entities, including the Saudi/Arab Peace Initiative (ratified by the Arab League in 2002 and renewed in 2007), United Nations Security Council Resolution 1397 (2002), the American Road Map (2003), and the Geneva Accords (2003). The existence of such agreements and plans, regardless of the extent to which they've been implemented, sustains the prevailing diplomatic goal of achieving a two-state solution peacefully. In a gesture toward this end, the UN recognized Palestine as a nonvoting, observer state in 2012.

Advocates of "two states for two nations" insist that, despite decades of difficulty, it is both the most just outcome and most optimal for preserving the Zionist aim of a Jewish democracy. Optimists hope that two separate states will allow both Jewish and

Palestinian national identities to not just survive but to thrive. Israel, and its army in which most Jewish citizens serve, would no longer administer a disenfranchised Palestinian population, and therefore, as journalist Ari Shavit has insisted, enacting a final peace plan "will serve us as a moral shield. We must make it clear to the world that we aren't a theocracy, we aren't an occupation state, and our hearts aren't closed."[22] Even though a two-state solution would require significant territorial sacrifices and possibly even security risks, it would also prevent the incorporation of the Palestinian population of those territories into the Israeli body politic and would thereby maintain a Jewish majority, considered by many to be a condition of a successful Zionist democracy. As Uri Avnery posited decades after his initial proposal for two states, "the desire for a state with a Jewish majority, where Jews are masters of their own fate, trumps all other aims, even the desire for a state in all of [The Land of] Israel."[23] With two states, both Israel and Palestine would each have their own government, state symbols, and cultural autonomy, particularly over areas of language, religion, and education. Perhaps most significantly, establishing two states would provide a place for each nation's diaspora to settle if they wished, which would partially fulfil the longtime Palestinian demand for the Right of Return. With borders finally agreed upon and refugees free to settle and obtain citizenship in a State of Palestine, the most volatile disputes between Jews and Palestinians in Israel/Palestine would be disarmed, and would unencumber the two independent states to pursue diplomatic relations as equal partners rather than combatants.

## One State

Many commentators insist that the longer the two-state solution languishes, the more inextricable Israelis and Palestinians become and the less a two-state framework remains viable. The alternative would mean some form of single-state arrangement. Many argue that a single governing entity and society already exists, employing different terms for this phenomenon: Jewish American journalist Peter Beinart warned that "the green line is fading," Israeli sociologist Yehouda Shenhav termed the current situation between Israel and the Palestinian Territories a "bi-national reality," Israeli politician and historian Meron Benvenisti called the region a "de facto binational state," and political scientist Ian Lustick identifies a "one state reality," entitling his 2019 book on the subject *Paradigm Lost*.[24] Some observers speculate (or in the more poetic words of one journalist, "eulogize") that while two states may have been possible at the time the Oslo agreements were drafted and signed, too much has changed both geographically and politically for a two-state arrangement to remain feasible.[25] Many critics have dismissed these conclusions, asserting that a single-state framework is either pathetic naivety of the possibility of coexistence or a strong-arm tactic to force a final achievement of two states by threatening the possibility of one.[26] Nevertheless, many commentators substantiate their diagnosis—or even their aspirations—of one state on logistical, moral, and political grounds.

Many claims of a "one-state reality" rest on logistical interconnectedness between the two nations: they currently occupy the same territory/borders with Jewish and Arab neighborhoods and cities interspersed throughout (indeed many maps of Israel—or Palestine for that matter—depict the 1947 borders of historic Mandate Palestine rather than the 1949 armistice borders). There is also considerable infrastructural overlap; the Jewish settlements in the West Bank are included under the same utilities services, road works and engineers, and electric grid as the rest of Israel.[27] Meron Benvenisti argues that, even on a geographical level, "you can erect all the walls in the world here, but you won't be able to overcome the fact there is only one aquifer here and the same sea."[28] Not only are environment and infrastructure intertwined, but so are social, economic, military, and political institutions—the IDF operates on both sides of the Green Line and the Israeli government has the final say on border closures and population movement. The Israeli Jews who live inside the Palestinian Territories work, learn, socialize, and receive health care on both sides of the Green Line. Despite these diagnoses of a one-state reality, there is of course not officially one state, and the proposals (or warnings) regarding a one-state outcome have a range of nationalist, democratic, and/or annihilationist possibilities. Each of these arrangements pose their own challenges and opportunities for the future of Zionism.

ONE STATE FOR ONE NATION

One version of a possible one-state arrangement is a crude "zero-sum" outcome for Israel or Palestine: all the land between the Jordan River and Mediterranean Sea would belong either to the State of Israel or the State of Palestine, as explicitly Jewish or Arab states, respectively. There would be one government over the land and its population, and minorities in each of these states would have varying degrees of individual rights and responsibilities.

In some of the most extreme visions for a one-state solution, minorities would not exist or would have significantly curtailed rights or representation. This exclusionary framework can be found in both Jewish and Palestinian political streams. In 1968, Uri Avnery had observed, "there may be some on the lunatic fringe of the annexation idea who believe the Arabs should and could be evicted in due course from the country, enabling all of [Israel] to become a homogenous state."[29] What Avnery called a "lunatic fringe" has sustained itself over the decades, such as in the political platform of 1980s right-wing leader Meir Kahane (outlined in his lengthy manifesto with the less-than-subtle title *They Must Go*), or the more recent party Otzama Yehudit (Hebrew for *"Jewish Strength"*), with a similar platform of official annexation of the West Bank into the Jewish State and possibly even the segregation or expulsion of Arabs. Another recurring Zionist proposal is for Jordan to be declared the Palestinian state—an arrangement predictably contested by Jordanian government officials, non-Palestinian Jordanians, and Palestinians who demand a Palestinian state on at least some of the territory of historic Palestine.[30]

While some more fringe Jewish Israeli platforms propose a Jewish state over all of Greater Israel, some Palestinian platforms envision a state of Palestine without Jews, or at least without Jews who claim any kind of national identity. Palestinian historian Walid Khalidi explained that, for many Palestinians before the 1967 War, "Palestinian and Arab opinion was not prepared" to consider the existence of two states; "it aspired to the recovery of the whole of Palestine or the establishment of a democratic secular state in it. Acceptance of partition or a state on the West Bank and in the Gaza Strip was treason. In some Palestinian and Arab quarters, it still is."[31] Khalidi wrote this in 1978 but it would still apply in some circles today. Hamas, for instance, has consistently demanded the right to control the entire land under an Islamic framework.[32] Their platforms ostensibly allow for the inclusion of Jews (or Christians) in this state but only if they "stop disputing the sovereignty of Islam in this region."[33] Jews would be welcome to live as a religious minority in an Islamic Palestinian state, but Jewish national identity would have no place in the government or society.

Some Zionist proposals for a Jewish nation-state on the entire land do include civil rights for individual Palestinians. Politicians from the Likud Party, and other further Right leaders such as those in the Yesha Council of settlement municipalities, have suggested, instead of partitioning the land in two, annexing the Palestinian Territories and population outright. In 2014 right-wing journalist and political activist Caroline Glick outlined a version of this framework in her book *The Israeli Solution: A One-State Plan for Peace in the Middle East.* Proposals include granting Palestinians the same ID cards, license plates, and insurance as the rest of Israel, and offering them either citizenship or permanent residency. One former Yesha Council spokesperson envisioned, "one land in which the children of settlers and the children of Palestinians will be bused to school together."[34] This framework is consonant with the ideology of Revisionist founder Jabotinsky, who accepted the fact Arabs would always live in the country, even proclaiming in a poem that, "From the wealth of our land there shall prosper / The Arab, the Christian, and the Jew."[35] But this type of coexistence would be predicated on Palestinian acceptance of a Jewish state over the entire territory. Likud politician Tzipi Hotovely clarified what she and her colleagues envision: "I do not recognize national rights of Palestinians in the Land of Israel. I recognize their human rights and their individual rights, and also their individual political rights—but between the sea and the Jordan there is room for one state, a Jewish state."[36] These proposals for one state for one nation, even when guaranteeing individual rights of minority citizens, still require national minorities to relinquish any nationalist identity or claims within the state.

ONE DEMOCRATIC CIVIC STATE

Another model for one state does not favor or identify either a Jewish or Palestinian nationality but would be, as became popularly known in the 1990s, "a state for all its citizens." The state would have a constitution endowing identical rights, responsibilities, and legal jurisdictions to every person in both Israel and Palestine regardless of national, religious, ethnic, or gender identity. In the mid-1980s there were just flickers of such a prospect; a Palestinian Israeli lawmaker proposed declaring Israel "a home and homeland for all its Jewish and Arab citizens," and Sari Nusseibeh, Palestinian intellectual and activist for an independent Palestinian state on 1967 borders, had—more out of exasperation than an actual political program— considered, "instead of seeking independence why not seek equal rights within Israel? After all Israel is controlling our land, resources, and lives."[37] In 1996, Palestinian Israeli politician Azmi Bishara established a party called National Democratic Assembly (known as Balad, which is both the Hebrew acronym and the Arabic word for "land" or "country"). This party existed to "struggle to transform the State of Israel into a democracy for all its citizens, irrespective of national or ethnic identity."[38] The party was banned multiple times for its possible violation of the 1985 amendment of Basic Law: Knesset, which prohibited candidates or parties that "[deny] the existence of the State of Israel as the state of the Jewish people."[39] However, the Supreme Court has overturned these bans, ruling the demand for democracy irrespective of national identity did not automatically preclude Israel remaining as the state of the Jewish people. Later activists and intellectuals have outlined similar platforms for a single constitutional democracy across all Israeli-controlled territories, in both Israel and Palestine.[40]

The creation of a single democratic state would enable the classification and cultivation of an Israeli national identification distinct from Jewish, Palestinian, or Arab national identities. Many Israeli Palestinians and Jews have already expressed a feeling of Israeli cultural identification based on a number of culinary, musical, social, and linguistic commonalities. Palestinian Israeli journalist and activist Nazir Majali termed the impact of this shared identity as "Israelization," that makes Palestinian Israelis distinct from other Arabs. "If we shake off our Israeliness day and night, if we deny it and abuse it, we'll fail. It will peek from every word we say, from every opinion we state; from the speech, the way of thinking, ways of life and conduct, opinions and costumes," Majali claims.[41] A series of documents released by various Palestinian Israeli groups in 2006–7, collectively known as the Vision Documents, also expresses this interdependence of Arabs and Jews in Israel: "We speak the Hebrew language fluently. We listen to Jewish rhetoric and provide them our rhetoric. We translate Israeli books into Arabic."[42] Despite "Israelization" of Palestinian and Jewish Israelis, a formal Israeli national identity does not bureaucratically exist. In 2013 a handful of Israeli politicians and scholars petitioned the state to be able to register nationality as "Israeli" (instead of Jewish or Arab), but the Supreme Court rejected this option, since, among other things, it would rupture the national link between Jews in Israel and Jews in the Diaspora. Associates in the Israel Democracy Institute applauded the court's decision. "Israeli Jews and Israeli Arabs share a common citizenship. They are both Israeli, and are therefore entitled to and must be accorded the same civil rights. But they are not members of the same nation," the IDI published in response to the ruling.[43] In the framework of a civic democratic state, however, citizens might be incentivized to cultivate a shared Israeli national identity based on common citizenship and history rather than shared ethnicity or religion.

Critics fear that a civic democratic state would become a Trojan Horse for a demographic race to ethnic domination. In this scenario, instead of the government by an electorate with the interests of a civic Israeli nation at heart, the ethnic majority would elect leaders and policies that put their own group in power. As early as the Mandate-era Brit Shalom movement for one binational state, Labor Zionist leader Berl Katznelson criticized that one state "is camouflage for an Arab state," since there were far more Arabs than Jews in Mandate Palestine.[44] The demographic makeup of Israel and Palestine still stokes the same fears, as the population between the Jordan River and the Mediterranean is now roughly the same number of Arabs and Jews but with a higher birthrate among Arabs. Perhaps even more significantly, a Palestinian electoral majority could potentially legislate a Palestinian Right of Return, in which case the Palestinian population might rise by an even more significant number. As prominent American lawyer Alan Dershowitz argues, the Palestinian demand for a Right of Return for refugees "is nothing less than a veiled 'right' to destroy Israel by demographic, rather than by terroristic, means."[45]

For understandable reasons, discourse on the possibility of a Jewish minority among a majority with which they have decades of strife frequently takes on existential dimensions (as Dershowitz's claim illustrates). An Israeli columnist warned in 2021 that, "the one-state idea posits a danger not only for Jewish identity but also for the Jewish (and Palestinian) body—the danger of a Bosnian or Rwandan, Yemeni or Syrian reality: a lethal, blood-drenched civil war, with tens of thousands or even hundreds of thousands killed."[46] And in a controversial article broaching support for a one-state solution, Peter Beinart went so far as to grimly posit that Zionism has been reduced to the fear that if Israel were a civic democratic state for all its citizens instead of a Jewish nation-state, Israeli Jews would risk genocide.[47] Beinart received a rash of criticism for his article; one editorial claimed that his proposal for a civic democratic state in Israel/Palestine amounted to "transforming it into yet another Arab-Muslim majority state."[48] Another strong response, by author and historian Daniel Gordis, outlined reasons why Zionism is more than, as Beinart suggested, a fear of genocide, but he still considered it a plausible fear: "Jews would quickly become a minority here, just as they were in Europe. They would be surrounded by hostile masses, just as they were in Europe, and that would certainly (and rapidly) destroy the Jewish confidence that has been at the core of [Judaism's] revitalization in Israel."[49] Gordis's reference to the hostile masses Jews faced as minorities in Europe is a clear reference to the Holocaust, and while he posits that in a civic state Jews "might not well be annihilated," they would still "commit national suicide."[50] In light of existing conflicts between Israelis and Palestinians, a government suddenly shared equally between the two (as compared to the establishment of two separate Israeli and Palestinian states) would, critics fear, create a vehicle for ethnic majoritarian oppression of the minority, and open the possibility for inter-ethnic civil violence or even genocide.

## One Binational State of Two Nations

The fears of annihilationist one-state arrangements have led an increasingly vocal contingent to envision single-state arrangements that would accommodate national identities in a way that a simple "one person one vote" government would not. A binational model attempts to merge the civic and territorial inclusiveness of a one-state solution with existing nationalist aspirations and identities. The model would establish the constitutional safeguards deemed necessary to avoid a majoritarian demographic race that many fear would result from a single democratic state. While the language of a single civic state and a single binational state is often used interchangeably in discourse, the two have key practical and ideological differences. Proponents of this approach have proposed a range of possible configurations to achieve national autonomy within a shared state, but the configurations all include some formal recognition of both Jewish and Palestinian national identities along with institutions to equitably cultivate and preserve these. The state would be a form of democracy that is not normal majority rule, and establishment of national autonomy that is not based on territorial separation—as Palestinian Israeli lawmaker Ahmad Tibi described it, "a state for all its nationalities" rather than "a state for all its citizens."[51]

Advocates of binationalism point to earlier precedents, such as the binationalist wing of the early Zionist movement Brit Shalom. Even the Zionist Democratic Faction 1906 Helsingfors Program for "present work" could be considered an example of the promotion of national autonomy within a larger state structure. While in that case it was for the Jews of eastern Europe and not for the context of a future Jewish state, the notion of some kind of national autonomy separate from the framework of a nation-state certainly had a place in early Zionist discourse. Possibilities for a binational state continued with the establishment of the political party Ichud in 1942; and in 1947 the UNSCOP committee that ultimately proposed partitioning British Mandate Palestine into separate Jewish and Arab states drafted a minority report suggesting a "federated state with full citizenship for Jews and Arabs."[52] This proposal even received 50 percent of the vote in the UN General Assembly, but was jettisoned in favor of two separate states. The Israeli Palestinian organization Al-Ard was established in 1959 to promote a binational state as well.[53] Since these various movements did not gain popular or political traction, Daniel Gordis described binationalism as relegated to the "dustbin of history"; however, binationalism has generated more discourse since the turn of the twenty-first century, especially as successful implementation of agreements for two states has tarried.[54]

Proponents offer different reasons for why a binational state may be the best prospect for both Jewish and Palestinian nationalism, the foremost being its potential to preserve national rights and identity for both in the framework of a constitutional democracy. Palestinian American journalist Ali Abunimah asserts that the "one country" he proposes can be considered "equally and simultaneously a Jewish state and a Palestinian state . . . It will provide a place for each of its communities to fulfill its national, cultural, and spiritual aspirations and needs"—not a democratic state void of national meaning.[55] Binationalism would thus expand the existing state sponsorship of Jewish national identity to include Palestinian nationality as well, instead of requiring one or both nations to relinquish their national identification.

Moving toward a government recognition of both nationalities, advocates hope, would create stronger foundations for justice and peace between the conflicting Jewish and Palestinian populations. National desires are strong enough that force would be necessary to convince a sizeable minority (let alone majority) population to relinquish them and, conversely, allowing both to exercise national autonomy could defuse this need for force. Early Zionist Hans Kohn believed binationalism was Zionism's only alternative to military subjugation of Arabs, and Martin Buber worried that a Jewish nation-state rather than binational state "will find itself in a state of war for generations, which will oblige it to militant, totalitarian behavior."[56] Celebrated Israeli author A. B. Yehoshua came to a similar conclusion after decades of energetically supporting a two-state model, claiming that "we are not Americans in Vietnam, the French in Algeria or the Soviets in Afghanistan, who one day get up and leave. We will live with the Palestinians for eternity, and every wound and bruise in relations between the two peoples will be engraved in the memory and passed on from one generation to the next."[57] A binational government of both Jewish and Palestinian nations could instead officially acknowledge the heavy significance of each nation's identity, history, and traumas. Peter Beinart urges liberal Zionists to acknowledge the Palestinians' traumas and national attachments to their land, contending that "in our bones, Jews know that when you tell a people to forget its past you are not proposing peace. You are proposing extinction."[58] In an even more bald statement of insisting on a binational framework that would include Palestinian refugees, Beinart insists, "If Palestinians have no right to return to their homeland, neither do we." "The return of Palestinian refugees . . . could be a kind of return for us as well, a return to traditions of memory and justice that the Nakba has evicted from organized Jewish life."[59] Codifying a binational government for both Israelis and Palestinians could promote peace by ensuring the equal citizenship of a civic democratic state alongside formal recognition of and degrees of autonomy for each national group.

MODELS OF BINATIONALISM
In 2003, Meron Benvenisti posited that "the question is no longer whether [Israel] will be binational, but which model to choose."[60] Some activists and political scientists have already outlined specific models or draft constitutions for how binationalism would work. Many other advocates have been far less programmatic and instead emphasize guiding principles, such as the recognition of both Hebrew and Arabic as official languages, some form of shared government, and the need for a constitution that guarantees equal national and individual rights. Some proposals underscore structural reform in budget and land allocation and, significantly, immigration policies.

Even the nomenclature of a binational state would possibly change—some proposals have still referred to a binational state as the State of Israel, but others have used Israel-Palestine, "Israstine," or even the "State of Jerusalem."[61] Ali Abunimah suggests "citizens of the state can call it a Jewish state or a Palestinian state if they wish to identify it as such."[62]

Most frameworks for a binational government involve some type of confederation, in which Jews and Palestinians have shared governing institutions alongside their own representative bodies. The national bodies would have autonomy in areas of culture, education, and religious institutions. A bicameral legislature (similar to the US Senate/House of Representatives) would incorporate both proportional representation (based on population) and a fixed equal number of each nationality. These branches of government would be secured through a constitution guaranteeing not only equal individual rights, but also minority veto rights and/or ensuring a very high percentage necessary for constitutional amendments (meaning a simple government majority could not overturn the binational nature of the state or the specific national protections for either Jews or Palestinians). Other countries have been cited as possible exemplars, such as Belgium's three linguistic groups that share power in a federal constitutional monarchy, or the 1998 agreement between Ireland and the United Kingdom establishing a government for Northern Ireland, effectively calming decades of Irish civil strife.

Along with establishing a binational constitution and government, proponents of binationalism stress that it would require a major economic and administrative overhaul. One of the ways this could take place is by allowing a return for Palestinians. In tandem with this would be some form of reparations, such as providing homes or compensation for Palestinian refugees. The Vision Documents offer some concrete examples of what this restitution could entail.[63] Significantly, many high-profile Palestinian proponents of binationalism reject the possibility of expelling Jews from homes or towns in order to accommodate these returning Palestinians. The Palestinian Right of Return could exist alongside the Law of Return for Jews, so that both diasporic Jews and Palestinians, as well as their descendants and dependents, would be eligible for citizenship.[64]

Other institutions that commentators have flagged as in possible need of revision in a binational state are the Jewish National Fund and Jewish Agency. The Jewish National Fund has significant economic and even geographic impact in Israel since it owns over 10 percent of Israeli land, and has almost half of the seats on the public Israel Land Administration. Even though it has this authority over public land allocation and management, it is not an institution of the Israeli State but rather formally of "the Jewish People," and therefore outside the access of non-Jewish Israeli citizens.[65] As the Haifa Declaration argued, a binational arrangement should cancel "participation of non-Israeli [institutions] and representatives" in "fields of land planning and housing."[66] Conversely, the Palestinian Liberation Organization would similarly need either reform or dissolution. Diaspora relations could be formally recognized or even equitably funded by a binational state, but would need to be subject to some oversight of the shared government and not just one of the national groups.

## IN-BETWEEN STATE

While two states for two nations remains the diplomatic status quo amid growing calls for one-state arrangements, some have proposed what Sammy Smooha has called an "in-between state"—a novel combination of aspects of two-state and one-state models.[67] Many feel that, given the unique challenges and opportunities for Israel and Palestine, existing options have been exhausted and some kind of unprecedented configuration is necessary. Bestselling Israeli author and journalist Ari Shavit, who espouses fairly centrist politics and is a staunch supporter of a two-state solution, himself insisted "we urgently need a novel idea. The paradigm of the right is outdated. But the paradigm of the center-left is also no longer relevant . . . it's time to think outside the box. It's time to think outside both boxes."[68] Yehouda Shenhav similarly calls for "creating new spheres of overlapping political, communal, municipal and theological sovereignties."[69] The Israeli–Palestinian Creative Regional Initiative, an association that aims to "ignite political imagination," placed the need for creative novelty in its organization's name. The Israeli intercommunal association Shaharit pledges to find "a new political language, to create new social networks, and to encourage new initiatives, for the benefit of all of Israel's communities, and . . . Israeli society as a whole."[70] One state versus two states or Left versus Right is not, according to these stakeholders, going to be sufficient in the Palestinian–Israeli context, which instead needs to adopt and adapt aspects of existing models to create an "in-between" version.

Some of the earliest proposals for two states already exhibited elements of both two-state and binational proposals. Not long after the 1967 War, Uri Avnery, as a Member of the Knesset, proposed to establish a Palestinian Republic on the captured territory, on the basis that "the whole of Palestine is the homeland of two nations— the Hebrew nation and the Arab-Palestinian nation."[71] While this proposal was for a separate state, it was also to establish a federation between the countries, and therefore it was not for two purely unrelated states but states created for the purpose of federation. Walid Khalidi's 1978 proposal of a Palestinian state resembled aspects of binational proposals as well, such as his suggestion for "freedom of movement and residence" between the two states, as well as a shared Jerusalem that "could remain open between the capital of Israel in West Jerusalem and the capital of Arab Palestine in East Jerusalem."[72]

More recent stakeholders have offered proposals for how more creative models may function. In Smooha's version of an "in-between state" Israel would still be formally recognized as a Jewish state but would establish a constitutional democratic government along the lines of most binational proposals, including dissolving the Jewish National Fund and the Jewish Agency. The activist organization "Land for All" issued a program for "Two States, One Homeland," in which Israel and Palestine would be independent states, both of which would have Jerusalem as the capital. The states would be linked in ways similar to the European Union, with shared economic, legal, and environmental institutions and agreements, and across which "citizens of both countries are free to move and live in all parts of the land."[73] The organization explains that its "idea is neither absolute separation nor absolute integration"; it adopts "the positive aspects of the two-state solution, such as the national expression of each nation and each nation's ability to manage its own affairs, while adopting the positive aspects of the one-state solution [like] equality [and] freedom of movement" under a federated system.[74] In a different vein, historian Rachel Havrelock has proposed "resource sovereignty" for Jews and Palestinians on both sides of the Green Line, with equal and shared decision-making powers over their shared watershed.[75] These are just a few proposals and principles that activists, many of whom come from across the political spectrum of both Israelis and Palestinians, have put forth in more recent years.

## FROM NATION-STATE TO NATION IN A STATE

Cultivating and cementing some kind of government shared by Jewish and Palestinian nations would, as both advocates and critics emphasize, compel Jews and Palestinians to revise their understandings of the relationships between nation and state, and of what Zionism means in a binationalist context. On a political level this would involve "downshifting of the collective goal from total control over a group's political destiny (sovereignty) to partial forms of such control."[76] Some oppose binationalism for the very reason that it would require a redefinition of Israel's political identity. Israeli legal scholar Yedidia Stern speculates that a civic democratic state would erode Israel's identity as a center of Jewish life and culture, and Progressive Zionist journalist Zach Beauchamp warns that changing Israel from being a specifically Jewish state to a general civic democratic one would "give up on Zionism wholesale" by overturning the one government "that exists to protect Jews in a hostile world."[77] Even some who support a single state have undertaken this alternative with a heavy heart; A. B. Yehoshua reluctantly concluded that "we need to deploy for a different way of thinking about our identity in the binational state we already are in, whether we like it or not."[78] Peter Beinart affirms that "even in the best of circumstances, such a transformation [from a nation-state model] would be profoundly jarring to many Jews," as it would mean "reconsidering cherished myths about the Israeli and Zionist past."[79] Beinart confessed that he had viewed "questioning Israel's existence as a Jewish state [as] . . . akin to spitting in the face of people I love and betraying institutions that give my life meaning and joy."[80] Palestinians would similarly face cultural and political adjustments in the context of a binational state. American Palestinian activist Michael Tarazi observed that "no Palestinian leader seems ready . . . to start confronting the sacred cow and saying 'Wait a minute, we got it all wrong, maybe the age of nation-states has passed us by, so let's jump to the next phase.'"[81] Political scientist Leila Farsakh observes that even among Palestinians who support a single-state arrangement, they have not considered "how far to engage with present Israelis and their ethnic concerns," or with "the complexity of Jewish identity and history."[82] Palestinian support for a binational state "clearly repudiates Zionism, but it seeks to incorporate the Jewish person as a neutral repentant entity," and Palestinians would need to start grappling with "what to do with the Israeli culture that has developed over the past 60 years."[83]

Both Jewish and Palestinian proponents of binationalism suggest that despite the difficulties of adapting nationalist identity to a binationalist state instead of a nation-state, it is still both possible and desirable. Beinart argues in his article "Yavne: A Jewish Case for Equality in Israel-Palestine" that a binational state "doesn't require abandoning Zionism," but instead "requires distinguishing between form and essence. The essence of Zionism is not a Jewish state in the land of Israel; it is a Jewish *home* in the land of Israel, a thriving Jewish society that both offers Jews refuge and enriches the entire Jewish world."[84] Beinart believes a Jewish home is still possible without a Jewish state, even elevating this reformulation of Zionism to be historically comparable to the shift after the destruction of the Second Temple in Jerusalem when Jews reoriented from a sacrificial system in Jerusalem to a rabbinical tradition rooted in Yavne. "Our task in this moment is to imagine a new Jewish identity," Beinart urges; "one that sees Palestinian liberation as integral to our own. That's what Yavne means today."[85] Israeli author Daniel Gavron, having shifted from a two-state to one-state paradigm, similarly suggested that a one-state arrangement is a return to different aspects of Jewish and Zionist history instead of an abandonment. He highlights the Bible's description of ancient Israelites living in a multiethnic society, noting that "King David . . . made use of Canaanite officials, had a Hittite general, enjoyed good relations with the Phoenicians, and (after some bloody conflicts with them) deployed Philistine units in his army."[86] Gavron concludes that "one can argue, then, that the establishment of a multicultural nation, rather than a specifically Jewish state, is a true expression of Zionism in that it is reconstructing a model similar to the historical entities of ancient Israel and Judea."[87] As with Zionists, a binational framework would also require Palestinians to revisit their own history in order to adapt the goals of their nationalist aspirations. Saleh Hijazi, a deputy regional director in Amnesty International, surmises that "our modern [Palestinian] story has been tied from the start to the story of the Jews [since] we were forced to pay the price for Europe's treatment of Jews." He urges Palestinians to self-reflectively acknowledge this history in order to "begin to weave new approaches to the place of the Jews in our movement's discourse."[88] Hijazi challenges Palestinians to "open up our collective imagination and allow us a vision of a way forward . . . to a different kind of politics."[89] Many observers consider the nationalist revision required for both Jews and Palestinians to be, if not impossible, "difficult to imagine."[90] "At this juncture in history, it is impossible to know how so fundamental a transition might occur, or if it ever will," Beinart wrote.[91] Caroline Glick has deemed it a "pipe dream." But some show more optimism; Daniel Gavron, for instance, says, "I think the miracle of Israel [in 1948] was a greater miracle than the one now required to create [one state]. The creation of the state was much less likely, much more fraught with danger, and much harder to achieve. What I'm proposing is simply a switch in thinking and conception. This is much, much easier to achieve."[92] Those who find this switch in conception possible venture that the resources to achieve it can be found within the respective national histories rather than by rejecting them.

## CONCLUSION

Many hope that Jewish national identity (and Palestinian identity for that matter) can be preserved and cultivated regardless of government structure or changing party majorities and coalitions. Pundits and activists have placed bets or hopes on different types of state structures. The satirical newspaper *The Onion* published an article called "Everyone in Middle East Given Own Country in 317,000,000-State Solution," obviously jesting at the notion of statehood resolving disputes ("Frankly, giving every Middle Eastern citizen a country of his or her own is long overdue," 49-year-old Naseer Khalidi told reporters from his newly formed 400-square-foot independent state along the former West Bank, which is adjacent to nations populated by his wife and two children").[93] There are extremes on both poles, but a broad overview of the various perspectives on the future of

Zionism shows that it is an ideology and policy with perhaps as many variations as when it started. Between these extremes, what one person may consider the end of Zionism another considers its fulfilment, or at least a new beginning. While structural political arrangements still hang in the balance—especially a constitution and a resolution of borders—various possibilities remain open, and others become more or less feasible with changing circumstances. Many Israelis, like the fictional families in the delivery room depicted in Kashua's *Arab Labor*, look to create as secure a reality as possible amidst the various political realities and possibilities. Original questions like whether Zionism aims to create a state for the Jews or a Jewish state, whether it should be a light to the nations or a state like any other, and how any of that is achieved, continue even today.

# EPILOGUE
### Zionism and Christians in Israel/Palestine

Examining Zionism in its historical contexts is like looking through a kaleidoscope in which various cultural, religious, and social components overlap into intricate permutations, some of which barely resemble another. Martin Buber and Vladimir Jabotinksy, two prominent Zionist leaders, for example, had quite different interpretations for the same movement they both espoused. Refusing to look through the prism of historical context, however, can make the kaleidoscope of Zionism look like an altogether different object—to some maybe a magic wand conjuring a form of redemption, to others maybe a cudgel for violence. Context and analysis are therefore critical to better understand these permutations of Zionism and to approach new perspectives and information on Zionism with more productive questions and more receptive ears.

While Zionism emerged from of a broad and rich Jewish history, Christians have not been absent from Zionist history and they would therefore be remiss to be ignorant of it. Theodor Herzl himself experienced the intersections of Zionism and Christianity in a number of ways, sometimes painfully so. Herzl's pronounced willingness to overlook religious and political differences helped him to appeal to just about anyone for his cause—a Russian minister of the interior who instigated pogroms, the pope, the Ottoman sultan, the anti-Zionist

Hasidic rebbe of Gur, and of course his close colleague and friend Reverend William Hechler. Herzl's strongest words are generally reserved for those who want to detract from his movement, regardless of their background. However, his reflections on his first (and ultimately last) visit to Jerusalem include an uncharacteristically bitter aside: "When I remember thee in days to come, O Jerusalem, it will not be with delight. The musty deposits of two thousand years of inhumanity, intolerance, and foulness lie in your reeking alleys. The one man who has been present here all this while, the lovable dreamer of Nazareth, has done nothing but help increase the hate."[1] Herzl's association of Jesus (the "dreamer of Nazareth") with destruction, bloodshed, and even inhumanity are a heartbreaking passing detail in his engrossing diaries. Indeed, Herzl had experienced hostility in church circles; Pope Pius X told Herzl, "we are unable to favor this movement [for a Jewish state] . . . We cannot prevent the Jews from going to Jerusalem—but we could never sanction it. The Jews have not recognized our Lord, therefore we cannot recognize the Jewish people."[2] This was certainly not the first or only time Herzl experienced for himself the prejudice that Christians could have toward him and his community as Jews, and his diary entry revealed one small point of contact of many between the history of Zionism and Christianity. Since Israel was established in 1948, the intersections between Christianity and Zionism still pose significant questions and challenges.

## CHRISTIANITY IN THE JEWISH STATE

In Israel itself, freedom of religion and of conscience is enshrined in the Declaration of Independence. Christianity is recognized as one of Israel's official religions; in fact there are ten officially recognized Christian denominations. These recognized denominations can register marriages and burials and can own and manage property. Christians from other denominations have freedom of worship in Israel as well, even if they are not administratively recognized by the state. These include Jews who believe in Jesus, also known as Messianic Jews (or generally in their own parlance, "believers"). While some Jewish religious political parties and organizations in Israel have introduced legislation prohibiting Christian proselytizing, none have passed, and evangelism is still legally permitted in Israel (though not if directed toward minors). Among some ultraorthodox communities there is still considerable opposition to missionary efforts and Messianic Jewish activity, including protests near Messianic congregations and homes, and even some instances of vigilante acts of vandalism and occasional violence, such as a bomb that a right-wing Jewish extremist delivered to an Israeli Messianic Jewish family in 2008.[3] This level of opposition generally does not target Messianic Jews exclusively, but groups them together with other perceived social ills.

Israeli Jewish believers in Jesus, like other converts to Christianity under the British Mandate or even earlier in the Zionist movement, have served as a kind of test case of the tenets of the Zionist movement that espouse Jewish national or ethnic identity as being separate from religion. Zionist attitudes toward converts have been mixed from the beginning. A 1914 controversy erupted among Zionist writers when author Yosef Haim Brenner upheld the New Testament as a Jewish text and claimed that even a Jew who believed in Jesus would still be Jewish if they adopted and cultivated Modern Hebrew to advance the Zionist project. A similar debate took place when Hans Herzl, the son of Theodor Herzl, converted to Christianity in 1925 but still identified with his Jewish national identity and his late father's project. Hans Herzl tragically died of suicide, and did not get to see his father's dream realized. Hans was a polarizing figure among Zionist leaders at the time, but many Zionist colleagues still accepted him, especially those who differentiated between ethnic and religious Jewish national identity.[4]

When Israel guaranteed religious freedoms upon its establishment, some commentators pointed to the status of converts as a gauge for the strength of the new Israeli democracy. Just a few months into Israeli independence, the newspaper *Palestine Post* editorialized that Israelis need not be categorized by their religion like they were under the British mandate: "Israel . . . has citizens of Moslem, Christian and Jewish denominations and it also has citizens of Arab, Greek, Armenian and Jewish race of no religious denomination. It may have Arab citizens of the Jewish faith and Jewish citizens of the Christian faith or of no faith at all. The fact that the word 'Jewish' has several connotations should not be allowed any longer to bedevil the issues."[5] However, the establishment of the state did not clear up the ambiguity of national identity, as was laid bare during the 1958 controversy over how the state would register who is a Jew. British philosopher Isaiah Berlin, one of the dozens whom Prime Minister Ben Gurion solicited for advice during this episode, asserted that, "there must exist a category of persons who will be entitled to register themselves as Jews by nationality, but not by religion."[6] Berlin believed that using religion to determine nationality would be a mild form of "religious coercion" that would infringe on individual liberty. "It should in principle be possible," Berlin continued, "for a man to be nationally a Jew and by religion a Christian, a Moslem, or whatever he pleases."[7] Nevertheless, the 1958 amendment to the Law of Return disqualifying Jews who have converted to another religion still stands, and the Israel Democracy Institute's draft constitution as well as the (nonbinding) Gavison–Medan Covenant retain the conversion stipulation for future state policy recommendations. This exception brought Brother Daniel to the famous Israeli Supreme Court case, where the difference between "status" and "identification" was stark: Rufeisen was legally denied Jewish nationality, while simultaneously affirmed as a fellow Jew by the judges deciding his case. He was able to become a naturalized citizen and live a full life in Israel as a Jewish Catholic priest to the end of his days.

Like Brother Daniel, the general integration of Messianic Jews in Israeli life speaks to the ambiguous boundaries of Jewish national identity and state bureaucracy. Israel has a small but active population of Israeli Jewish believers in Jesus. In the early 1960s one Hebrew Christian source claimed the size of this community in Israel was around several hundred, and estimates today range between 10,000 and 50,000, with a 2017 US State Department estimate at 20,000.[8] These groups have developed over the decades and there are now an estimated 240 congregations (*kehillot*, singular *kehillah*)—a term that is used instead of the formal word for "church" (*knessiyah*), which is generally reserved as a term for the church as a historical institution or for an actual church building. Many of these congregations espouse evangelical theology and congregational styles of church governance, though these fall along a broad spectrum, from charismatic to Reformed, and/or from heavily incorporating Jewish traditions or even *halakha* (like keeping kosher) to repudiating customs that originate in Judaism.[9] There is also an even smaller "Hebrew Catholic" community, nurtured by Brother Daniel and others, such as Jewish convert to Catholicism Elias Friedman, who in 1979 helped establish the Association of Hebrew Catholics.[10] Israeli Messianic Jewish *kehillot* have primarily Jewish and international expatriate attendance and their services are generally conducted in Hebrew, often with translation (or separate services) in Russian, English, or other languages.

Messianic Jews participate in all areas of secular Israeli Jewish life; they serve in the army, go to public Jewish schools, and work in every sector of the Israeli economy. In times of war, they are under as much threat as any other citizens of Israel. They also are free to develop their Messianic Jewish community at large, and hold regular conferences, summer camps, and concerts. Grace and Truth Congregation became the first congregation in Israel to construct its own building (after many years of bureaucratic red tape, international fundraising and volunteer efforts, and tireless prayer and flexibility by congregation leaders and members).[11] There are Messianic institutions including a Messianic kibbutz (Yad HaShmona), publishing houses like HaGefen (which publishes both original works and translations into Hebrew, Russian, Amharic, and other languages), the Caspari Center for Biblical and Jewish Studies, and even coffee houses and hostels. The inconspicuous Alliance Church International Cemetery in Jerusalem's German Colony is the resting place of several prominent Israeli Jewish believers in Jesus, including Dola Ben Yehuda, the daughter of the "Father of Modern Hebrew" Eliezer Ben Yehuda.

Many if not most Messianic Jews support the Zionist principle of Israel as a Jewish state, resonating as an important concept for their faith, ethnicity, or both. Gershon Nerel, an Israeli Messianic Jewish historian, has emphasized that both Messianic Judaism and Zionism "highlight the idea of bridging a historical gap between modern times and biblical times," and claim a connection to Jewish history despite a departure from rabbinic Judaism.[12] Keri Zelson Warshawsky similarly identifies Israel as what Messianic Jews "believe to be their Scriptural and historical homeland," and they thus support the Zionist tenet of the "ingathering of exiles" instrumentalized with the Law of Return.[13] Additionally, Israeli Messianic Jews typically "show a concern for security and peace that largely reflects current Israeli and Jewish political views."[14] As a 2016 statement of Israeli and Palestinian Christians noted, "many [Israeli Messianic Jews] see Israel's control over the territories as necessary to maintain security and prevent further escalation, and some see it as part of God's promise to greater Israel, and view military service as a duty to their country."[15] Within the Zionism of Israeli Messianic Jews are political and cultural leanings nearly as diverse as Zionism itself. Richard Harvey, scholar and analyst of Messianic Jewish communities and a Messianic Jew himself, has discerned a significant range of eschatological beliefs among Israeli Messianic Jews, along with varying interpretations of whether or how these eschatological beliefs have political implications in Israel.[16]

Israel/Palestine also has a sizeable population of Palestinian Christians. Most belong to Eastern Orthodox or Catholic branches of Christianity (such as Melkite Catholic and Armenian Orthodox), though there are many Protestant Palestinian Christians as well, with congregations and ministry organizations on both sides of the Green Line. Palestinian Christians share many of the social, economic, and cultural experiences of other Palestinians—living in exclusively Arab towns and neighborhoods (this was especially the case during the military administration through 1966, but has persisted), speaking Arabic as their mother tongue and in schools, not generally serving in the IDF, and marrying other (Christian) Palestinians. Like other Palestinians in 1948 and 1967, many lost their homes and villages or have in their displacement been separated from family members. These difficult experiences, and the markedly less Zionist history of the Orthodox and Catholic churches to which most belong (the Vatican did not even officially recognize Israel or open diplomatic relations until 1993), have fostered an inclination toward more critical positions toward Zionism among Palestinian Christians. Many of these Christian critics object not only to Israeli policies but to the theology of Christian Zionism, some even condemning it as heresy. Like Messianic Jews in Israel, Palestinian Christians in Israel/Palestine do not share a uniform political orientation in Israeli and/or Palestinian politics.[17]

Congregations in Israel are generally ethnically homogenous, not only because Jewish and Palestinian Christians identify with their respective national identities (noting, of course, the extensive variations amid both), but because of demographic factors. As Keri Zelson Warshawsky summarized, "most Messianic Jews and Arab Christians seem to have their hands full maintaining their own congregations and local communities, and must truly make a concerted effort to expand these circles to include" other communities.[18] Other than in big cities, most towns and villages in Israel are ethnically homogenous, and thus either worship predominantly in Hebrew or Arabic. Additionally, the populations' respective official days of rest on which to worship do not coincide, as Messianic Jews generally worship on Saturday (Israel's official day of rest) and go to school and work on Sunday, while Palestinian Christians generally worship on Sunday, recognized in Israel as an official day of rest for Christians, who start the work/school week on Monday. The trend of separation of Jewish and Palestinian Christians into separate congregations thus follows many of the same structural reasons for separation between Palestinians and Jews in Israel and Palestine more broadly.

## FELLOWSHIP

Regardless of where they stand on Zionism, there are many faithful Jewish and Palestinian Christians in Israel, the Palestinian Territories, and the Arab world who prioritize their shared faith in Christ ahead of their political aspirations. In a 1997 questionnaire of Israeli Messianic Jews, 94 percent responded that there should be more fellowship between Jewish and Arab Christians, and 85 percent thought that "developing this fellowship was more important than land issues."[19] Attempts at cultivating fellowship, edification, and reconciliation between Christian Palestinians and Messianic Jews have been developed in a variety of ways. For instance, the organization Musalaha was founded as "a forum which . . . allows believers, regardless of background, ethnicity and theology pertaining to the Holy Land and concepts of justice, to come together to express and voice their concerns and opinions in a safe and secure environment."[20] They organize summer camps, outdoor youth trips, and discussion groups, and publish material on national identity, reconciliation, and theology. They base their efforts on Romans 12:18—"if it is possible, as far as it depends on you, live at peace with everyone." In 2016, thirty Messianic Jews and Christian Palestinians met in Larnaca, Cyprus, under the auspices of the international evangelical Lausanne Movement, where they drafted and signed the Larnaca Statement. The statement "affirms our unity as believers in Jesus (section 1), calls for mutual commitment to live out that unity in the midst of conflict and division (section 2), recognizes areas of challenge and theological disagreement and identifies where further work needs to be done (section 3), proposes practical actions that express hope for the future, especially amongst the next generation of believers in both communities (section 4), and calls for prayer and support for this initiative from the wider family of believers."[21] The Larnaca Statement thus acknowledged the differences and even conflicts between the communities while committing to address them for the sake of a shared faith in Jesus and love for the Body of Christ as a whole.

These efforts are met with challenges both from within these communities and from wider sociopolitical realities. Some efforts face political and bureaucratic limitations; Musalaha for instance struggles to gather Israelis and Palestinians together across the Green Line. Furthermore, both Messianic Jews and Palestinian Christians are religious minorities within their respective nations, which can come with its own challenges that may be compounded by initiating overt efforts to blend communities. As Richard Harvey writes, Messianic Jews feel their Christian faith already makes them suspect in Israeli society, and thus to take on other social aims with potentially controversial reception—like building Jewish and Arab unity—could further marginalize them, and possibly even hamper "their rights as citizens, their status as immigrants, and their ability to speak into the political debate."[22] Furthermore, perhaps not unlike Christians in other divided nations, there is not always a general will for confronting difficulties between communities, especially if these are waved away as "political" or "worldly" distractions from the mission of the church. Musalaha is careful to note that when Jewish and Palestinian Christians confront national experiences and differences in the context of shared faith in Christ, "divisive issues are not neutralised or considered unimportant, but rather they are articulated in a loving and understanding environment which allows participants to enter into a process of reconciliation with each other."[23] Conflicting communities must address both the political and spiritual aspects of their division and reconciliation, which requires an honest acknowledgment of each other's traumas, wrongdoings, and assumptions. It is easier to end discussion with a surface-level affirmation of similar theological beliefs than to explore how those beliefs are applied or tested in a contentious social and political context.

Another problem these fellowship efforts face is the conditions and expectations that each group brings to the other. Mutually suspicious or hostile perspectives toward the other nation's narratives discourage direct engagement, let alone warm fellowship. One Musalaha newsletter observed that "some believe that the process of reconciliation can only begin once Jewish restoration to the land of Israel is declared as objective [theological] truth by all involved. In this context, reconciliation has come to mean that my true interpretation of Scripture must over-ride your false interpretation of Scripture, before we can enter into a process of reconciliation." On the other hand, some "argue that a pre-condition for reconciliation is that the dictates of justice are met, including the end of the Israeli occupation of the territories. They believe that to meet before this is to co-operate with the 'normalisation process' which accepts the status quo and legitimises the confiscation of land, the settlements and the multi-layered legal system which keeps the Palestinians as second class citizens."[24] These kind of totalizing prerequisites for fellowship stop a process of mutual understanding before it can start.[25] Messianic Jewish scholar Judith Mendelssohn Rood (who is not Israeli, but has spent significant stretches of time in Israel) expressed plainly that "in the years of my engagement with Palestinian evangelicals, I have never felt accepted for who I am: a Zionist Jew."[26] While she insists that Jewish and Arab Christians must love unconditionally as God does, these feelings of unacceptance—on both sides—can and do linger. The signatories of the abovementioned Larnaca Statement recognized the challenge

of polarization and thus vowed "not [to] require others to change
their position and accept ours as a pre-condition of our fellowship."
The Larnaca Statement tried to address existing differences by including side-by-side columns with summaries of each group's narratives
and perspectives, a format depicting that even if Jewish and Palestinian Christians do not share or synthesize perspectives on their current
political situation they will at least acknowledge them.[27]

Yet another challenge for fellowship between Jewish and Arab
Christians in the Jewish State is the presence of polarizing theology
in which positions on Zionism can become a litmus test for a Christian's belief in the authority of Scripture.[28] Palestinian pastor Mitri
Raheb, for instance, wrote in an issue of Sabeel's publication *Cornerstone* that "the State of Israel is like the empires of the Bible and that
the Palestinians of today are like the Israelites of the Bible."[29] Raheb's
vivid claim directly implicates Israel with the same fate and sins that
God condemned in the Bible, and conversely the Palestinians with the
same trajectory of righteous redemption of the Israelites. By extension
Raheb implies that anyone who concludes otherwise about Israel or
the Palestinians would be contradicting the teachings of God's word.
On the other hand, Israeli Messianic Jew Hannah Nesher, founder
of the Voice for Israel ministries, wrote that "with regards to Israel, it
is vital that we view the situation through God's eyes, and not judge
by what we see taking place in the natural realm . . . [C]rucial to our
survival will be our unconditional commitment to stand with Israel."[30]
Sweeping schematics that equate Israel to "the empires" of the Bible
or demand "unconditional commitment" to Israel are generally not
conducive to meaningful fellowship, or even cursory contact. Instead,
totalizing views on Zionism as indications of faithfulness to Scripture
dismiss Christians who think differently as inauthentic and thus outside the family of believers called to live in unity.

Some Jewish and Palestinian Christians have framed these
challenges as an opportunity for theological growth.[31] The drafters

of the Larnaca Statement, for instance, call Christians to resist temp-
tations to reject fellow believers based on their positions on Zionism,
and to instead utilize "a generous theological stance, which makes
room for and respects the conscientious convictions of others that
they sincerely derive from their reading of Scripture."[32] In the midst
of this acceptance, however, the Larnaca Statement writers challenged themselves "to clarify our positions in situations where they
might be interpreted in a way that harms or excludes others."[33] This
burden of clarification and interpretation requires those with different perspectives to actually test their opinions against the weight
of Scripture and their impact toward others, rather than forcing
those with opposing views to keep quiet in the name of respect-
ability. Other Messianic Jewish and Palestinian Christian scholars
and leaders have identified areas in which believers can engage in
deeper theological engagement with their social and political positions. Richard Harvey urges fellow Messianic Jews to push their theology beyond eschatological or hermeneutical stances to seek also
"a practical theology of reconciliation with Arab Christians and the
Arab population in light of the Israel–Palestine conflict."[34] Phillip
Ben-Shmuel similarly proposes that Messianic Jews must pursue
"an authentically Israeli Zionism that is also genuinely Christ-like
and Christ-centered," and work to distinguish "Christ-like Zionism" from the existing phenomena of Christian Zionism and the
"State-Zionism" prevalent in Israeli society.[35] Palestinian Christian
Yohanna Katanacho calls his fellow Palestinian Christians to expand
discussions on justice from "a philosophical or political point of
view" to also "define justice biblically." Katanacho asserts, "I don't
want to separate righteousness from justice; the horizontal, and the
vertical perspectives of justice. The relation with God and the relation with our fellow neighbours are intrinsically linked."[36] Instead of
seeking only to determine if one side is more right or more wronged,
Christians can instead ask how their relationship to Zionism can
inform or be informed by their faith.

Some believers have also asked how their presence in the Holy Land does or can testify to God's work among his people. Ben-Shmuel asserts that "as the ecclesial community that embodies the Messiah in the land, we must speak prophetically to the nations, calling them to serve and keep the land as a place of holiness, justice, and peace as exemplified by Yeshua himself."[37] Similarly, Musalaha founder Salim Munayer writes that "the Holy Land and the holy city of Jerusalem remain a highly suggestive and emblematic symbol for the rest of the earth and for all of humanity. For if we are called to reconcile with our enemies, to love God and love truth, to live in peace and in joy of our deliverance in order to bring about the kingdom of heaven, we can judge how far we are from reaching these goals by observing the Holy Land. That this particular spot of land should be so filled with hatred, violence, and rebellion against God is a telling sign of how far we still have to go."[38] This orientation asks how believers can embody the gospel regardless of the "correct" theology of the role of the land in the eschaton, or whether the modern State of Israel is or isn't a fulfilment of Old Testament prophecies about the ingathering of exiles. Ben-Shmuel suggests that sharing the Eucharist, for instance, can be a fruitful starting place for Jewish–Palestinian Christian fellowship.[39]

Both Jewish and Arab Christians grappling with the national identity of the other in a Jewish State would likely strike Theodor Herzl as—aside from being a curiosity—a source of pride and accomplishment for the existence of a state that can host such questions. As Jewish and Arab believers grapple with intersections of Zionism and faith, they face some unique challenges but also illuminate unique possibilities.

# ACKNOWLEDGMENTS

This book could not exist without the care, expertise, or support (both material and moral) of many people.

First and foremost, I want to thank the editorial team at Fortress Press, including Scott Tunseth who brought the project together, and Bethany Dickerson who provided deeply beneficial editorial insight and intervention.

It has been a long journey full of twists and turns, both professionally and personally, that led me to write this book about Zionism for a Christian publisher. I want to acknowledge some of the most influential people on that journey, without whom this book would never have existed. My professors and mentors at the University of California, San Diego, especially Deborah Hertz, Amelia Glaser, and Michael Provence, paved the way for me to pursue a graduate education in Modern Jewish History and the Modern Middle East. My dear friend Vicki, the most detailed, generous, and passionate Hebrew tutor anyone could ask for, laid my foundation in Hebrew that became the basis of travel in Israel, friendships in the US, and perhaps most significantly, graduate research (the rest of her family became part of my heart in the process as well). I want to thank my Arabic teachers, especially Maissam, for opening fuller linguistic and cultural literacy for me in Israel, Palestine, and Lebanon.

I am grateful to dear friends and colleagues who made various study and research trips in Israel possible over the years. Thank you to the Zadoks for including me in your family, your congregation, and the many summers in your home, with meals, laughs, rides, introductions to colleagues, and general friendship. You all tirelessly personify faithfulness to God and people in a unique way, and I am inspired and humbled by you. Thank you so much to Benny and to Alona (and Gavriel), for your hosting and warm and sincere companionship through many visits. I owe special thanks to Shoshi Norman and Galilee College, which offered a summer study program with incredible breadth and depth, opening my eyes (and personal connections) to diverse networks in Israel and Palestine.

I owe profound thanks to my seminary professors, especially Glen Scorgie and James Smith III, for equipping me to think about history, theology, spirituality, ministry, and leadership in interconnected ways. The professional society the Conference for Faith and History has also facilitated the integration of faith and historical scholarship, and while life circumstances have thus far kept me from getting to participate in CFH activity to the extent I wish I could, the mission of the organization and work of its members and leaders are a huge encouragement and motivation for me. The very idea of writing a book drawing from my research expertise in a way that would be edifying for nonspecialists came from the work of Beth Allison Barr, John Fea, Jemar Tisby, and many others in CFH.

There is no way I would have had the ability or platform to pursue this project if not for my professors and colleagues at the University of California, Davis. Many thanks to my mentor David Biale for teaching me to how to approach a field of literature, how to grasp the scope of a project and, most of all, how to write (and to make writing part of who you are instead of just something you do—a constant work in progress, but a work in progress nonetheless). Further thanks to David (and Rachel Biale as well) for believing and demonstrating that a scholarly vocation can take different forms than that of traditional academia, and that the demands of work, family, activism, and life can vacillate in different seasons while one maintains a purposeful center of gravity. I owe thanks to the guidance of my exam and dissertation committee members Susan Miller, Eran Kaplan, Sudipta Sen, and David Myers (at UCLA). Colleagues in the UCD Jewish Studies program committee, especially Diane Wolf, included me in the life of the program, with its fantastic visiting lecturers and students. I drew and still draw inspiration from the research, teaching, and general way of being of Davis professors and graduate student colleagues: Rachel Feldman, Ian Campbell, Clarence Walker, Noha Radwan, Baki Tezcan, Omnia al-Shakry, Carrie Alexander, Yesika Ordaz, Rebecca Egli, Heather Jennings, Griselda Jarquin, Jamiella Brooks, Mike Mortimer, and Natalie Esteban Collin, whose light in our lives was cut way too short. I am also indebted to colleagues in the Association for Israel Studies, Association for Jewish Studies, American Society of Church History, and the Posen Fellowship of Scholars. Of these I especially want to thank Geraldine Gudefin for offering encouragement and accountability at key junctures. Thank you Deanna Feree Womack for your overall guidance and mentorship, and for facilitating opportunities to bridge my research with the study of church history.

Special thanks to Emile Chabal for arranging a visiting research associate position at the University of Edinburgh, where I could access library materials to craft my proposal for this project.

I want to thank those who read drafts throughout different stages of this project. Thank you to those who gave feedback on the early proposal-stages of this book: Kelly, Hollis, Juan, Jane, Kirk, Teri, and Sandra. Thank you so much Kelly Gilbert, Tim Kim, Daniel Hummel, and Jonathan Pérez for reading and commenting on drafts along the way.

The most thanks are owed to my family and friends who provided incalculable support, encouragement, and inspiration through the process of planning and writing this book. Thank you to my church communities—you know who you are. Thanks to my siblings for the love, laughter, and commiseration, and for being, among many other things, a hype man and history/academia sounding board (guess who is which). Kelly, thank you for being not only a best friend but true partner in all things writer/mom/American Christian/lockdown and the concoction that is all of the above. My parents' unconditional love and steady support for me as I have followed my interests—even when doing so was costly or far away or not very promising from a lucrative standpoint—has been and continues to be one of the pillars of my life, and this book wouldn't be possible without that. I want to thank my parents and in-laws for tracking progress, offering support throughout this writing process, and of course for being invested grandparents. My grandma, to whom this book is dedicated, gave me and the rest of her world tireless love, support, and pride—may we all hope for peace as much as she did.

To my children, you provided the highest concentration of life (to put it mildly) throughout the journey of writing this book. Thank you for constantly putting your joy, imagination, sense of right and wrong, affection, and discoveries on full display. Jonathan, the most gratitude belongs to you. There's supportive, and then there's partner-writing-a-book-during-an-international-move-with-two-small-kids-and-pandemic supportive. I love you and I like you.

# NOTES

## INTRODUCTION

1 Faydra L. Shapiro, "To the Apple of God's Eye: Christian Zionist Travel to Israel," *Journal of Contemporary Religion* 23, no. 3 (2008): 308. For closer discussion on Christian Zionism in the Global South, see Daniel G. Hummel, "Global Christian Zionism," chap. 9 in *Covenant Brothers: Evangelicals, Jews, and US–Israeli Relations* (Philadelphia: University of Philadelphia Press, 2019).

2 Jackie Feldman, "Abraham the Settler, Jesus the Refugee: Contemporary Conflict and Christianity on the Road to Bethlehem," *History & Memory* 23, no. 1 (2011): 69.

3 Raymond P. Scheindlin, *A Short History of the Jewish People: From Legendary Times to Modern Statehood* (New York: Oxford University Press, 1988), 10.

4 Babylonian Talmud Tractate Sanhedrin 44a.

5 For good examples of a contextualized history of the cultures of the Jews, see David Biale, ed., *Cultures of the Jews: A New History* (New York: Schocken Books, 2002) and Paul Mendes-Flohr and Jehuda Reinharz, eds., *The Jew in the Modern World: A Documentary History* (New York: Oxford University Press, 1995).

6 For an excellent short summary of the historical method, see Thomas Andrews and Flannery Burke, "What Does It Mean to Think Historically?" *Perspectives on History* 45, no. 1 (January 2007), https://tinyurl.com/yckmb548.

## CHAPTER 1

1 Theodor Herzl, *The Diaries of Theodor Herzl*, trans. and ed. Marvin Lowenthal (New York: The Dial Press, 1956), 224.

2 Quoted in Herzl, *Diaries of Theodor Herzl*, 214.

3 For more on key terminology like *Land of Israel* and *Palestine*, see this book's Introduction.

4 The seventeenth-century failed messiah Shabbtai Zevi and his followers were a noteworthy exception of an organized movement of Jews to immigrate to the Holy Land, but if anything their destabilizing movement cast any aspirations for a premature return in an even less favorable light among many Jews.

5 Babylonian Talmud Ketubot 111a.

6 See, for example, Charles D. Smith, "The Islahat Fermani [Hatti Humayoun] of February 1856," in *Palestine and the Arab–Israeli Conflict: A History with Documents*, 6th ed. (Boston: Bedford/St. Martin's, 2007), 49–52.

7 For more on early Palestinian society and national identity, see Rashid Khalidi, *Palestinian Identity: The Construction of Modern National Consciousness* (New York: Columbia University Press, 1997); Baruch Kimmerling and Joel S. Migdal, *The Palestinian People: A History* (Cambridge: Harvard University Press, 2003).

8 Quoted in Gil Troy, *The Zionist Ideas: Visions for the Jewish Homeland—Then, Now, Tomorrow* (Philadelphia: Jewish Publication Society, 2018), xxxvi.

9 See Benedict Anderson's seminal text *Imagined Communities* (1983), as well as the work of Rogers Brubaker and Anthony Smith, who have also expounded upon the broader causes and trajectories of the development of nationalism. Eugen Weber's *Peasants into Frenchmen* (1976) is another early and influential example of the development of nationalism in the French case, and Baki Tezcan's chapter, "Ethnicity, Race, Religion and Social Class: Ottoman Markers of Difference," in *The Ottoman World*, ed. Christine Woodhead (Abingdon: Routledge, 2011), is another instructive example.

10 Zvi Hirsch Kalischer, "Seeking Zion," in *The Zionist Idea: A Historical Analysis and Reader*, ed. Arthur Hertzberg (Philadelphia: Jewish Publication Society, 1997), 114.

11 Theodor Herzl, "The Jewish State," in Hertzberg, *Zionist Idea*, 222; Tom Segev, *Elvis in Jerusalem: Post-Zionism and the Americanization of Israel*, trans. Haim Watzman (New York: Metropolitan Books, 2002), 33.

12 Quoted in David Vital, *Zionism: The Formative Years* (New York: Oxford University Press, 1988), 439.

13 Moses Hess, "Rome and Jerusalem," in Hertzberg, *Zionist Idea*, 134.

14 Hess in Hertzberg, 120.

15 Wilhelm Marr, "The Victory of Judaism over Germandom," in Mendes-Flohr and Reinharz, *The Jew in the Modern World*, 271.

16 Moshe Leib Lilienblum, "The Future of Our People," in Hertzberg, *Zionist Idea*, 173.

17 Max Nordau, "Speech to the First Zionist Congress," in Hertzberg, 239.

18 Leo Pinsker, "Auto-Emancipation: An Appeal to His People by a Russian Jew," in Hertzberg, 187 (emphasis in original).

19 Pinsker in Hertzberg, 184.

20 Pinsker in Hertzberg, 193.

21 Herzl in Hertzberg, 205.

22 Eliezer Ben Yehuda, "*Introduction to The Complete Dictionary of Ancient and Modern Hebrew*," in Troy, *Zionist Ideas*, 106.

23 Ahad HaAm, "The Law of the Heart," in Hertzberg, *Zionist Idea*, 251.

24 Ahad HaAm in Hertzberg, 252.

25 Ahad HaAm in Hertzberg, 254–55.

26 Ahad HaAm in Hertzberg, 255.

27 Ahad HaAm in Hertzberg, 255.

28 "The Manifesto of the Bilu," in *The Israel–Arab Reader: A Documentary History of the Middle East*, 4th ed., ed. Walter Laqueur and Barry Rubin (New York: Penguin Books, 1984), 3.

29 Quoted in Laqueur and Rubin, 4.

30 For more on early religious opposition to Zionism, see Ehud Luz, *Parallels Meet* (Philadelphia: Jewish Publication Society, 1988), and Aviezer Ravitzky, *Messianism, Zionism, and Jewish Religious Radicalism* (Chicago: University of Chicago Press, 1996).

31 Quoted in Vital, *Zionism*, 212.

32 See "Protest against Zionism," in Mendes-Flohr and Reinharz, *The Jew in the Modern World*, 427.

33 Samuel Mohilever, "Message to the First Zionist Congress," in Hertzberg, *Zionist Idea*, 402.

34 Yehiel Michael Pines, "Religion Is the Source of Jewish Nationalism," in Hertzberg, 413.

35 Moshe HaCohen, "Mateh Moshe," in Troy, *Zionist Ideas*, 98.

36 Joshua Shanes, "Ahron Marcus: Portrait of a Zionist Hasid," *Jewish Social Studies: History, Culture, and Society* 16, no. 3 (2010): 124.

37 Herzl in Hertzberg, *Zionist Idea*, 206.

38 Herzl in Hertzberg, 220.

39 "The Basel Program," in Smith, *Palestine and the Arab–Israeli Conflict*, 57.

40 "The Basel Program," in Smith, 57.

41 "The Basel Program," in Smith, 57.

42 Ian S. Lustick, *Paradigm Lost: From Two-State Solution to One-State Reality* (Philadelphia: University of Pennsylvania Press, 2019), 11.

## CHAPTER 2

1 Vital, *Zionism*, 285n28.

2 This episode was and still is commonly but incorrectly referred to as the Uganda Affair, since the protectorate of Uganda bordered (and was temporarily included in) the British East Africa Protectorate.

3 Quoted in Vital, *Zionism*, 161.

4 Quoted in Vital, 275.

5 Quoted in Vital, 367.

6 Quoted in Vital, 305.

7 Gideon Shimoni, *The Zionist Ideology* (Hanover, NH: Brandeis University Press, 1995), 52.

8 Quoted in *Vital*, Zionism, 357.

9 Ahad HaAm, "Negation of the Diaspora," in Hertzberg, *Zionist Idea*, 273.

10 "Texts Concerning Zionism: 'The Jewish State and the Jewish Problem' by Ahad HaAm (1897)," Jewish Virtual Library, https://tinyurl.com/49jk7t26.

11 Ahad HaAm, "Negation of the Diaspora," in Hertzberg, *Zionist Idea*, 271.

12 Ahad HaAm, "Negation of the Diaspora," in Hertzberg, 271. Ahad HaAm expressed similar arguments in Ahad HaAm, "The First Zionist Congress," in Mendes-Flohr and Reinharz, *The Jew in the Modern World*, 430–2.

13 Quoted in "Gordon, Yehudah Leib," *The YIVO Encyclopedia of Jews in Eastern Europe*, https://tinyurl.com/2s4m6r5m.

14 Herzl in Hertzberg, *Zionist Idea*, 214.

15 Theodor Herzl, "A Solution to the Jewish Question," in Mendes-Flohr and Reinharz, *The Jew in the Modern World*, 425.

16 Herzl in Hertzberg, *Zionist Idea*, 214.

17 Herzl, "A Solution to the Jewish Question," in Mendes-Flohr and Reinharz, *The Jew in the Modern World*, 423.

18 Herzl in Hertzberg, *Zionist Idea*, 227.

19  Herzl in Mendes-Flohr and Reinharz, *The Jew in the Modern World*, 425; Theodor Herzl, *The Jewish State*, Jewish Virtual Library, https://tinyurl.com/scwjyxmh.

20  Vital, *Zionism*, 192.

21  Quoted in Vital, *Zionism*, 191.

22  Quoted in Vital, 203.

23  Vital, 43.

24  Isaac Jacob Reines, "A New Light on Zion," in Troy, *Zionist Ideas*, 91.

25  Quoted in Troy, 91.

26  Quoted in Shlomo Avineri, *The Making of Modern Zionism: The Intellectual Origins of the Jewish State* (New York: Basic Books, 1981), 195.

27  Quoted in Troy, *Zionist Ideas*, 96.

28  Quoted in Troy, *Zionist Ideas*, 95.

29  Micah Joseph Berdichevski, "Wrecking and Building," in Hertzberg, *Zionist Idea*, 295.

30  Berdichevski in Hertzberg, 294.

31  A. D. Gordon, "Some Observations," in Hertzberg, 377.

32  Jacob Klatzkin, "Boundaries," in Hertzberg, 325.

33  "Our World View," in Mendes-Flohr and Reinharz, *The Jew in the Modern World*, 455.

34  Haim Nahman Bialik, "The City of Slaughter," in Mendes-Flohr and Reinharz, 330.

35  Max Nordau, "Jewry of Muscle," in Troy, *Zionist Ideas*, 21.

36  "Our World View," in Mendes-Flohr and Reinharz, *The Jew in the Modern World*, 455.

37  Bialik in Mendes-Flohr and Reinharz, 331.

38  "Our World View," in Mendes-Flohr and Reinharz, 455.

39  "Our World View," in Mendes-Flohr and Reinharz, 455.

40  Micah Joseph Berdichevski, "The Question of Our Past," in Hertzberg, *Zionist Idea*, 299.

41  A. D. Gordon, "People and Labor," in Hertzberg, *Zionist Idea*, 374.

42  Gordon, "Our Task Ahead," in Hertzberg, 379.

43  Gordon in Hertzberg, 373.

44  Quoted in Gershon Shafir, *Land, Labor and the Origins of the Israeli–Palestinian Conflict, 1882–1914* (Berkeley: University of California Press, 1996), 60.

45  Quoted in Ian Black, *Enemies and Neighbors: Arabs and Jews in Palestine and Israel, 1917–2017* (New York: Atlantic Monthly Press, 2017), 34.

46 Uri Avnery, *Israel without Zionists: A Plea for Peace in the Middle East* (New York: Macmillan Company, 1968), 8–9.

47 Naguib Azoury, "From *The Awakening of the Arab Nation*," in Smith, *Palestine and the Arab–Israeli Conflict*, 58.

48 Quoted in Black, *Enemies and Neighbors*, 32.

49 Quoted in Smith, *Palestine and the Arab–Israeli Conflict*, 80.

50 See for example Smith, 74.

51 For more on the legacy of the Balfour Declaration, see David M. Halbfinger, "Balfour Declaration of Support for Jewish Homeland Still Divisive at 100," *The New York Times*, November 2, 2017, https://tinyurl.com/bdeaha32.

52 Shimoni, *The Zionist Ideology*, 286, 292–3.

## CHAPTER 3

1 "The Feisal–Weizmann Agreement and Feisal–Frankfurter Letters," in Laqueur and Rubin, *The Israel–Arab Reader*, 19.

2 Quoted in Laqueur and Rubin, 21.

3 Laqueur and Rubin, 18.

4 David Fromkin, *A Peace to End All Peace: The Fall of the Ottoman Empire and the Creation of the Modern Middle East* (New York: Henry Holt, 1989).

5 "Resolutions of the General Syrian Congress," in Smith, *Palestine in the Arab–Israeli Conflict*, 106–7.

6 Smith, 106–7.

7 "Article 22 of the Covenant of the League of Nations," in Smith, 108.

8 "The Mandate for Palestine," in Smith, 109–10.

9 Smith, 110.

10 "The Mandate for Palestine," in Smith, 109.

11 "The Mandate for Palestine," in Smith, 110.

12 For more on Arab Christians during the British Mandate period, see Noah Haiduc-Dale, *Arab Christians in British Mandate Palestine* (Edinburgh: Edinburgh University Press, 2013), and Laura Robson, *Colonialism and Christianity in Mandate Palestine* (Austin: University of Texas Press, 2011).

13 Yosef Haim Brenner, "Tel Hai," in *The Origins of Israel, 1882–1948: A Documentary History*, ed. Eran Kaplan and Derek J. Penslar (Madison: University of Wisconsin Press, 2011), 214–15.

14 "The Churchill White Paper," in Smith, *Palestine and the Arab–Israeli Conflict*, 159.

15 Quoted in Avineri, *The Making of Modern Zionism*, 205–6.

16 Smith, *Palestine and the Arab–Israeli Conflict*, 140.

17 Troy, *Zionist Ideas*, 66.

18 Quoted in Smith, *Palestine and the Arab–Israeli Conflict*, 122; "The Fundamentals of the Beitarian World Outlook," in Troy, *Zionist Ideas*, 70; see also Vladimir Jabotinsky, "Thou Shall Not Wear *Sha'atnez*," in Kaplan and Penslar, *Origins of Israel*, 141–4.

19 See Vladimir Jabotinsky, "What the Revisionist Zionists Want," in Mendes-Flohr and Reinharz, *The Jew in the Modern World*, 462.

20 Yaakov Shavit, "Fire and Water: Ze'ev Jabotinsky and the Revisionist Movement," in *Essential Papers on Zionism*, ed. Jehuda Reinharz and Anita Shapira (New York: New York University Press, 1996), 555.

21 See Jabotinsky in Mendes-Flohr and Reinharz, *The Jew in the Modern World*, 462; "Declaration of the Central Committee of the Union of Zionists-Revisionists," in Troy, *Zionist Ideas*, 66.

22 Vladimir Jabotinsky, "On the Iron Wall," in Kaplan and Penslar, *Origins of Israel*, 257.

23 Jabotinsky in Mendes-Flohr and Reinharz, *The Jew in the Modern World*, 464; "Declaration" in Troy, *Zionist Ideas*, 66.

24 Jabotinsky in Mendes-Flohr and Reinharz, 464.

25 Jabotinsky in Kaplan and Penslar, *Origins of Israel*, 258.

26 "Declaration," in Troy, *Zionist Ideas*, 66.

27 Kaplan and Penslar, *Origins of Israel*, 257.

28 Jabotinsky, "The Iron Wall," in Troy, *Zionist Ideas*, 73.

29 Jabotinsky in Troy, 73.

30 Jabotinsky in Troy, 74.

31 Jabotinsky in Troy, 74.

32 "Proclamation of the Irgun Zvai Leumi," in Troy, 78.

33 "Eighteen Principles of Rebirth," in Troy, 81.

34 Hagit Lavsky, "German Zionists and the Emergence of Brit Shalom," in Reinharz and Shapira, *Essential Papers*, 665.

35 Martin Buber, "The Bi-National Approach to Zionism" and "Facts and Demands: A Reply to Gideon Freudenberg," in Paul Mendes-Flohr, *A Land of Two Peoples: Martin Buber on Jews and Arabs* (New York: Oxford University Press, 1983), 207–14, 236–8.

36 See, for example, Martin Buber, "The National Home and National Policy in Palestine," in Mendes-Flohr, *A Land of Two Peoples*, 81–91.

37 "The Case for a Bi-National Palestine," in Mendes-Flohr and Reinharz, *The Jew in the Modern World*, 472.

38 See Black, *Enemies and Neighbors*, 60.

39 Avnery, *Israel without Zionists*, 8–9.

40 David Ben Gurion, "On the Partition of Palestine," in Kaplan and Penslar, *Origins of Israel*, 241.

41 Quoted in Walter Laqueur, *A History of Zionism: From the French Revolution to the Establishment of the State of Israel* (New York: Schocken Books, 2003), 266.

42 "The 1939 White Paper," in Smith, *Palestine and the Arab–Israeli Conflict*, 167.

43 See "Radio Broadcasts from the Force of Fighting Zion," in Kaplan and Penslar, *Origins of Israel*, 358–65.

44 "UNSCOP's Plan of Partition with Economic Union," in Smith, *Palestine and the Arab–Israeli Conflict*, 218.

45 Quoted in Black, *Enemies and Neighbors*, 108.

46 Perhaps the most controversial aspect of the debate regarding ethnic cleansing is "Plan Dalet" (or Plan D), the name of the Haganah' evolving military strategy in Palestine. Historians debate the interpretation of the text of this plan and its influence on other Zionist military operations. Some scholars, including but not limited to Walid Khalidi and Ilan Pappé, have concluded Plan Dalet is proof of a Zionist plan of "ethnic cleansing" of Palestine; Benny Morris takes a more moderated approach in which Plan Dalet did not express an explicit plan for ethnic cleansing but rather strategic aim for territorial expansion and military dominance; whereas Yoav Gelber argues it reflected a defensive military strategy. See Walid Khalidi, "Plan Dalet Revisited," *Journal of Palestine Studies* 18 (1988): 3–70; Ilan Pappé, *The Ethnic Cleansing of Palestine* (Oxford: Oneworld, 2006); Benny Morris, *Righteous Victims: A History of the Zionist-Arab Conflict, 1881–2001* (New York: Vintage Books, 2001), 205–11, 256; Yoav Gelber, "Appendix I: History and Invention: Was Plan D a Blueprint for 'Ethnic Cleansing'?" in *Palestine 1948: War, Escape, and the Emergence of the Palestinian Refugee Problem* (Portland, OR: Sussex University Press, 2001), 303–6.

## CHAPTER 4

1 State of Israel, the Supreme Court, *Judgment: High Court Application of Oswald Rufeisen v. The Minister of Interior*, 57, 60. For more see Michael Stanislawski, "A Jewish Monk? A Legal and Ideological Analysis of the Origins of the

'Who Is a Jew' Controversy in Israel," in *Text and Context: Essays in Modern Jewish History and Historiography in Honor of Ismar Schorsch*, ed. Eli Lederhendler and Jack Wertheimer (New York: Jewish Theological Seminary of America, 2005), 548–77.

2 "Declaration of Independence," the Knesset website, https://tinyurl.com/yny966h8.

3 "Declaration of Independence," https://tinyurl.com/yny966h8.

4 "Declaration of Independence," https://tinyurl.com/yny966h8. This 1950 law deferring a constitution was known as the Harari Law.

5 "The Law of Return," the Knesset website, https://tinyurl.com/5fthssep.

6 Ari Shavit, *My Promised Land: The Triumph and Tragedy of Israel* (New York: Spiegel & Grau, 2013), 148.

7 Shavit, *My Promised Land*, 139.

8 See Tom Segev, *The Seventh Million: The Israelis and the Holocaust*, trans. Haim Watzman (New York: Henry Holt, 2000).

9 Quoted in Shavit, *My Promised Land*, 148. Sasson Somekh's memoir *Baghdad, Yesterday* also presents a portrait of this transition.

10 For more on Israeli control of Palestinian refugees and particularly their ability to document their social and political situation, see Salim J. Munayer and Lisa Loden, "Israeli-Palestinian Historiography," in *Through My Enemy's Eyes: Envisioning Reconciliation in Israel-Palestine* (Milton Keynes, England: Paternoster, 2014).

11 See, for example "A Protest against Expropriation of Arab Lands," "We Must Grant the Arabs Truly Equal Rights," and "Memorandum on the Military Government," in Mendes-Flohr, *A Land of Two Peoples*, 261–2, 283–8, 297–9.

12 Mitchell Bard, "The Status of Arabs in Israel," Jewish Virtual Library, https://tinyurl.com/2p95terw.

13 Peter Beinart, *The Crisis of Zionism* (New York: Times Books, 2012), 16.

14 Tom Segev, *1949: The First Israelis* (London: Macmillan, 1998).

15 "The Imperatives of the Jewish Revolution," in Hertzberg, *Zionist Idea*, 606–7.

16 Ben Gurion in Hertzberg, 613.

17 David B. Green, "This Day in Jewish History: 1952: Ben Gurion Visits a Wizened Torah Sage," *Haaretz*, October 20, 2013, https://tinyurl.com/ykf96ma8.

18 Quoted in Green, "Ben Gurion Visits a Wizened Torah Sage."

19 Colin Shindler, *A History of Modern Israel* (New York: Cambridge University Press, 2008), 8.

20 See Yair Ettinger, "Peres: Number of Haredi Men Exempt from Army Service Reaching 'Impossible' Level," *Haaretz*, July 15, 2012, https://tinyurl.com/23a9bv9n.

21 Gad Barzilai, "Conversion Crisis: Who Decides Who Is a Jew?" *Jerusalem Post*, March 15, 2021, https://tinyurl.com/pmycytsu.

22 Peter Y. Medding, *The Founding of Israeli Democracy, 1948–1967* (New York: Oxford University Press, 1990), 16.

23 Quoted in Eliezer Ben-Rafael, *Jewish Identities: Fifty Intellectuals Answer Ben Gurion* (Leiden: Brill, 2002), 1.

24 Quoted in Ben-Rafael, *Jewish Identities*, 1.

25 David Ellenson, "'Who Is a Jew?': Issues of Jewish Status and Identity and Their Relationship to the Nature of Jewish Identity in the Modern World," in *Berit Milah in a Reform Context*, ed. Lewis Barth (Cincinnati: Berit Milah Board of Reform Judaism, 1990), 70.

26 See Elise K. Burton, "An Assimilating Majority? Israeli Marriage Law and Identity in the Jewish State," *Journal of Jewish Identities* 8, no. 1 (2015): 73–94; Anne Perez, "Social Inclusion and Legal Exclusion in a Jewish or Democratic State: Intermarriage in the Zionist Movement and the Early State of Israel," *British Journal of Middle Eastern Studies* 48, no. 5 (2021): 908–26.

27 Nitzan Horowitz, "On the Steps of Boorishness," in Troy, *Zionist Ideas*, 377.

28 "Declaration of Independence," the Knesset website, https://tinyurl.com/yny966h8.

29 "Basic Law: Human Dignity and Liberty," Israel Ministry of Foreign Affairs, https://tinyurl.com/yckt9ucd.

30 "Basic Law: The Knesset," Israel Ministry of Foreign Affairs, https://tinyurl.com/4f3afnpt.

31 Quoted in Wikipedia contributors, "Jewish and Democratic State," *Wikipedia, The Free Encyclopedia*, https://tinyurl.com/mryvjy47. For the original Hebrew text, see https://tinyurl.com/2vydn63t, 13.

32 Quoted in Wikipedia contributors, "Jewish and Democratic State," *Wikipedia, The Free Encyclopedia*, https://tinyurl.com/mryvjy47. For original Hebrew text, see https://tinyurl.com/2vydn63t, 15.

33 Israel Democracy Institute, "Constitution by Consensus," https://tinyurl.com/4kwz45zs, 37.

34 For more on ethnocracy in Israel, see Sammy Smooha, "A Zionist State, a Binationalist State, and an In-Between Jewish and Democratic State," Israel Democracy Institute, March 12, 2013, https://tinyurl.com/yckcru29; The National Committee for the Heads of Arab Local Authorities in Israel, "The Future Vision of the Palestinian Arabs in Israel," 2006, https://tinyurl.com/ypz62z58, 9.

35 "Constitution by Consensus," 33.

36 "Constitution by Consensus," 33.

37 Quoted in Jonathan Nis and Noa Landau, "Israel Passes Controversial Jewish Nation-State Bill After Stormy Debate," *Haaretz*, July 19, 2018, https://tinyurl.com/mvbmauek.

38 Lahav Harkov, "Gutted Jewish Nation-State Bill Heads to First Reading in Knesset," *Jerusalem Post*, March 13, 2018, https://tinyurl.com/rj4kpth.

39 Avner Inbar, "Jewish, or Democratic? The True Aim of Israel's 'Nation-State' Law," *World Politics Review*, August 9, 2018, https://tinyurl.com/yckm4x4a.

40 Quoted in Nis and Landau, "Israel Passes Controversial Jewish Nation-State Bill after Stormy Debate."

41 " 'Yes' to a Nation-State, 'No' to a Nationalistic State!" Israel Democracy Institute, July 26, 2017, https://tinyurl.com/p2ck5w9z.

42 Alon Harel, "How the Proposed Basic Law: Israel—Nation-State of the Jewish People Actually Impairs Judaism," Molad Center for the Renewal of Israeli Democracy, August 26, 2013, https://tinyurl.com/bdnhws7y.

43 "The Importance of the Nation State Law," Kohelet Policy Institute, August 16, 2021, https://tinyurl.com/4jktvhf2.

44 *Times of Israel* Staff, "Netanyahu Cheers Jewish Nation State Law as a 'Pivotal Moment' in Zionist History," *Times of Israel*, July 19, 2018, https://tinyurl.com/ytx9cxza.

45 See Gershom Gorenberg, *Accidental Empire: Israel and the Birth of the Settlements, 1967–1977* (New York: Times Books, 2006).

46 "United Nations General Assembly Resolution 2625 (XXV) Declaration on Principles of International Law Concerning Friendly Relations and Co-Operation among States in Accordance with the Charter of the United Nations," *American Journal of International Law* 65, no. 1 (1971): 243–51, https://doi.org/10.2307/2199350. See also United Nations Security Council Resolution 446, United Nations Digital Library, https://tinyurl.com/bdeb4frm; United Nations Security Council Resolution 465, United Nations Digital Library, https://tinyurl.com/eprdwesj.

47 See Black, *Enemies and Neighbors*, 208.

48 "Israeli Settlements and International Law," Israel Ministry of Foreign Affairs, https://tinyurl.com/cebn56e9.

49 See Shenhav, *Beyond the Two-State Solution: A Jewish Political Essay* (Cambridge: Polity Press, 2012), 19.

50 Quoted in Beinart, *The Crisis of Zionism*, 20.

51 Zvi Yehuda Kook, "On the 19th Anniversary of Israel's Independence," in Troy, *Zionist Ideas*, 244.

52 Beinart, *The Crisis of Zionism*, 14.

53 Quoted in Black, *Enemies and Neighbors*, 249.

54 "About B'Tselem," B'Tselem The Israeli Information Center for Human Rights in the Occupied Territories, https://tinyurl.com/ykbcanrd.

55 "Who We Are: Aims of Gush Shalom," https://tinyurl.com/2p99e5k7.

56 "About: Organization," Breaking the Silence, https://tinyurl.com/w5s96vt9.

57 "About: FAQ," Breaking the Silence, https://tinyurl.com/3zcs5jsy. Other Jewish Israeli organizations have formed to oppose various aspects of the occupation as well, including Women in Black, Israeli Coalition against House Demolitions (ICAHD), Yesh Gvul ("There is a Limit/Border"), Machsom (Checkpoint) Watch, and Yesh Din: Volunteers for Human Rights. The New Israel Fund also promotes the end of the occupation as a cornerstone of their work, along with wide range of progressive initiatives in Israel.

58 Eran Kaplan, "Post-Post-Zionism: A Paradigm Shift in Israel Studies?" *Israel Studies Review* 28, no. 1 (2013): 145.

59 Segev, *Elvis in Jerusalem*, 5.

60 "Remembering Israeli Author and Peace Activist Amos Oz," *NPR*, January 4, 2019, https://tinyurl.com/4dahupva.

## CHAPTER 5

1 Herzl, *Diaries*, 104. See also Shalom Goldman, *Zeal for Zion: Christians, Jews, and the Idea of the Promised Land* (Chapel Hill: University of North Carolina Press, 2009), 103.

2 Herzl, *Diaries*, 105, 113.

3 While there are several earlier works on Christian Zionism, there has been a proliferation of writing on Christian Zionism since the mid-2000s. Perhaps the most comprehensive book to date is Donald M. Lewis, *A Short History*

*of Christian Zionism: From the Reformation to the Twenty-First Century* (Downers Grove, IL: IVP Academic, 2021). Shalom Goldman's article, "Christians and Zionism: A Review Essay," in *American Jewish History* summarizes the state of scholarly literature on Zionism as of 2007. Some of the most recent academic work by Daniel Hummel, *Covenant Brothers: Evangelicals, Jews, and US–Israeli Relations* (Philadelphia: University of Pennsylvania Press, 2019), and Aron Engberg, *Walking on the Pages of the Word of God* (Leiden: Brill, 2019), has successfully synthesized, built upon, and redirected much of this literature.

4 W. D. Davies, *The Gospel and the Land: Early Christianity and Jewish Territorial Doctrine* (Berkeley: University of California Press, 1974), 367.

5 R. Todd Mangum and R. S. Sweetnam, *The Scofield Bible: Its History and Impact on the Evangelical Church* (Colorado Springs, CO: Paternoster, 2009), 113.

6 Mangum and Sweetnam, *The Scofield Bible*, 174–5.

7 Hal Lindsey, *The Late Great Planet Earth* (Grand Rapids, MI: Zondervan, 1970), 56, 179.

8 See, for instance, Gary Burge, *Whose Land? Whose Promise? What Christians Are Not Being Told about Israel and the Palestinians* (Cleveland, OH: The Pilgrim Press, 2003).

9 Richard Harvey, *Mapping Messianic Jewish Theology: A Constructive Approach* (Milton Keynes: Paternoster, 2009), 246; Mangum and Sweetnam, *The Scofield Bible*, 185.

10 William Blackstone, *Jesus Is Coming* (New York: Fleming H. Revell, 1898), 158, 172, 175.

11 Lindsey, *The Late Great Planet Earth*, 112.

12 David Brog, *Standing with Israel* (Lake Mary, FL: FrontLine, 2006), 205.

13 Judith Mendelsohn Rood, "Shoah/Nakba: Offerings of Memory and History," in *History (1933–1948): What We Choose to Remember*, ed. Margaret Monahan and James M. Lies (Portland, OR: University of Portland, 2011), 437.

14 Judith Mendelsohn Rood and Paul W. Rood, "Is Christian Zionism Based on Bad Theology?," *A Journal for the Theology of Culture* 7, no. 1 (2011): 48.

15 John S. Feinberg, "Dispensationalism and Support for the State of Israel," in *The Land Cries Out: Theology of the Land in the Israeli–Palestinian Context*, ed. Salim J. Munayer and Lisa Loden (Eugene, OR: Cascade Books, 2012), 109.

16 Mark Tooley and Gerald McDermott, "The 21st Century Case for Christian Zionism," FoxNews.com, May 6, 2015, https://tinyurl.com/2p9bb69b. See also Gerald R. McDermott, ed., *The New Christian Zionism: Fresh Perspectives on Israel and the Land* (Downers Grove, IL: IVP Academic, 2016).

17 Bill Adams, "Christian Zionism in the New Testament," Bridges for Peace website, https://tinyurl.com/42aj6tpr.

18 Engberg, *Walking on the Pages of the Word of God* (Leiden: Brill, 2019), 120.

19 Engberg, 17.

20 Salim Munayer, "Theology of the Land: From a Land of Strife to a Land of Reconciliation," in Munayer and Loden, *The Land Cries Out*, 243.

21 These types of inclusive "from/to" formulations are known as "merism phrases." See Munayer, "Theology of the Land," 243–4.

22 Quoted in Munayer, "Theology of the Land," 245.

23 P. W. L. Walker, *Holy City, Holy Places? Christian Attitudes to Jerusalem in the Holy Land in the Fourth Century* (Oxford: Oxford University Press, 1990), 295.

24 Walker, *Holy City, Holy Places?*, 293.

25 See Burge, *Whose Land? Whose Promise?* Colin Chapman raises similar arguments in *Whose Promised Land? The Continuing Conflict in Israel and Palestine* (Oxford: Lion Books, 1983).

26 Phillip D. Ben-Shmuel, "Hagshamah: A Theology for an Alternate Messianic Jewish Zionism," in Munayer and Loden, *The Land Cries Out*, 170–1.

27 Quoted in Yaakov Ariel, *On Behalf of Israel: American Fundamentalist Attitudes Toward Jews, Judaism, and Zionism, 1865–1945* (Brooklyn, NY: Carlson Publishing, 1991), 55.

28 Quoted in Ariel, *On Behalf of Israel*, 71.

29 Robert Benne, "Theology and Politics: Reinhold Niebuhr's Christian Zionism," in McDermott, *The New Christian Zionism*, 223.

30 Reinhold Niebuhr, "Jews after the War: Parts I & II," in *Love and Justice: Selections from the Shorter Writings of Reinhold Niebuhr*, ed. D. Robertson (Gloucester, MA: Peter Smith, 1957), 132–42.

31 Quoted in Clayborne Carson with Rev. Dr. Troy Jackson, "Martin Luther King Jr.'s Hope for a Better Israel," in *A Land Full of God: Christian Perspectives on the Holy Land*, ed. Mae Elise Cannon (Eugene, OR: Cascade Books, 2017), 101.

32 Carl Hermann Voss and David A. Rausch, "American Christians and Israel, 1948–1988," *American Jewish Archives* 40, no. 1 (1988): 68.

33 Quoted in Colin Chapman, *Whose Promised Land?*, 83–4.

34 Brog, *Standing with Israel*, 6.

35 *Why Israel? The Jewish State's Biblical Roots, Miraculous Rebirth, and Modern Trials* (San Antonio: Christians United for Israel, 2019), https://tinyurl.com/2p865fh5.

36 See Hummel, *Covenant Brothers*, 30; Goldman, *Zeal for Zion*, 117.

37 Mark Tooley, "Theology and the Churches: Mainline Protestant Zionism and Anti-Zionism," in McDermott, *The New Christian Zionism*, 218.

38 Adams, "Christian Zionism in the New Testament," https://tinyurl.com/42aj6tpr.

39 See, for example, "A CUFI Primer: The Biblical Foundation of Christian Zionism," https://tinyurl.com/4ztsk8kk.

40 Geoffrey Wigoder, *Jewish–Christian Relations since the Second World War* (Manchester: Manchester University Press, 1988), 109.

41 Quoted in Daniel F. Rice, *Reinhold Niebuhr and His Circle of Influence* (Cambridge: Cambridge University Press, 2013), 108.

42 Clayborne Carson, "Martin Luther King Jr.'s Hope for a Better Israel," in Cannon, *A Land Full of God*, 106.

43 Brog, *Standing with Israel*, 253.

44 Benne, "Theology and Politics," 228.

45 Quoted in Stephen Spector, *Evangelicals and Israel: The Story of American Christian Zionism* (Oxford Scholarship Online, 2009), 72, https://doi.org/10.1093/acprof:oso/9780195368024.001.0001.

46 Quoted in Spector, *Evangelicals and Israel*, 65.

47 Quoted in Brog, *Standing with Israel*, 138.

48 Quoted in Spector, *Evangelicals and Israel*, 140.

49 Hummel, *Covenant Brothers*, 3.

50 "Love the Jewish People," Chick Publications, https://tinyurl.com/3w9sxp7.

51 Quoted in Spector, *Evangelicals and Israel*, 24.

52 Spector, *Evangelicals and Israel*, 150–1, 154.

53 Tony Maalouf, "The Holy Land and the Larger Family of Abraham," in Cannon, *A Land Full of God*, 59. Bible scholar Tony Maalouf explains that this verse should be translated as "in proximity to all his brothers" (indeed, the Jewish Publication Society Hebrew Bible translation reads that Ishmael "shall dwell alongside of all his kinsmen").

54 "Scofield Reference Notes: Genesis 9," Bible Hub, https://tinyurl.com/2p9dnhxu.

55 See Andrews and Burke, "What Does It Mean to Think Historically?" https://tinyurl.com/yckmb548.

56 See Tony Maalouf, *Arabs in the Shadow of Israel: The Unfolding of God's Prophetic Plan for Ishmael's Line* (Grand Rapids, MI: Kregel Academic, 2003).

57 Maalouf, "The Holy Land," 64.

58 Maalouf, 64.

59 Spector, *Evangelicals and Israel*, 146.

60 International Christian Embassy Jerusalem brochure, 2007.

61 "Stand for Israel," International Fellowship of Christians and Jews website, https://tinyurl.com/2z78ww7t.

62 "Impact: Making Israel Stronger and Her People Safer," Christians United for Israel website, https://cufi.org/about/about-us/.

63 Quoted in *Why Israel?*, https://tinyurl.com/2p865fh5.

64 Aaron Hecht, "The Ariel-Evangelical Special Connection," *The Jerusalem Post* Christian Edition, August 2007, 28.

65 Hecht, "The Ariel-Evangelical Special Connection," 29.

66 See Yaakov Ariel, "Contemporary Christianity and Israel," in *Essential Israel: Essays for the 21st Century*, ed. S. Ilan Troen and Rachel Fish (Bloomington: Indiana University Press, 2017), 296–7.

67 "Approaching the Millennium: Mississippi Preacher Devotes Life to Birthing Red Heifer in Israel," *Jewish Telegraphic Agency*, September 3, 1999, https://tinyurl.com/2vnas6tu.

68 "Donors Wall," Temple Institute website, https://templeinstitute.org/donors-wall-2/.

69 Adams, "Christian Zionism in the New Testament," https://tinyurl.com/42aj6tpr.

70 International Christian Embassy Jerusalem brochure, 2007.

71 See Judy Maltz, "Despite COVID-19 Travel Ban, Israel Lets in 70 Evangelicals to Volunteer in Settlements," *Haaretz*, September 8, 2020, https://tinyurl.com/2emcxajt.

72 See Engberg, *Walking on the Pages of the Word of God*, 59.

73 Judy Maltz, "How an Obscure TV Channel Drove a Wedge between Israeli Settlers and Their Evangelical Allies," *Haaretz*, May 6, 2020, https://tinyurl.com/2y5xekcd.

74 See the Day of Prayer for the Peace of Jerusalem website, https://tinyurl.com/598kdzft.

75 Voss and Rausch, "American Christians and Israel," 47.

76 "Issue Analysis," Christians United for Israel website, https://tinyurl.com/4ty4skmz.

77 Adams, "Christian Zionism in the New Testament," https://tinyurl .com/42aj6tpr.

78 See for example "Christian Tourists to Israel," Israel Ministry of Foreign Affairs website, https://tinyurl.com/mrx4rmtr.

79 "About Passages," Passages website, https://passagesisrael.org/about-us/.

80 These include but are not limited to programs with the Philos Project; Christ at the Checkpoint conference; programs by the Sabeel Ecumenical Liberation Theology Center; Pilgrims of Ibillin; Telos; and Christians for Middle East Peace young adult education summit CMEP1835.

81 Pilgrim Tours website, https://tinyurl.com/46a5mrbs.

## CHAPTER 6

1 "Natalie Portman Refuses to Visit Israel to Accept Prize, Citing 'Recent Events,'" *Times of Israel*, April 20, 2018, https://tinyurl.com/5c5psdzf.

2 Judy Maltz, "Natalie Portman to Donate $2m Genesis Prize Despite Boycotting Israel Ceremony, Foundation Source Says; Portman Rep Denies," *Haaretz*, April 20, 2018, https://tinyurl.com/3ktytzhx.

3 Gil Hoffman, "Israeli Minister: Natalie Portman's Decision Borders on Antisemitism," *The Jerusalem Post*, April 22, 2018, https://tinyurl .com/2p8puh5m.

4 Tom Porter, "Natalie Portman Has Turned to the 'Dark Side' Like Anakin Skywalker: Israeli Minister," *Newsweek*, April 23, 2018, https://tinyurl .com/y454bx8a.

5 Maltz, "Natalie Portman to Donate $2m Genesis Prize," https://tinyurl .com/3ktytzhx.

6 Later that year Portman also publicly condemned the Israeli Nation State Law (see Chapter 4 in this book).

7 Eric Levitz, "Natalie Portman and the Crisis of Liberal Zionism," *New York Magazine*, Intelligencer, April 26, 2018, https://tinyurl.com/4tj4dm3p.

8 Daniella Greenbaum, "Natalie Portman Is Wrong about Israel—Here's Why," *Business Insider*, April 24, 2018, https://tinyurl.com/yw78wfz4.

9 Yousef Munayyer, "Actually, Natalie Portman, You ARE Practicing BDS," *Forward*, April 21, 2018, https://tinyurl.com/2p96v9yt.

10 "Our Approach to Zionism," Jewish Voice for Peace, https://tinyurl .com/2p8p2s2k; "What Is . . . Anti-Israel, Anti-Semitic, Anti-Zionist?," Anti-Defamation League, https://tinyurl.com/yc4xsp4s.

11  Edward W. Said, "Zionism from the Standpoint of Its Victims," *Social Text* 1 (Winter, 1979): 25.

12  Said, "Zionism from the Standpoint of Its Victims," 22.

13  "Palestine Liberation Organization: The Original Palestine Charter," Jewish Virtual Library, https://tinyurl.com/2p8z862y.

14  "Palestinian National Charter," The Avalon Project, https://tinyurl .com/ymypx2kr.

15  See Frantz Fanon, *The Wretched of the Earth* (New York: Grove Press, 2004).

16  Shindler, *A History of Modern Israel*, 210; *LA Times* Archives, "Full Text of Arafat's Statement to News Conference," *Los Angeles Times*, December 15, 1988, https://tinyurl.com/yeyprzc3.

17  "Israel–PLO Recognition: Exchange of Letters between PM Rabin and Chairman Arafat," Israel Ministry of Foreign Affairs, https://tinyurl.com/3hakaajj.

18  Black, *Enemies and Neighbors*, 321.

19  Shindler, *A History of Modern Israel*, 311.

20  "Communique No. 1 of the Intifada Issued by the Unified National Leadership," in Smith, *Palestine and the Arab–Israeli Conflict*, 444.

21  "The Covenant of the Islamic Resistance Movement," The Avalon Project, https://tinyurl.com/2p8sfzad.

22  "The Covenant of the Islamic Resistance Movement."

23  "The Covenant of the Islamic Resistance Movement."

24  "Anthem of the Neturei Karta," Neturei Karta International, https://www.nkusa.org/aboutus/anthem.cfm.

25  "Neturei Karta," ADL, https://tinyurl.com/3ukp9cap.

26  See Gustavo Gutiérrez, *A Theology of Liberation: History, Politics, Salvation* (Maryknoll, NY: Orbis Books, 1973).

27  Quoted in William C. Placher, *Readings in the History of Christian Theology, Vol. 2: From the Reformation to the Present* (Philadelphia: Westminster Press: 1988), 173–5.

28  "About," Sabeel website, https://sabeel.org/.

29  For more on the controversy surrounding Stephen Sizer, see Richard Harvey, "Toward a Messianic Jewish Theology of Reconciliation in the Light of the Arab–Israeli Conflict," in Munayer and Loden, *The Land Cries Out*, 85–6; Stephen Sizer's personal website, https://www.stephensizer.com/.

30  "Kairos Palestine Document," World Council of Churches, https://tinyurl .com/8w9yddz3.

31  "Kairos Palestine Document."

32 "Christ at the Checkpoint: Seven Affirmations," Stephen Sizer personal website, https://tinyurl.com/mwbsp8uk.

33 "Policy Guidelines," Churches for Middle East Peace, https://tinyurl .com/572bxfyd.

34 "Policy Guidelines," Churches for Middle East Peace.

35 Daniel Patrick Moynihan, "Response to United Nations Resolution 3379," American Rhetoric Online Speech Bank, https://tinyurl.com/mry5f8wr.

36 See Ron Kampeas, "20 Years Ago, the UN Durban Conference Aimed to Combat Racism: It Devolved into a 'Festival of Hate' against Jews," *Jewish Telegraphic Agency*, September 9, 2021, https://tinyurl.com/mrxkmmat.

37 "Mission," Jewish Voice for Peace website, https://tinyurl.com/2p954bf4.

38 "Defunding Occupation," If Not Now website, https://tinyurl.com/ 27bvtvz3.

39 Fayez A. Sayegh, *Zionist Colonialism in Palestine* (Beirut: Research Center Palestine Liberation Organization, 1965), 27.

40 Said, "Zionism from the Standpoint of Its Victims," 33.

41 Black, *Enemies and Neighbors*, 244.

42 See "A Threshold Crossed: Israeli Authorities and the Crimes of Apartheid and Persecution," Human Rights Watch website, April 27, 2021, https://tinyurl.com/bp679r6w.

43 See "International Convention on the Suppression and Punishment of the Crime of Apartheid," https://tinyurl.com/356vv54p; for more background on the convention see John Dugard, "Convention on the Suppression and Punishment of the Crime of Apartheid," UN Audiovisual Library of International Law, https://tinyurl.com/7s9t5j8e.

44 "International Convention on the Suppression and Punishment of the Crime of Apartheid."

45 "International Convention on the Suppression and Punishment of the Crime of Apartheid."

46 "Our Approach to Zionism," Jewish Voice for Peace, https://tinyurl .com/2p8p2s2k.

47 "FAQs," New Israel Fund Website, https://www.nif.org/about/faqs/.

48 Sari Nusseibeh, *Once Upon a Country: A Palestinian Life* (New York: Farrar, Straus, & Giroux, 2007), 524.

49 "Who We Are: List of Actions," Gush Shalom website, https://tinyurl .com/yj25yuak.

50 "What Is BDS?," BDS Movement website, https://tinyurl.com/mthsrxj2.

51 "What Is BDS?," BDS Movement website.

52 Palestinian Campaign for the Academic and Cultural Boycott against Israel, "On BDS Bashers and Their Search for Palestinian Fig Leaves," BDS Movement website, March 6, 2011, https://tinyurl.com/2p94uew6.

53 Yonatan Levi, "Updated Analysis: Economic Boycotts against Israel," Molad Center for the Renewal of Israeli Democracy website, January 21, 2014, https://tinyurl.com/msz9j8ah.

54 "Policy Guidelines," Churches for Middle East Peace, https://tinyurl .com/572bxfyd.

55 "JVP Policy Briefing: Applying the Leahy Law to Israel," Jewish Voice for Peace, June 2015. https://tinyurl.com/3p8axe92; see also "Jewish Voice for Peace on Peace, US Military Aid, and Israel," Jewish Voice for Peace website, August 4, 2004, https://tinyurl.com/2uhp9hnv.

56 See for instance "The Boycott, Divestment, and Sanctions (BDS) Movement Unmasked," Creative Community for Peace website, https://tinyurl .com/2p8vhe8a.

57 Glenn Greenwald and Ryan Grim, "US Lawmakers Seek to Criminally Outlaw Support for Boycott Campaign against Israel," *The Intercept*, July 19, 2017, https://tinyurl.com/yckwbnmy.

58 See Josh Nathan-Kazis, "REVEALED: Secret ADL Memo Slammed Anti-BDS Laws as 'Harmful to Jews,'" December 13, 2018, *The Forward*, https://tinyurl.com/596m7np6.

59 See Tamar Pileggi, "Jewish Groups Decry Fresh Presbyterian Divestment Efforts," *The Times of Israel*, June 28, 2016, https://tinyurl.com/yckzsvtf.

60 Beinart, *The Crisis of Zionism*, 193.

61 Mouin Rabbani, "Reflections on a Lifetime of Engagement with Zionism, the Palestine Question, and American Empire: An Interview with Noam Chomsky," *Journal of Palestine Studies* 41, no. 3 (2012): 118–19.

62 Zack Beauchamp, "What's behind the Anti-Semitism Surge in the US," *Vox*, June 2, 2021, https://tinyurl.com/mr3an2z6.

63 Deborah Lipstadt, *Antisemitism: Here and Now* (New York: Schocken Books, 2019), 103.

64 See for example Stand With Us, "The Nazi Roots of Middle Eastern Anti-Semitism," Center for Combating Anti-Semitism Vol. 15, https://tinyurl.com/mrymhnep.

65 Black, *Enemies and Neighbors*, 111.

66 Gershon Nerel, *Anti-Zionism in the "Electronic Church" of Palestinian Christianity*, No. 27 (Jerusalem: Hebrew University of Jerusalem, Vidal Sassoon International Center for the Study of Antisemitism, 2006), 3, 28.

67 "Contemporary Way of the Cross," Sabeel website, March 23, 2015, https://tinyurl.com/mr3cua32; *Contemporary Way of the Cross: A Liturgical Journey along the Palestinian Via Dolorosa* (Jerusalem: Sabeel Ecumenical Liberation Theology Center, 2005).

68 Quoted in Dexter Van Zile, "Sabeel's Rhetoric Questioned by Jewish Peace Activists," CAMERA website, March 28, 2008, https://tinyurl.com/yr8xv7um.

69 Quoted in Van Zile, "Sabeel's Rhetoric Questioned by Jewish Peace Activists," https://tinyurl.com/yr8xv7um.

70 "You Can Stand Firmly against Antisemitism & Palestinian Human Rights Says Rabbil Sikdar," Muslims against Antisemitism website, November 5, 2018, https://tinyurl.com/2b2muuvh.

71 "Farrakhan: In His Own Words," Anti-Defamation League, March 20, 2015, https://tinyurl.com/2p97kcbu.

72 "The Covenant of the Islamic Resistance Movement," The Avalon Project, https://tinyurl.com/2p8sfzad.

73 "Document of General Principles and Policies," Palestinian Islamic Resistance Movement website, May 1, 2017, https://tinyurl.com/2p98tvdh.

74 "Document of General Principles and Policies," https://tinyurl.com/2p98tvdh.

75 "Document of General Principles and Policies."

76 John Gage, "Senior Hamas Official Urges Palestinians Worldwide to Kill 'Every Jew on the Globe,'" *Washington Examiner*, July 15, 2019, https://tinyurl.com/2p9d6f4j.

77 Seth J. Frantzman, "Anti-Trump Antisemitism: The Link between Pittsburgh and Poway," *The Jerusalem Post*, April 28, 2019, https://tinyurl.com/yzmexycd.

78 *Haaretz* Staff, "Durban University Student Council Issues Call to Expel Jewish Students," *Haaretz*, February 12, 2015, https://tinyurl.com/yc88ct8p.

79 Lipstadt, *Antisemitism*, 202–3.

80 Salim Vally, "Solidarity with Palestine: Confronting the 'Whataboutery' Argument and the Bantustan Denouement," in *Apartheid Israel: The Politics of an Analogy*, ed. Jon Soske and Sean Jacobs (Chicago: Haymarket Books, 2015), 47.

81  See Michael G. Schechter, *United Nations Global Conferences* (New York: Rout-ledge, 2005), 177–82.

82  Atalia Omer quoted in Rebecca Burns, "Israel and Palestine: One State or Two?" Al-Shabaka Palestine Policy Network, February 5, 2013, https://tinyurl.com/a3yfmh7s.

83  Smith, *Palestine and the Arab–Israeli Conflict*, 183.

84  Smith, 220.

85  Voss and Rausch, "American Christians and Israel," 49–50.

86  "What Is Antisemitism?," International Holocaust Remembrance Alliance website, https://tinyurl.com/22hvc3z4.

87  "What Is Antisemitism?," International Holocaust Remembrance Alliance website.

88  "First-Ever: 40+ Jewish Groups Worldwide Oppose Equating Antisemitism with Criticism of Israel," Jewish Voice for Peace website, July 17, 2018, https://tinyurl.com/mu964fa9.

89  "Palestinian Rights and the IHRA Definition of Antisemitism," *The Guardian*, November 29, 2020, https://tinyurl.com/yckkjker.

90  "The Jerusalem Declaration on Antisemitism," www.jerusalemdeclaration.org.

91  "The Jerusalem Declaration on Antisemitism."

92  "The Jerusalem Declaration on Antisemitism."

93  "The Jerusalem Declaration on Antisemitism."

94  "The Jerusalem Declaration on Antisemitism."

95  "The Jerusalem Declaration on Antisemitism."

96  "The Jerusalem Declaration on Antisemitism."

97  Stand with Us, "Explaining the BDS Movement," https://tinyurl.com/2p8mauzs; J'Accuse Coalition for Justice, https://www.jaccusecoalition.org/issues.

98  Uri Avnery, "One State: Solution or Utopia?," *Palestine–Israel Journal of Politics, Economics, and Culture* 14, no. 2 (2007), https://tinyurl.com/49k83pr6.

99  "The Jerusalem Declaration on Antisemitism."

100 "Palestinian Rights and the IHRA Definition of Antisemitism," https://tinyurl.com/yckkjker.

101 "The Jerusalem Declaration on Antisemitism."

## CHAPTER 7

1  "Israel 2048," Shaharit, https://tinyurl.com/5de3pxd3; Basma Ghalayni, ed., *Palestine +100: Stories from a Century after the Nakba* (Manchester: Comma

Press, 2019); Ronen Shoval, *Herzl's Vision 2.0: Im Tirtzu: A Manifesto for Renewed Zionism* (Jerusalem: Rubin Mass Publishers, 2013).

2 The *Nakba*, meaning "catastrophe" in Arabic, is the term commonly used among Arabs for the creation of Israel and the Palestinian Diaspora in 1948. See Chapter 4 for more on this phenomenon and term.

3 See Troy, *Zionist Ideas*.

4 Quoted in Philippa Strum, "The Road Not Taken: Constitutional Non-Decision Making in 1948–1950 and Its Impact on Civil Liberties in the Israeli Political Culture," in *Israel: The First Decade of Independence* , ed. Ilan Troen and Noah Lucas (Albany: State University of New York, 1995), 83.

5 "About: Constitution by Consensus," Israel Democracy Institute, https://tinyurl.com/4r8cwkwz.

6 Uri Dromi, "We, the Israeli People: The Push for a Document to Bind a Fractured Society," Israel Democracy Institute, June 14, 2006, https://tinyurl.com/mrxwzezx.

7 "Constitution by Consensus," Israel Democracy Institute, https://tinyurl.com/4kwz45zs, 14.

8 "Constitution by Consensus," 102.

9 Dromi, "We the Israeli People."

10 "Constitution by Consensus," 100.

11 "Constitution by Consensus," 101.

12 "Constitution by Consensus," 101.

13 "Constitution by Consensus," 101.

14 For the details of how this compromise would be instrumentalized, see Yoav Artsieli, *The Gavison–Medan Covenant: Main Points and Principles* ( Jerusalem: Israel Democracy Institute, 2004), https://tinyurl.com/yckwufs5.

15 Artsieli, *Gavison–Medan Covenant*, 16.

16 Artsieli, 19.

17 Artsieli, 81.

18 Artsieli, 49.

19 See Avnery, *Israel without Zionists*, 184.

20 Walid Khalidi, "Thinking the Unthinkable: A Sovereign Palestinian State," *Foreign Affairs* 56 (1977).

21 "Document of General Principles and Policies," Palestinian Islamic Resistance Movement website, May 1, 2017, https://tinyurl.com/2p98tvdh.

22 Ari Shavit, "Back to Liberal Zionism," in Troy, *Zionist Ideas*, 383.

23 Uri Avnery, "One State: Solution or Utopia?" *Palestine–Israel Journal of Politics, Economics, and Culture* 14, no. 2 (2007), https://tinyurl.com/49k83pr6.

24  Beinart, *The Crisis of Zionism*, 19; Shenhav, *Beyond the Two-State Solution*, 38; Meron Benvenisti, "The Case for Shared Sovereignty," *The Nation*, May 31, 2007, https://tinyurl.com/y2evnauz; Lustick, *Paradigm Lost*, 127.

25  Dahlia Scheindlin, "The Confederation Alternative for Israel and Palestine," The Century Foundation, February 3, 2020, https://tinyurl.com/yxyxa96e; Gideon Levy, "The Real Radical Left," *Haaretz*, April 5, 2012, https://tinyurl.com/24expnyf; Peter Hirschberg, "One-State Awakening," *Haaretz*, December 10, 2003, https://tinyurl.com/48fs7z8z.

26  Assaf Sharon, "Half a Loaf," *Boston Review*, October 12, 2015, https://tinyurl.com/2p95f7ur; Avnery, "One State: Solution or Utopia?," https://tinyurl.com/49k83pr6.

27  Shenhav, *Beyond the Two-State Solution*, 31.

28  Quoted in Ari Shavit, "Cry the Beloved Two-State Solution," *Haaretz*, August 6, 2003, https://www.haaretz.com/1.5356751.

29  Avnery, *Israel without Zionists*, 186.

30  See Daniel Douek, "Lawmaker Backs Segregated Jewish, Arab Maternity Wards," *The Times of Israel*, April 5, 2016, https://tinyurl.com/3knvb8f7; Lamis Andoni, "Jordan Is Not Palestine," *Aljazeera*, July 4, 2010, https://tinyurl.com/yc38jmy7.

31  Khalidi, "Thinking the Unthinkable."

32  Especially articles 2, 3, and 7 in "Document of General Principles," May 1, 2017, https://tinyurl.com/2p98tvdh.

33  See article 31 in "The Covenant of the Islamic Resistance Movement," The Avalon Project, https://tinyurl.com/2p8sfzad.

34  Noam Sheizaf, "Endgame," *Haaretz*, July 15, 2010, https://tinyurl.com/ycks8nkm.

35  "Ze'ev (Vladimir) Jabotinsky," Zionist Freedom Alliance, https://tinyurl.com/mhannp2x.

36  Sheizaf, "Endgame," https://tinyurl.com/ycks8nkm.

37  Quoted in Yousef T. Jabareen, *"An Equal Constitution for All? On a Constitution and Collective Rights for Arab Citizens in Israel"* (Mossawa Center, May 2007), https://tinyurl.com/2p93aphp, 34; Nusseibeh, *Once Upon a Country*, 240.

38  Sammy Smooha, "A Zionist State, a Binationalist State, and an In-Between Jewish and Democratic State," Israel Democracy Institute, March 12, 2013, https://tinyurl.com/yckcru29.

39  "Basic Law: The Knesset," Israel Ministry of Foreign Affairs, https://tinyurl.com/4f3afnpt. For more on this Basic Law see Chapter 4.

40  See for example Palestinian American journalist Ali Abunimah's 2001 book
     *One Country: A Bold Proposal to End the Palestinian–Israeli Impasse*, as well as the
     website he cofounded, Electronic Intifada, which frequently features arti-
     cles with variations of this platform; Hirschberg, "One-State Awakening,"
     https://tinyurl.com/48fs7z8z; and the platform of the One Democratic
     State Campaign formed in 2018 at "About Us," One Democratic State
     Campaign, https://tinyurl.com/3nbe3hfk.

41  Quoted in Shenhav, *Beyond the Two-State Solution*, 91.

42  "The Future Vision of the Palestinian Arabs in Israel," 2006,
     https://tinyurl.com/ypz62z58, 10.

43  Jay Ruderman and Yedidia Stern, "Is 'Israeli' a Nationality?" Israel Democ-
     racy Institute, March 9, 2014, https://tinyurl.com/2p894xvj.

44  Laqueur, *A History of Zionism*, 253.

45  Alan Dershowitz, *The Case for Israel* (Hoboken, NJ: Wiley, 2003), 240.

46  Avi Garfinkel, "Why Did Israel's Greatest Living Writer Turn on the Two-
     State Solution?" *Haaretz*, December 17, 2021, https://tinyurl.com/2p8dcdjk.

47  Peter Beinart, "Yavne: A Jewish Case for Equality in Israel-Palestine," *Jewish
     Currents*, July 7, 2020, https://tinyurl.com/3hefxez2.

48  Petra Marquardt-Bigman, "The Increasing Radicalism of Peter Beinart Must
     Be Confronted," *The Algemeiner*, July 9, 2020, https://tinyurl.com/533e5j2y.

49  Daniel Gordis, "End of the Jewish State? Let's Try Some Honesty, First,"
     *Times of Israel*, July 8, 2020, https://tinyurl.com/yv79az8n.

50  Gordis, "End of the Jewish State?"

51  Ali Waked, "Tibi: Israel Should Not Be a Jewish State," *Ynet News*, January
     16, 2006, https://tinyurl.com/mr2e3cys.

52  Leila Farsakh, "The One-State Solution and the Israeli–Palestinian Con-
     flict: Palestinian Challenges and Prospects," *The Middle East Journal* 65, no. 1
     (2011): 63.

53  Shenhav, *Beyond the Two-State Solution*, 84.

54  Gordis, "End the Jewish State?"

55  Abunimah, *One Country*, 16.

56  Quoted in Shenhav, *Beyond the Two-State Solution*, 161–2.

57  A. B. Yehoshua, "Time to Say Goodbye to the Two-State Solution: Here's
     the Alternative," *Haaretz*, April 19, 2018, https://tinyurl.com/2p82daft.

58  Peter Beinart, "Teshuvah: A Jewish Case for Palestinian Refugee Return,"
     *Jewish Currents*, May 11, 2021, https://tinyurl.com/mwuwbbur.

59  Beinart, "Teshuvah."

60  Meron Benvenisti, "Which Kind of Binational State?," *Haaretz*, November 20, 2003, https://www.haaretz.com/1.4765955.

61  See Sheizaf, "Endgame," https://tinyurl.com/ycks8nkm; Hirschberg, "One-State Awakening," https://tinyurl.com/48fs7z8z.

62  Abunimah, *One Country*, 110.

63  See for example, "*The Democratic Constitution*" (Adalah, The Legal Center for Arab Minority Rights in Israel, 2007), 13–16, https://tinyurl.com/2p8wr7we; "The Future Vision of the Palestinian Arabs in Israel" (The National Committee for the Heads of Arab Local Authorities in Israel, 2006), 10, https://tinyurl.com/ypz62z58.

64  Beinart, "Teshuvah: A Jewish Case for Palestinian Refugee Return."

65  See "About KKL-JNF," Jewish National Fund website, https://tinyurl.com/54y6hyyt.

66  "The Haifa Declaration," https://tinyurl.com/2p98axbb.

67  Sammy Smooha, "A Zionist State, a Binationalist State, and an In-Between Jewish and Democratic State," Israel Democracy Institute, March 12, 2013, https://tinyurl.com/yckcru29. See also Khaled Elgindy, "After Oslo: Rethinking the Two-State Solution," Brookings Institution, June 2018, 1.

68  Quoted in Shenhav, *Beyond the Two-State Solution*, 37.

69  Shenhav, 38.

70  "About Us," Shaharit, https://tinyurl.com/bdf382sc.

71  Avnery, *Israel without Zionists*, 184–5.

72  Khalidi, "Thinking the Unthinkable."

73  "Shared and Agreed Principles," Two States, One Homeland, A Land for All, https://tinyurl.com/yw4thsuc.

74  "Good Answers to Tough Questions," https://tinyurl.com/2a6m3pcm.

75  See Rachel Havrelock, *Joshua Generation: Israeli Occupation and the Bible* (Princeton, NJ: Princeton University Press, 2020).

76  Nadav G. Shelef, "Israel, Palestine, and the Prospects for Denationalization," Project on Middle East Political Science, https://tinyurl.com/wh73hktp.

77  Zack Beauchamp, "In Defense of the Two-State Solution," https://tinyurl.com/y3ccxk33; Yedidia Z. Stern, "A Jewish and Undemocratic State?," Israel Democracy Institute, November 9, 2011, https://tinyurl.com/3xhbhxbc.

78  Yehoshua, "Time to Say Goodbye," https://tinyurl.com/2p82daft; see also Hirschberg, "One-State Awakening," https://tinyurl.com/48fs7z8z.

79  Beinart, "Yavne: A Jewish Case for Equality in Israel-Palestine," https://tinyurl.com/3hefxez2.

80 Beinart, "Yavne."

81 Quoted in Abunimah, *One Country*, 162.

82 Farsakh, "The One-State Solution and the Israeli–Palestinian Conflict," 64.

83 Farsakh, 70.

84 Beinart, "Yavne."

85 Beinart, "Yavne." For more on Yavne in the history of Judaism, see this book's Introduction.

86 Hirschberg, "One-State Awakening," https://tinyurl.com/48fs7z8z.

87 Hirschberg, "One-State Awakening."

88 "How to Reclaim the Palestinian Narrative," Al-Shabaka, February 20, 2013, https://tinyurl.com/2x7pva8t.

89 "How to Reclaim the Palestinian Narrative."

90 Beauchamp, "In Defense of the Two-State Solution," https://tinyurl.com/y3ccxk33.

91 Beinart, "Yavne."

92 Hirschberg, "One-State Awakening."

93 "Everyone in Middle East Given Own Country in 317,000,000-State Solution," *The Onion*, July 17, 2014, https://tinyurl.com/mr2rczu5.

## EPILOGUE

1 Herzl, *Diaries*, 283.

2 Herzl, *Diaries*, 427–30. For more on relations between Israel and the Catholic Church, see Uri Bialer, *The Cross on the Star of David: The Christian World in Israel's Foreign Policy, 1948–1967* (Bloomington: Indiana University Press, 2005).

3 Amos Harel, "Settler Admits to Murder, Series of Bomb Attacks," *Haaretz*, November 1, 2009, https://tinyurl.com/48px9bha; "Bomber of Israeli Messianic Family Sentenced," Baptist Press website, April 22, 2013, https://tinyurl.com/4xrvnumt.

4 See Anne Perez, "Apostasy of a Prince: Hans Herzl and the Boundaries of Jewish Nationalism," *AJS Review* 42, no. 1 (2018): 89–110.

5 Quoted in R. G. Allison to Buksbazen, October 5, 1948, Dep. C.M.J. c 219, Papers of the Church Missions to the Jews (CMJ), Weston Library, Bodleian Libraries, Oxford.

6 Quoted in Ben-Rafael, *Jewish Identities*, 172.

7 Quoted in Ben-Rafael, 172.

8 Arthur W. Kac, "Israel's Fifteenth Anniversary: Lights and Shadows," *The Hebrew Christian* 36, no. 2 (Summer 1963): 52; "2017 Report on International Religious Freedom: Israel, Golan Heights, West Bank and Gaza," US Department of State website, https://tinyurl.com/4s4ck9xa.

9 For more on the Messianic Jewish communities in Israel see Richard Harvey, "Messianic Jews in the State of Israel 1948–2017: Mapping the Contours of Theological, Political and Social Engagement" (paper presented at the 17th World Congress of Jewish Studies, Hebrew University of Jerusalem, August 8, 2017), https://tinyurl.com/5n7jcy26; Harvey, *Mapping Messianic Jewish Theology*; Munayer and Loden, "An Introduction to Israeli Messianic Jewish Identity" in *Through My Enemy's Eyes*; Kai Kjær-Hansen and Bodil F. Skjøtt, *Facts and Myths about the Messianic Congregations in Israel* (Jerusalem: United Christian Council in Israel, 1999); Akiva Cohen, "Messianic Jews in the Land of Israel," in *Introduction to Messianic Judaism: Its Ecclesial Context and Biblical Foundations*, ed. David J. Rudolph and Joel Willetts (Grand Rapids, MI: Zondervan, 2013), 107–15; Kehilla News website, https://news.kehila.org/.

10 Emma O'Donnell Polyakov, "Jewish–Christian Identities in Conflict: The Cases of Fr. Daniel Rufeisen and Fr. Elias Friedman," *Religions* 12, no. 12 (2021): 1101.

11 "Our History," Grace and Truth Christian Congregation, https://tinyurl.com/2p8vy2ek.

12 Gershon Nerel quoted in Harvey, "Messianic Jews in the State of Israel 1948–2017."

13 Keri Zelson Warshawsky quoted in Harvey, "Messianic Jews in the State of Israel 1948–2017."

14 Harvey, "Toward a Messianic Jewish Theology of Reconciliation in the Light of the Arab–Israeli Conflict," in Munayer and Loden, *The Land Cries Out*, 83.

15 "The Larnaca Statement," Lausanne Movement website, January 2016, https://tinyurl.com/ycjfre5x.

16 Harvey, "Toward a Messianic Jewish Theology of Reconciliation in the Light of the Arab–Israeli Conflict," in Munayer and Loden, *The Land Cries Out*, 83.

17 Haiduc-Dale, *Arab Christians in British Mandate Palestine*, 200. For more on Palestinian Christians, see "An Introduction to Palestinian Christianity" in Munayer and Loden, *Through My Enemy's Eyes*; Elias Chacour with Mary E. Jensen, *We Belong to the Land: The Story of a Palestinian Israeli Who Lives for*

*Peace and Reconciliation* (Notre Dame, IN: University of Notre Dame Press, 2015); Elias Chacour with David Hazard, *Blood Brothers* (Grand Rapids, MI: Chosen Books, 2003).

18 Keri Zelson Warshawsky quoted in Harvey, "Messianic Jews in the State of Israel 1948–2017."

19 Harvey, "Toward a Messianic Jewish Theology of Reconciliation," in Munayer and Loden, *The Land Cries Out*, 95.

20 "From Dominance to Humility: Reflections on the Ethics of Reconciliation," Musalaha mailing list, July 30, 2010.

21 "The Larnaca Statement," Lausanne Movement website, January 2016, https://tinyurl.com/ycjfre5x.

22 Harvey, "Toward a Messianic Jewish Theology of Reconciliation," 84.

23 "From Dominance to Humility," Musalaha mailing list, July 30, 2010; Salim Munayer, "Theology of the Land," in Munayer and Loden, *The Land Cries Out*, 256.

24 "From Dominance to Humility," Musalaha mailing list, July 30, 2010.

25 See also Harvey, "Toward a Messianic Jewish Theology of Reconciliation," 92.

26 Judith Mendelsohn Rood, "I Am Jewish: Reflections on Jewish Identity in the Holy Land," in *A Land Full of God: Christian Perspectives on the Holy Land*, ed. Mae Elise Cannon (Eugene, OR: Cascade Books, 2017), 54.

27 "The Larnaca Statement," https://tinyurl.com/ycjfre5x.

28 Faydra L. Shapiro, "'Thank You Israel, for Supporting America': The Transnational Flow of Christian Zionist Resources," *Identities* 19, no. 5 (2012): 621.

29 Mitri Raheb, in "Theologies of Palestine," *Cornerstone: A Publication by Sabeel Ecumenical Liberation Theology Center* 81 (Winter 2019/2020): 4.

30 Hannah Nesher, "Standing with Israel: Yom Ha'atzma'ut (Israeli Independence Day)," https://tinyurl.com/52j59n88.

31 For an excellent volume on Israeli Messianic Jewish and Palestinian Christian approaches to the challenges of national identity and narrative, theology, and fellowship, see Munayer and Loden, *Through My Enemy's Eyes*.

32 "The Larnaca Statement," https://tinyurl.com/ycjfre5x.

33 "The Larnaca Statement."

34 Harvey, "Toward a Messianic Jewish Theology of Reconciliation," 100.

35 Phillip D. Ben-Shmuel, "Hagshamah: A Theology for an Alternate Messianic Jewish Zionism," in Munayer and Loden, *The Land Cries Out*, 142.

36 Yohanna Katanacho, in "Theologies of Palestine," *Cornerstone: A Publication by Sabeel Ecumenical Liberation Theology Center* 81 (Winter 2019/2020): 13.

37 Ben-Shmuel, "Hagshamah," in Munayer and Loden, 154.

38 Munayer, "Theology of the Land," 251–2.

39 Ben-Shmuel, "Hagshamah," 166.

# SELECTED BIBLIOGRAPHY

The following represent most of the books, journal articles, and pamphlets (along with a limited selection of especially influential internet articles) cited in this book. Most internet articles cited in footnotes throughout this book are not included here; however, some of the commonly used websites are listed below.

Abunimah, Ali. *One Country: A Bold Proposal to End the Israeli–Palestinian Impasse.* New York: Metropolitan Books, 2006.

Andrews, Thomas, and Flannery Burke. "What Does It Mean to Think Historically?" *Perspectives on History* 45, no. 1 (January 2007). https://tinyurl.com/yckmb548.

Ariel, Yaakov. *On Behalf of Israel: American Fundamentalist Attitudes toward Jews, Judaism, and Zionism, 1865–1945.* Brooklyn, NY: Carlson Publishing, 1991.

———. "Contemporary Christianity and Israel." In *Essential Israel: Essays for the 21st Century*, edited by S. Ilan Troen and Rachel Fish, 280–310. Bloomington: Indiana University Press, 2017.

Artsieli, Yoav. *The Gavison–Medan Covenant: Main Points and Principles.* Jerusalem: Israel Democracy Institute, 2004. https://tinyurl.com/yckwufs5.

Avineri, Shlomo. *The Making of Modern Zionism: The Intellectual Origins of the Jewish State.* New York: Basic Books, 1981.

Avnery, Uri. *Israel without Zionism: A Plea for Peace in the Middle East.* New York: Macmillan Company, 1968.

———. "One State: Solution or Utopia?" *Palestine–Israel Journal of Politics, Economics, and Culture* 14, no. 2 (2007). https://tinyurl.com/49k83pr6.

Beinart, Peter. *The Crisis of Zionism*. New York: Times Books, 2012.

———. "Teshuvah: A Jewish Case for Palestinian Refugee Return." *Jewish Currents*, May 11, 2021. https://tinyurl.com/mwuwbbur.

———. "Yavne: A Jewish Case for Equality in Israel-Palestine." *Jewish Currents*, July 7, 2020. https://tinyurl.com/3hefxez2.

Ben-Rafael, Eliezer. *Jewish Identities: Fifty Intellectuals Answer Ben Gurion*. Leiden: Brill, 2002.

Benvenisti, Meron. "The Case for Shared Sovereignty." *The Nation*, May 31, 2007. https://tinyurl.com/y2evnauz.

Berent, Moshe. *Nation Like All Nations: Towards the Establishment of an Israeli Republic*. New Rochelle, NY: Israel Academic Press, 2015.

Biale, Rachel. *Growing Up below Sea Level: A Kibbutz Childhood*. Simsbury, CT: Mandel Vilar Press, 2020.

Bialer, Uri. *The Cross on the Star of David: The Christian World in Israel's Foreign Policy, 1948–1967*. Bloomington: Indiana University Press, 2005.

Black, Ian. *Enemies and Neighbors: Arabs and Jews in Palestine and Israel, 1917–2017*. New York: Atlantic Monthly Press, 2017.

Brog, David. *Standing with Israel*. Lake Mary, FL: FrontLine, 2006.

Burge, Gary. *Whose Land? Whose Promise? What Christians Are Not Being Told about Israel and the Palestinians*. Cleveland, OH: The Pilgrim Press, 2003.

Burton, Elise K. "An Assimilating Majority? Israeli Marriage Law and Identity in the Jewish State." *Journal of Jewish Identities* 8, no. 1 (2015): 73–94.

Cannon, Mae Elise, ed. *A Land Full of God: Christian Perspectives on the Holy Land*. Eugene, OR: Cascade Books, 2017.

Cohen, Akiva. "Messianic Jews in the Land of Israel." In *Introduction to Messianic Judaism: Its Ecclesial Context and Biblical Foundations*, edited by David J. Rudolph and Joel Willetts. Grand Rapids, MI: Zondervan, 2013.

Davies, W. D. *The Gospel and the Land: Early Christianity and Jewish Territorial Doctrine*. Berkeley: University of California Press, 1974.

D'Costa, Gavin. "Catholic Zionism." *First Things*, January 2020. https://tinyurl.com/2p8p6b8d.

*The Democratic Constitution*. Adalah: The Legal Center for Arab Minority Rights in Israel, 2007. https://tinyurl.com/2p8wr7we.

Dershowitz, Alan. *The Case for Israel*. Hoboken, NJ: Wiley, 2003.

Elgindy, Khaled. "After Oslo: Rethinking the Two-State Solution." Brookings Institution, June 2018.

Ellenson, David. "'Who Is a Jew?' Issues of Jewish Status and Identity and Their Relationship to the Nature of Jewish Identity in the Modern World." In *Berit Milah in a Reform Context*, edited by Lewis Barth, 69–81. Cincinnati: Berit Milah Board of Reform Judaism, 1990.

Engberg, Aron. *Walking on the Pages of the Word of God: Self, Land, and Text among Evangelical Volunteers in Jerusalem*. Boston: Brill, 2019.

Farsakh, Leila. "The One-State Solution and the Israeli–Palestinian Conflict: Palestinian Challenges and Prospects." *The Middle East Journal* 65, no. 1 (2011): 55–71.

Feldman, Jackie. "Abraham the Settler, Jesus the Refugee: Contemporary Conflict and Christianity on the Road to Bethlehem." *History & Memory* 23, no. 1 (2011): 62–95.

Goldman, Shalom. *Zeal for Zion: Christians, Jews, and the Idea of the Promised Land*. Chapel Hill: University of North Carolina Press, 2009.

Gorenberg, Gershom. *Accidental Empire: Israel and the Birth of the Settlements, 1967–1977*. New York: Times Books, 2006.

Grinberg, Lev. "The Israeli–Palestinian Union: The '1-2-7 States' Vision of the Future." *Journal of Palestine Studies* 39, no. 2 (2010): 46–53.

Haiduc-Dale, Noah. *Arab Christians in British Mandate Palestine*. Edinburgh: Edinburgh University Press, 2013.

*The Haifa Declaration*. Haifa: Al-Mada Arab Center for Applied Social Research, 2007. https://tinyurl.com/2p98axbb.

Harvey, Richard. *Mapping Messianic Jewish Theology: A Constructive Approach*. Milton Keynes: Paternoster, 2009.

———. "Messianic Jews in the State of Israel 1948–2017: Mapping the Contours of Theological, Political and Social Engagement." Paper presented at the 17th World Congress of Jewish Studies, Hebrew University of Jerusalem, August 8, 2017. https://tinyurl.com/5n7jcy26.

Havrelock, Rachel. *Joshua Generation: Israeli Occupation and the Bible*. Princeton, NJ: Princeton University Press, 2020.

Herberg, Will. *Protestant, Catholic, Jew: An Essay in American Religious Sociology*. Chicago: University of Chicago Press, 1983.

Hertzberg, Arthur. *The Zionist Idea: A Historical Analysis and Reader*. Philadelphia: Jewish Publication Society, 1997.

Herzl, Theodor. *The Diaries of Theodor Herzl*. Translated and edited by Marvin Lowenthal. New York: The Dial Press, 1956.

Hummel, Daniel. *Covenant Brothers: Evangelicals, Jews, and US–Israeli Relations*. Philadelphia: University of Pennsylvania Press, 2019.

Jabareen, Yousef T. *"An Equal Constitution for All? On a Constitution and Collective Rights for Arab Citizens in Israel."* Mossawa Center, May 2007. https://tinyurl.com/2p93aphp.

Kaplan, Eran. *Beyond Post-Zionism.* Albany: State University of New York Press, 2015.

———. "Post-Post-Zionism: A Paradigm Shift in Israel Studies?" *Israel Studies Review* 28, no. 1 (2013): 142–55.

Kaplan, Eran, and Derek J. Penslar, eds. *The Origins of Israel, 1882–1948: A Documentary History.* Madison: University of Wisconsin Press, 2011.

Khalidi, Walid. "Thinking the Unthinkable: A Sovereign Palestinian State." *Foreign Affairs* 56 (1977): 695–713.

Kjær-Hansen, Kai, and Bodil F. Skjøtt. *Facts and Myths about the Messianic Congregations in Israel.* Jerusalem: United Christian Council in Israel, 1999.

Laqueur, Walter. *A History of Zionism: From the French Revolution to the Establishment of the State of Israel.* New York: Schocken Books, 2003.

Laqueur, Walter, and Barry Rubin, eds. *The Israel–Arab Reader: A Documentary History of the Middle East,* 4th ed. New York: Penguin Books, 1984.

Lewis, Donald M. *A Short History of Christian Zionism: From the Reformation to the Twenty-First Century.* Downers Grove, IL: IVP Academic, 2021.

Lindsey, Hal. *The Late Great Planet Earth.* Grand Rapids, MI: Zondervan, 1970.

Lipstadt, Deborah. *Antisemitism: Here and Now.* New York: Schocken Books, 2019.

Lustick, Ian S. *Paradigm Lost: From Two-State Solution to One-State Reality.* Philadelphia: University of Pennsylvania Press, 2019.

Luz, Ehud. *Parallels Meet: Religion and Nationalism in the Early Zionist Movement.* Philadelphia: Jewish Publication Society, 1988.

Maalouf, Tony. *Arabs in the Shadow of Israel: The Unfolding of God's Prophetic Plan for Ishmael's Line.* Grand Rapids, MI: Kregel, 2003.

Mangum, R. Todd, and R. S. Sweetnam. *The Scofield Bible: Its History and Impact on the Evangelical Church.* Colorado Springs, CO: Paternoster, 2009.

McDermott, Gerald R., ed. *The New Christian Zionism: Fresh Perspectives on Israel and the Land.* Downers Grove, IL: IVP Academic, 2016.

Medding, Peter Y. *The Founding of Israeli Democracy, 1948–1967.* New York: Oxford University Press, 1990.

Mendes-Flohr, Paul. *A Land of Two Peoples: Martin Buber on Jews and Arabs.* New York: Oxford University Press, 1983.

Mendes-Flohr, Paul, and Jehuda Reinharz, eds. *The Jew in the Modern World: A Documentary History*. New York: Oxford University Press, 1995.

Munayer, Salim, and Lisa Loden. *Through My Enemy's Eyes: Envisioning Reconciliation in Israel-Palestine*. Milton Keynes, England: Paternoster, 2014.

Munayer, Salim J., and Lisa Loden, eds. *The Land Cries Out: Theology of the Land in the Israeli–Palestinian Context*. Eugene, OR: Cascade Books, 2012.

The National Committee for the Heads of Arab Local Authorities in Israel. "The Future Vision of the Palestinian Arabs in Israel." 2006. https://tinyurl.com/ypz62z58.

Nerel, Gershon. *"Anti-Zionism in the "Electronic Church" of Palestinian Christianity.*" Hebrew University of Jerusalem, Vidal Sassoon International Center for the Study of Antisemitism, 2006.

Niebuhr, Reinhold. "Jews after the War: Parts I & II." In *Love and Justice: Selections from the Shorter Writings of Reinhold Niebuhr*, edited by D. Robertson, 132–42. Gloucester, MA: Peter Smith, 1957.

Nusseibeh, Sari. *Once Upon a Country: A Palestinian Life*. New York: Farrar, Straus, & Giroux, 2007.

Perez, Anne. "Apostasy of a Prince: Hans Herzl and the Boundaries of Jewish Nationalism." *AJS Review* 42, no. 1 (2018): 89–110.

Placher, William C. *Readings in the History of Christian Theology, Vol. 2, From the Reformation to the Present*. Philadelphia: Westminster Press: 1988.

Polyakov, Emma O'Donnell. "Jewish-Christian Identities in Conflict: The Cases of Fr. Daniel Rufeisen and Fr. Elias Friedman." *Religions* 12, no. 12 (2021): 1101. https://doi.org/10.3390/rel12121101.

Rabbani, Mouin. "Reflections on a Lifetime of Engagement with Zionism, the Palestine Question, and American Empire: An Interview with Noam Chomsky." *Journal of Palestine Studies* 41, no. 3 (2012): 92–120.

Ravitzky, Eliezer. *Messianism, Zionism, and Jewish Religious Radicalism*. Chicago: The University of Chicago Press, 1996.

Reinharz, Jehuda, and Anita Shapira, eds. *Essential Papers on Zionism*. New York: New York University Press, 1996.

Rice, Daniel F. *Reinhold Niebuhr and His Circle of Influence*. New York: Cambridge University Press, 2013.

Robson, Laura. *Colonialism and Christianity in Mandate Palestine*. Austin: University of Texas Press, 2011.

Rood, Judith Mendelsohn. "Shoah/Nakba: Offerings of Memory and History." In *History (1933–1948): What We Choose to Remember*, edited by

Margaret Monahan and James M. Lies, 411–48. Portland, OR: University of Portland, 2011.

Rood, Judith Mendelsohn, and Paul W. Rood. "Is Christian Zionism Based on Bad Theology?" *A Journal for the Theology of Culture* 7, no. 1 (2011): 37–48.

Said, Edward W. "Zionism from the Standpoint of Its Victims." *Social Text* 1 (1979): 7–58.

Sayegh, Fayez A. *Zionist Colonialism in Palestine.* Beirut: Research Center Palestine Liberation Organization, 1965.

Schechter, Michael G. *United Nations Global Conferences.* New York: Routledge, 2005.

Scheindlin, Raymond P. *A Short History of the Jewish People: From Legendary Times to Modern Statehood.* New York: Oxford University Press, 1988.

Segev, Tom. *Elvis in Jerusalem: Post-Zionism and the Americanization of Israel.* Translated by Haim Watzman. New York: Metropolitan Books, 2002.

Shafir, Gershon. *Land, Labor and the Origins of the Israeli–Palestinian Conflict, 1882–1914.* Berkeley: University of California Press, 1996.

Shanes, Joshua. "Ahron Marcus: Portrait of a Zionist Hasid." *Jewish Social Studies: History, Culture, and Society* 16, no. 3 (2010): 116–60.

Shapiro, Faydra L. "'Thank You Israel, for Supporting America': The Transnational Flow of Christian Zionist Resources." *Identities* 19, no. 5 (2012): 616–31.

———. "To the Apple of God's Eye: Christian Zionist Travel to Israel." *Journal of Contemporary Religion* 23, no. 3 (2008): 307–20.

Shavit, Ari. *My Promised Land: The Triumph and Tragedy of Israel.* New York: Spiegel & Grau, 2013.

Shenhav, Yehouda. *Beyond the Two-State Solution: A Jewish Political Essay.* Cambridge: Polity Press, 2012.

Shimoni, Gideon. *The Zionist Ideology.* Hanover, NH: Brandeis University Press, 1995.

Shindler, Colin. *A History of Modern Israel.* New York: Cambridge University Press, 2008.

Silberstein, Laurence. *The Postzionism Debates: Knowledge and Power in Israeli Culture.* New York: Routledge, 1999.

Smith, Charles D. *Palestine and the Arab–Israeli Conflict: A History with Documents,* 6th ed. Boston: Bedford/St. Martin's, 2007.

Spector, Stephen. *Evangelicals and Israel: The Story of American Christian Zionism.* Oxford Scholarship Online, 2009. https://doi.org/10.1093/acprof:oso/9780195368024.001.0001.

Stanislawski, Michael. "A Jewish Monk? A Legal and Ideological Analysis of the Origins of the 'Who Is a Jew' Controversy in Israel." In *Text and Context: Essays in Modern Jewish History and Historiography in Honor of Ismar Schorsch*, edited by Eli Lederhendler and Jack Wertheimer, 548–77. New York: Jewish Theological Seminary of America, 2005.

Troen, Ilan, and Noah Lucas, eds. *Israel: The First Decade of Independence.* Albany: State University of New York, 1995.

Troy, Gil. *The Zionist Ideas: Visions for the Jewish Homeland—Then, Now, Tomorrow.* Philadelphia: Jewish Publication Society, 2018.

Vally, Salim. "Solidarity with Palestine: Confronting the 'Whataboutery' Argument and the Bantustan Denouement." In *Apartheid Israel: The Politics of an Analogy*, edited by Jon Soske and Sean Jacobs, 43–52. Chicago: Haymarket Books, 2015.

Vital, David. *Zionism: The Formative Years.* New York: Oxford University Press, 1988.

Voss, Carl Hermann, and David A. Rausch. "American Christians and Israel, 1948–1988." *American Jewish Archives* 40, no.1 (1988): 41–81.

Walker, P. W. L. *Holy City, Holy Places? Christian Attitudes to Jerusalem in the Holy Land in the Fourth Century.* Oxford: Oxford University Press, 1990.

Wigoder, Geoffrey. *Jewish–Christian Relations since the Second World War.* Manchester: Manchester University Press, 1988.

# KEY WEBSITES

Al-Shabaka Palestine Policy Network, https://www.al-shabaka.org/.

The Avalon Project: Documents in Law, History, and Diplomacy, https://www.avalon.law.yale.edu/.

*The Forward*, https://www.forward.com.

*Haaretz*, https://www.haaretz.com.

Israel Democracy Institute, https://www.en.idi.org.il/.

Israel Ministry of Foreign Affairs, https://tinyurl.com/59kyzsua.

*The Jerusalem Post*, https://www.jpost.com.

*Jewish Telegraphic Agency*, https://www.jta.org.

Jewish Virtual Library, American Israeli Cooperative Enterprise, https://www.jewishvirtuallibrary.org.

The Knesset, https://tinyurl.com/mphpa2dz.

*The New York Times*, https://www.nytimes.com.

*The Times of Israel*, https://www.timesofisrael.com.

# INDEX